THE DOUBLE VISION OF
STAR TREK

THE DOUBLE VISION OF
STAR TREK

Half-Humans, Evil Twins,
and Science Fiction

MIKE HERTENSTEIN

Cornerstone Press Chicago
Chicago, Illinois

Copyright © 1998 Cornerstone Press Chicago. All rights reserved
First edition

Cornerstone Press Chicago
(a division of Jesus People USA Covenant Church)
939 W. Wilson Ave.
Chicago, IL 60640
www.cornerstonepress.com
cspress@jpusa.chi.il.us

Cover image, "Hourglass Nebula (STScI-PRC96-07)," by R. Sahai and J. Trauger (JPL), the WFPC2 Science Team and NASA. Material contained herein was created with support to Space Telescope Science Institute, operated by the Association of Universities for Research in Astronomy, Inc., from NASA contract NAS5-26555, and is reproduced here with permission from AURA/ST ScI. Any opinions, findings, or conclusions in this book are solely those of its authors and do not necessarily reflect the views of NASA, AURA, or ST ScI, or their employees. Used by permission.

Cover and inside design and layout by Pat Peterson/wheatsdesign
Printed in the United States of America
02 01 00 99 98 5 4 3 2 1

Library of Congress Cataloging in Publication Data

Hertenstein, Michael, 1960–
      The double vision of Star Trek : half-humans, evil twins, and
science fiction / Mike Hertenstein.
            p.   cm.
      Includes index.
      ISBN 0-940895-42-0
      1. Star Trek television programs. 2. Star Trek films. 3. Television
broadcasting—religious aspects.   I. Title.
PN1992.8.S74H47   1998
791.45'75—dc21   98-9932
                                                                      CIP

To Rod,
who rebaptized my imagination

Contents

Preface ix
Acknowledgements xiii

Introduction: Infinite Diversity and Unification 3
1. Happy Endings in the Final Frontier 17
2. Good Guys Versus Bad Guys
   (And a Few Shades of Gray) 39
3. The Heart Has Its Reasons
   (that Reason Thinks "Illogical") 63
4. Which Comes First: The Many or the One? 89
5. No Golden Rules Except for This One 113
6. "We've Got to Save Humanity" 139
7. Spirits, Bodies, and Other Alien Beings 165
8. Get a Life (Or a Reasonable Facsimile Thereof) 193
9. A Starship Named *Desire* 223
10. The Voyage Home 251

Notes 269
Select Bibliography 275
Index 277
Index of Episodes 283

Preface

 This book was born as an article idea for the late (and indeed lamented) *Wonder* magazine, which after that extraordinary publication's untimely demise saw print in *Cornerstone* magazine (where I am one of several senior editors). The same material was later expanded into a seminar series for "the Imaginarium" at the 1996 Cornerstone Festival, where we have found movies, books, old radio shows, comics, bubblegum wrappers and such cultural efflorescence to be a fine jumping-off place for serious discussion of the Big Questions. My studies also represent a reclaiming of territory of a world I enjoyed as a boy, but somehow lost track of for many years, and do so again, with pleasure and added perspective.

 Other readers will notice my frequent reference to another group of writers and thinkers I tend to gather irresponsibly under the name "Inklings," including C. S. Lewis, J. R. R. Tolkien (actual Inklings, i.e., writers who met at Lewis's house to read and drink), and G. K. Chesterton, George MacDonald, Dorothy Sayers (friends of or influences on Lewis), along with Flannery O'Connor and Walker Percy (can't let us Yanks be unrepresented among those Brits). My attempted grounding of the discussion in this circle of thinkers is deliberate, since the Imaginarium finds its bearings among these—imaginative writers, critics of culture, Christians all. Those readers who assume *Trek*'s incompatibility with religion will, of course, in the spirit of *Trek*ish tolerance be willing to give this odd and unexpected perspective a hearing.

Without a doubt I have occasionally put the insights of these various literary mentors to uses which may have appalled them: both Lewis and Tolkien were staunch defenders of the reading experience as against film (not to mention television.) I sympathize with their point that the essential core of the imaginative experience is assembling pictures in our heads, but I would no more classify film and television as "unimaginative" than I would music, paintings, sculpture, or theater. I attribute their views on the subject to having their formative imaginative experiences before film and television became part of the cultural air we breathe. (Indeed, in his negative remarks about film, Lewis goes against his own stricture of not criticizing art forms he has not personally enjoyed.) And as Lewis was willing to grant legitimacy to aesthetic experience for those who found it in pulp fiction, I apply that view to pulp TV.

Then again, it is probable that the only thing I've really learned from all these Inklings is Chesterton's tendency to wander away from the topic at hand and propensity for losing track of sources. There can be no doubt that what G. K. C. might have tossed off before breakfast has taken me considerable time and effort, with much waking in the middle of the night to scribble thoughts on paper scraps. But if this book can introduce *Trek* fans into the strange, new world of Lewis, et al, or get "Inklings" fans to apply (and build on) Lewis's critique to today's culture, this book will have indeed been worth losing sleep over.

Following the conventions of most *Trek* discussions, the "canon" here is limited to TV and film, with no cartoons, comic books, or novels included. I quickly found I needed to come up with a shorthand way of rendering frequently repeated terms. Hence, the reader will find *Star Trek* usually rendered simply as *Trek*. Science Fiction will often appear as SF. The Prime Directive may be abbreviated PD. The first *Trek* series may be rendered either as Classic *Trek* or *TOS*, short for "The Original Series." We'll abbreviate *Star Trek: The Next Generation* as simply *TNG*. *Star Trek: Deep Space Nine* shall be *DS9*, and we'll call *Star Trek: Voyager* just plain *Voyager*, abbreviated *VOY*. When it comes to the movies, since all the titles usually begin with the words *Star Trek*, we'll drop those words and just use the rest of the title to refer to each films, and sometimes just initials. For example, *Star Trek: The Motion Picture* will usually be rendered simply *TMP*. Every so often I go back to the long form to keep things clear. Also, any discussion of "aliens" necessarily includes plenty of references to "humans," but I got tired of "humankind," which didn't always connote right (no more than that brutally neutered business of going where "no one" has gone in the *TNG* prologue), and so I felt myself slipping occasionally into "Man" without the least bit of sexism intended.

Acknowledgments

Writing a book is a bit like going through Pon Farr. Thanks to all those in the community in which I live who put up with my recurring madness. Special thanks to *Cornerstone* editors Jon Trott, Curt and Dawn Mortimer, and Eric Pement for various realignments, remodulations and reconfiguring over the years, who with Chris Harold saw all of our office discussions for the past year traced back to *Trek;* to Dave Canfield, my Imaginarium pal; to Mark Fackler and his media studies classes at Wheaton; to Grace for watching lots of outer space stuff with me; to Jennifer Ingerson for superb copy editing, to Sally "the Salinator" Watkins, proofer extraordinaire, and to Pat "wheats" Peterson and Tom Montgomery at Cornerstone Press, which is also where my wife works—so I thank Jane profusely for hanging in there when *Trek* became part of both work and home: and also thanks for letting me monopolize the TV/VCR so long and trying not to laugh during the stupid parts.

Of course, it's one thing to discuss the Big Questions among friends into a hot summer night, another to put one's ideas into print. A few highly-qualified individuals graciously agreed to scan my manuscript in hopes of keeping me out of trouble; these include closet Trekkers and some folks who probably thought I needed to get a life—and I found both points of view helpful. Special thanks to Rod Bennett, Bill Backus, Sloan Lee, and Tom Peters. This group of readers saved me from foolish errors, spurred me to deeper thinking, and added insights of their own (a few marginal comments found their way directly into the text.) And if I managed to get myself into trouble despite such heroic efforts, the fault and mistakes must be credited to me, not them.

Mike Hertenstein

May, 1998

Introduction

Infinite Diversity or Unification?

According to the ancient Vulcan ideal of "Infinite Diversity in Infinite Combinations" (IDIC), the proper response to the magnificent multiplicity of the cosmos is one of unrestrained appreciation.

My own response tends toward dizziness and wanting to throw up.

On the other hand, who could fail to appreciate this sort of cosmic diversity: four television series, eight movies, Saturday morning cartoons, uncountable novels, comic books, commentaries, concordances, dictionaries, encyclopedias, trading cards, technical manuals, toothbrushes, watches, towels, sheets, pillowcases, posters, postcards, puzzles, calendars, coffee cups, cardboard cutouts, conventions, lunch boxes, uniforms, T-shirts, sweatshirts, shot glasses, shaving kits, limited-edition Franklin Mint castings, boxer shorts, personal checks, bumper stickers, computer games, mouse pads, screen savers, video- and audiotapes, fan clubs, E-mail discussion groups, plastic models, tribbles, tricorders, action figures, celebrity cruises, and a multi-million-dollar media-extravaganza "simulated adventure," star of the Spacequest Casino at the Las Vegas Hilton Hotel.

Of course, we all know this diversity isn't really *infinite*—for that would be mere anarchy, a disconnected flux. We're talking about a very *finite* diversity here, indeed a unity: a particular set of images and ideas held within specific borders, a single identity, a vision. Supply and demand can often be a chicken-versus-egg proposition, but what the people want, it seems, at this end of the twentieth century, is something very close to Vulcan idealism: that bundle of notions and emotions we grasp by the handle of a certain double-worded phrase, *Star Trek*.

In response to popular demand, the first American space shuttle bore the name of the most famous *Trek* flagship. Schools across the country bring kids by the busload to museums to see the traveling show *Federation Science*, real physics and astronomy combined with actual TV props. Other props from the series have joined the *Spirit of St. Louis* and the original Star-Spangled Banner on display at the Smithsonian Institution. Academics write books examining the "physics," "metaphysics," and "meaning" of *Trek*. Parents send their kids to Klingon-language summer camp, operated by the authors of *Good News for the Warrior Race*, a Bible translation for that guttural alien tongue.

British scientists studied a couple hundred *Trek* fans, finding five to ten percent virtual addicts who exhibited symptoms of withdrawal when deprived of the show. The kind who buy all that stuff listed above eat, sleep, and drink *Trek*. Yet the fans involved in the study were also found to be educated, intelligent, and employed: "not weirdos," it was concluded. [1]

But you can be the judge. Exhibit A: the juror who showed up at federal court dressed in a *Trek* uniform—her way of spreading the message of IDIC. Neither the prosecution nor His Honor was miffed by the wardrobe; the juror was dismissed because she couldn't stop talking to the media about *Trek*. Exhibit B is much more serious: the Heaven's Gate cult, devout *Trek* fans all, who believed the world was a "holodeck" (a reference to *Trek*'s virtual-reality playground) and "the true *Enterprise*" was a UFO which trailed the recently discovered comet Hale-Bopp, and who wore patches labeled "away team" when they finally "beamed up"— that is, left their physical "vehicles" in a mass suicide.

It's as if those nineteenth-century missionaries of art got their wish—sort of: religion has been replaced by pop culture. Indeed, despite its avowedly secular vision, *Trek* has trouble escaping the atmosphere it perpetually generates—a following with the earnestness of seekers of personal salvation. Devotees collect mass-marketed relics, sought and treasured like bones of the saints or a splinter of the True Cross (and sold with a familiar cynicism). The faces and other identifying images of *Trek* have become "cultural icons." And then there are the appearances of the saints: the highlight of the regular *Trek* conventions is the chance to see a cast member in a "live" question-and-answer session. The original *Trek*'s "Captain Kirk," William Shatner, once made no secret of his disdain of fanatic Trekkies—an attitude which climaxed in a notorious *Saturday Night Live* sketch. In the sketch, guest host Shatner played himself as the star attraction at a *Trek* convention. After being driven crazy by costume-wearing, trivia-spouting fans, Shatner thundered, "*Get a life!*"—a phrase most infamous throughout fandom ever since.

The Trekkies in the *Saturday Night Live* sketch were depicted as stereotypical sci-fi nerds, outsiders, aliens. Yet real *Trek* convention attendees might as easily include grey-haired ladies in duck-themed applique sweatshirts—one might first assume they're from the craft show next door—all wearing the orange sticker that means they've paid fifty bucks a head for reserved seats to see Kate Mulgrew, the captain on *Star Trek: Voyager*. Or the older man, with the tiny Federation insignia badge on his flannel-shirt collar, seeing the sights with his grandkids. Or the stout middle-aged guy stuffed into his Starfleet uniform, chatting with friends in the dealers' room about car payments.

Far from stereotypical, Trekkers are a diversity unto themselves. And here is the truth behind the praise of "Infinite Diversity": uniqueness is celebrated, yes, but within the friendly confines of a sharply defined cosmos. *Trek* is about vicarious adventures, yes; but more important, and like Frodo's much-loved "fellowship" of the ring, *Trek* is about feeling safe within a vicarious home.

A popular inscription on ancient tombs was *Et in Arcadia ego*—"I, too, lived in Arcadia." Arcady was a lovely rural place in ancient Greece which became idealized in a myth of a lost world of beauty, simplicity, and social harmony. To claim citizenship in Arcadia was to declare faith in a better world. And "Beam me up, Scotty" is a plea to be transported to Arcadia.

Even William Shatner made his peace with *Trek*—both in the *SNL* sketch and otherwise. Perhaps he decided it was unwise to bite the hand that fed him so well. Maybe *Trek* helped *him* get a life: *Who am I? T. J. Hooker? No! I'm a cultural icon. I'm Captain Kirk.* For even movie stars need a life. And *Trek* may turn out to be the most tangible evidence that a few of them ever had one.

Yet there is an irony in making oneself at home in the *Trek* cosmos: it is a cosmos afflicted with homelessness. One of the things that helps fans identify so closely with *Trek* is the abundance of characters who are searching for an identity: aliens and outsiders lost in the diversity, seeking unification, looking for their own friendly confines, longing for home.

THE ENEMY WITHIN

Every action-adventure show requires conflict, and *Trek* has always had plenty of good-guy-versus-bad-guy, the external kind.

But the most characteristic *Trek* conflict is internal: a single character at war with his or her self. *Trek* specializes in truly *alien*-ated characters, from the half-Vulcan Spock to the half-Klingon B'elanna Torres, and including such figuratively divided selves as the android Data, the shape-shifter Odo, the Trill Dax, *Voyager*'s holographic Doctor, and that vessel's new half-Borg character, Seven of Nine. A simpleminded adviser might say that all these characters needed was to "get a life"—but their chronic and agonized response would be: which one? And so they oscillate between their personal extremes, seeking the answer to the *Trek* question that seems to haunt us all: Who am I?

And since each of these characters is, in their own way, half-*human*, their question becomes, What does it mean to be human?

One answer *Trek* gives: to be human is to be divided. For it's not just *half*-humans who are split personalities. In the words of the schizoid title character of *Dr. Jekyll and Mr. Hyde*, man "is not truly one; he is truly two"—if not more, we might add. Yet the conflict usually plays best as dueling polarities: various anatomists from Plato to Freud, while dividing the psyche into more than two parts, could be said to draw the starkest line between what we might call "higher" and "lower" functions in a sort of "good guy/bad guy" conflict.

Freud warned that those elements of the psyche we repress find ways to emerge, as in dreams or neuroses. On *Trek*, submerged selves find their way to the surface through various ruses, including "space madness" and even technological means. In the *TOS* episode "The Enemy Within," James T. Kirk is split into component parts by a transporter malfunction. After the captain beams down to a planet, twin Kirks materialize in the chamber on the return trip—though not quite identical. One twin is the "lower" Kirk, an animalistic "Mr. Hyde." The other is that which remains of Kirk's psyche without this lower component: a "civilized" half. Thus, we see that Spock and the other divided alien characters are, in their way, merely symbols for all of human experience—which is, from the start, inescapably dual.

Human duality is itself experienced in multiple ways. There's the sense in which man is centaur, half man, half beast,—part of nature, and yet outsider; a "rational animal" who seems suspended between matter and mind, both eternal soul and vapor. The duality of our species includes the tragic simultaneity of human glory and human depravity: man is the creature who builds the gas chambers, says Victor Frankel, but also the one who enters them with head high and a prayer on his lips. And then there is the division between the "I" of self-consciousness, the "inside" view, and everything "out there," the "not-I," a division which draws the line between one self and another. Or that "inside" perspective against the "objective" view of science.

The classic way to explore the multiplicity of the human condition is that longtime staple of soap operas, the "evil twin." The doppelganger, or double, was also a key motif of German expressionism, an early twentieth-century art movement which specialized in externalizing internal conflicts. For an era newly bathed in Freud, German expressionism presented an opportunity to dredge up hidden impulses (usually sexual) and repress others (such as the reality of death) from the depths of the unconscious. Among the movement's classic iconography is the mirror: a sure sign a character has a hidden, dark side is if they stop and look at themselves in a mirror. The cinematic manifestation of expressionism found quick and natural affinity in the horror genre, with its battles against literal monsters. The monsters of science-fiction films, too, offered a chance to externalize the dark side: "My evil self is at that door, and I have no power to stop it!" cries Dr. Morbius, after unleashing a monster from his own unconscious in the film *Forbidden Planet*.

In other words, even the doubling is doubled on *Trek:* for along with half-humans, one is constantly running into evil twins.

Entire universes can have evil twins. In the fan-favorite *TOS* episode "Mirror, Mirror," another transporter accident switches landing parties from neighboring universes. Captain Kirk and his team find themselves in a dark, "Mr. Hyde" Federation, complete with an "evil" Spock (who sports a Mephistophelian goatee). Meantime, the "Hyde" crew must cope with our "Jekyll" universe.

In a variation of this idea, after the TV "death" of *TNG* regular character Tasha Yar (in "Symbiosis"), actress Denise Crosby was able to resurrect that character later in evil-twin fashion as an "evil" Romulan officer (in "Redemption," *TNG*, and elsewhere). Even androids can have evil twins. Honest and decent Commander Data turns out to have an identical, but evil, brother, Lore (seen in the episode "Datalore" and various *TNG* sequels later).

Spock's "evil" twin is—he thinks—his "human" half—though most of his friends might disagree with this diagnosis. For much of the series, Spock's solution to his duality is *segregation* from his unwanted self—not *integration*, which turns out to be Captain Kirk's solution to his own duality in "The Enemy Within."

These different solutions are implied in *Trek's* two kinds of doubling: half-humans seek to integrate, evil twins to segregate. And despite their different attitudes and approaches to their Other, the goal for Captain Kirk and Mr. Spock is one and the same: wholeness, a sense of completeness, that is, *integrity*.

Inasmuch as it involves "having all the parts," integrity is a matter of *inclusiveness*. To *integrate* is to combine elements to form an interrelated, unified whole. *Trek* certainly has always prided itself on inclusiveness. Unlike older science fiction, the message has always been that difference—the "alien"—is not necessarily a bad thing which must be excluded (and, in the case of fifties science fiction, the alien had to be destroyed). *Trek*, on the other hand, takes delight in "infinite diversity." But despite its emphasis on the different, on the individual, *Trek's* primary impulse has been to *unify*—to bring aliens and outsiders inside, to "embrace the Other," which one writer calls "*Star Trek's* essential credo," and defines as "becoming wholly ourselves"[2]—just as Kirk regained wholeness in "The Enemy Within": the happy ending of that story involved remodulating the transporter to "beam" Kirk's separated halves together as one.

But this strategy is not always the best solution. In the *Voyager* episode "Tuvix" another transporter accident causes two crewmen to be "beamed" together into a single individual, who must then be separated into component parts. Likewise, in *TNG's* "Second Chances," yet another transporter accident (and no wonder Doctor McCoy didn't trust these unreliable contraptions!) creates an identical double of Commander Will Riker. The solution, again, is not to integrate, but to *segregate*—the story ends with Riker's double inventing his own name and going off to lead his own life. We also recall those stories that involve Spock, armed with phaser, confronting twin Captain Kirks—one real, one an imposter. Once again, a *choice* between opposing doubles must be made. For sometimes one head *is* better: in "Time Squared," *(TNG)*, Captain Picard meets his double (from six hours in the future) whom he must phaser-stun to be singleminded enough to save his ship.

Thus, wholeness is not just a matter of inclusiveness, but also *exclusiveness*—which involves keeping out the wrong parts. A compromise of integrity introduces *something which does not belong*. And integrity is a matter of vital concern to those for whom compromise can mean disaster or death. Thomas Richards, in his insightful book, *The Meaning of Star Trek,* has suggested that maintaining integrity is perhaps the central *Trek* concern.[3] Of course, there is a sense in which every story is about integrity and compromise: All stories begin with a certain status quo, which is somehow breached, and finally end with some kind of restoration to changed status quo. But on *Trek* we hear constantly of literal breaches and restorations: the crisis often revolves around a temporal *rift,* a *rupture* in the space-time continuum, a *breach* of the hull or warp core, a *violation* of the Prime Directive (which is an *interference* in the integrity of a culture), an *intruder* alert—all of which mean borders have been crossed by something alien. The issue is security: in each case, safety involves keeping sealed barriers.

So far, so good, but by stopping here Richards leaves the reader with only a half-truth. For while it is true that *Trek* is vitally concerned about maintaining certain borders, *Trek* takes equal pride in smashing certain other borders—in *breaking down* walls and prejudices, from putting women and minorities on the crew (or in command), to *Trek*'s famous breach of racist notions of integrity in television's "first interracial kiss," to the very impulse to breach the final frontier and "go where no man" (or "no one") "has gone before." The need to tear down certain walls, such as the one in Berlin, spotlights the downside of certain kinds of integrity. For the desire for wholeness has led some to seek "racial purity" and "ethnic cleansing." Definite borders would seem the necessary prerequisite to having an identity at all—just ask Odo, the shape-shifter who is drawn to the society of "solids." Yet how often our need for identity degenerates into an imperialistic grasping for territory, a consolidation of our identity at the expense of the other.

The question is, where do we draw the lines? The difficulty is in knowing which examples of inclusiveness are necessary to achieve integrity, and which would be a destructive compromise. In fact, dealing with the Other is such a complicated business, and increasingly so, that many are throwing up their hands and saying the only solution is to give up the quest for identity and wholeness, and give in to the shapelessness of Odo.

But as we shall see, giving up drawing lines, surrendering to protean notions of human identity, ultimately places at risk the very possibility of identity—human, ethical, or otherwise.

Certainly one more method for dealing with doppelgangers on *Trek* is ignoring them and hoping they'll go away. In the seventh *Trek* film, *Star Trek: Generations*, Captain Picard enters a timeless limbo, called the Nexus, and then comes back out of the limbo to a moment in time just *before* he entered: in other words, there should have now been *two* Captain Picards, but apparently the filmmakers lost track of one and ignored the double altogether.

As tempting as that last option seems, we learn from Spock's agonized example and bear in mind the warning that repressed doppelgangers will, sooner or later, come back to haunt you.

And so we boldly go.

THE BEST OF BOTH WORLDS?

In the fifties, certain French film critics popularized what became known as the auteur theory, which gave primary credit for any given film to the director—the "author." Various commentators on *Trek* have spoken of its creator, producer Gene

Roddenberry, as an auteur in this sense, and treated *Trek* as if it were a grand, unified vision—a "conscious philosophy," writes one, "produced as a unity to communicate" a particular "world view and philosophy."[4] Such a judgment, however, shows not only a want of understanding of the history of this particular production, but also of film and television production in general: it overlooks the multiplicity of input from a constantly shifting retinue of writers, directors, and actors, as well as the role of studio politics, corporate economics, production logistics, the vagueries of ratings and demographics, and plain serendipity.

Indeed, you don't have to examine *Trek* very closely to find the inevitable contradictions in this "unified" vision—from the details of alien culture, a particular character's history, *Trek*'s "official" worldview, to the workings of its technology. Critics who have examined *Trek* with a specific end—such as teaching physics or metaphysics—have had to pick and choose among the material to create a semblance of coherence: smoothing gaps, ignoring contradictions, even disagreeing with *Trek* about what *Trek* "really" means in using scientific or other terms.

But instead of smoothing over these inner conflicts, this book aims right for them: the central theme shall be what SF film critic Vivian Sobchack calls "the aesthetics of collision."[5] Our thesis is this: that *Trek* is a bundle of unresolved tensions, and only by observing the collisions of these, or rather, following the ping-pong between extremes, can one understand *Trek*, and so its appeal—and maybe, along the way, better understand ourselves.

This is not to insist that the human psyche can be reduced to a duality. We focus on the doubleness of *Trek* because the most powerful of *Trek*'s inner conflicts are expressed as collisions between diametrically opposed forces, in the same way that *Trek*'s starships are powered by a collision between matter and antimatter. Duality, in fact, is a central notion in contemporary physics—where the truth has turned out to be as strange as science fiction. The revelations that space is "curved" and somehow connected to time, that the speed of time is relative to one's velocity in space, the proven existence of antiparticles and the straight-faced conjecture of some physicists that alternative universes may really exist—all seem quite as far-fetched as anything *Trek* has served up. The subatomic, or quantum, world, likewise defies our common-sense experience.

And for our purposes, quantum theory is especially pertinent: especially the "particle/wave duality" of light. Under certain conditions light behaves as if it were made up of particles. But under certain other conditions light behaves as if it were made up of waves. For a complete description of the behavior of light, one needs both understandings—one must, for practical purposes, accept the idea that light is *both* particle *and* wave.

Keeping that in mind, we'll examine whether *Trek* is particle or wave—or both. Is *Trek*'s imaginative utopia achieved by avoiding hard choices and negotiating forks in the road with double-talk? Or is the quantum nature of *Trek* itself a clue to what we go to *Trek* for? And can we answer that most classic *Trek* question: Who am I?—i.e., what can *Trek* tell us about human identity?

The Holy Grail of contemporary physics is the grand unified theory, the GUT. For not only is quantum theory seemingly at odds with itself, but the most fundamental theories of physics contradict one another. Albert Einstein spent his final years in quest of unity, a single set of equations that would explain everything. Some physicists are still looking; others have given up, resigned to the belief that reality at its core is illogical, or at least paradoxical.

This book does not presume to present any grand unified theories. Rather, we'll explore those key inner conflicts and try to find a provisional context within which to think about them. *Trek* fans may find our exploration helpful in understanding what it is they reach for in *Trek,* and whether there's any hope the *Trek* vision can deliver on its promises. This book is also for those who are already skeptical about *Trek*'s vision—both fans who find themselves drawn to *Trek* despite their reservations, and those skeptics who think *Trek* and its fans need to get a life. One warning: to presume to tell somebody to "get a life" suggests certain presuppositions about life, some of which *Trek*'s critics might be abashed to find they share in common with Trekkies.

Indeed, for all the science-fiction trappings, *Trek*'s double-jointed impulses echo both fundamental human paradoxes and our shared contemporary dilemmas. Likewise, *Trek*'s solutions to these puzzles, even if couched in technobabble, echo commonly held assumptions and beliefs about creating a just society. Anyone interested in the future, especially those who hope for "a better world," has a stake in probing *Trek*'s assumptions and goals.

One of my own hopes is that our approach to *Trek* might serve as a model for engaging with popular culture in general, in the context of another famous duality, that of baby and bath water— and here is proof positive that "both/and" might not always be the best way of dealing with doubles. For there are two mistakes people can make in their approach to culture: first, rejecting both baby and bath water, and thereby losing something valuable. And second, taking "unrestrained appreciation" of diversity to mean treating baby and bath water as fundamentally equal in value. In dealing with dualities, we'll see that one must employ *both* "both/and" *and* "either/or." This probably sounds like doubletalk at this point; yet my belief is that in this way lies true wholeness.

Meanwhile, let's begin where *Trek* begins—at the end: at the resolution of conflict, that is, with "happily ever after." The first chapter will explore *Trek*'s optimistic vision in the context of the age-old tension of optimistic and pessimistic strains of imaginative futures. We'll also explore a key term, *deus ex machina*, which is a way of making happy endings work that leaves many unhappy. All this will lead to a showdown with that two-headed beast at the center of our subject: science fiction.

1

Happy Endings in the Final Frontier

UTOPIA V. DYSTOPIA: FACT AND FANTASY

The usual explanation for *Trek*'s popularity, and certainly a key difference between the series and most other recent science fiction—literature and film—is that *Trek* presents an *optimistic* take on the world of tomorrow. *Trek* begins with a happy ending, so to speak. Gene Roddenberry's original vision of the future is set in the context of a human society which has eliminated poverty, disease, social conflict and war, and possesses (without being possessed by) a technology that extends human powers almost indefinitely. Who could ask for anything more?

The vision becomes especially appealing when one recalls the historical moment at which *Trek* premiered: the ugliest years of the most tumultuous American decade in living memory. The period between September of 1966 and March of 1969, the dates of the original series' run, includes some of the most bitter memories of "the sixties." The United States was mired in an escalating and increasingly unpopular proxy conflict of the cold war, with a nuclear Armageddon always waiting in the wings. The domestic scene featured protests, race riots, political assassinations, titanic social upheaval, and apocalyptic environmental warnings.

In some ways (depending on one's own circumstances, no doubt) the present seems calm in comparison—though our society has in no way reached Roddenberry's promised land. Indeed, as *Trek* continues to hold forth a vision of a brighter tomorrow, conflicts in the present seem to be multiplying: the world is now fragmenting into smaller but angrier and often violent culture wars, from heightened racial tensions to bloody ethnic cleansing. The threat of bipolar nuclear conflict has likewise splintered into a potential for mass destruction from a thousand sources, both known and of the sort we don't know about until the morning after. At least in the sixties there was some optimism about the government's ability to solve urban poverty and violence. *Trek*'s backstory, which suggests human history gets worse before it gets better, seems its most convincing prediction for the future.

So the chance to visit a future in which humanity's present is but dim memory remains inviting. Such a vision offers hope: both that humankind survives this tragic twentieth century into the twenty-third, and that humans are able to solve their social, political, and economic problems—the only way such survival seems possible. Better than that, in the *Trek* future, humans are shown to have finally created that just and stable society to which they always aspired, able now to face the rest of the universe and its challenges with confidence and grace. Finally, the moralistic thrust of the series suggests that if viewers could only learn the lessons of *Star Trek*, they might begin now to make such a future a reality.

To fully understand the significance of this now rare optimistic perspective, one must set *Trek* in the context of the history of imagined futures. Traditionally, these have oscillated between twin extremes, corresponding roughly to both optimistic and pessimistic views, drawing on both secular and religious visions.

The word *utopia* comes from two Greek words meaning *no place* (hence William Morris's utopian novel, *News from Nowhere*). And yet *utopia* is pronounced the same as Greek words meaning *good place*. So utopia is *the good place which is no place*.[1] Utopia represents the ancient dream of humanity, the ideal state, the promised land—Arcadia. Human experience has always been haunted by the dim memory of a lost golden age, to be reclaimed in some future reign of justice and peace. For some, such dreams can only be fulfilled in the next life. Others have always believed that, if not exactly heaven, then at least the ideal commonwealth, could be constructed on Earth. Accordingly, blueprints for building some form of Nowhere Land here and now have been put forward since the Hebrew Zion and Plato's Republic.

In the Western religious tradition, utopia was the Garden of Eden, from which mankind was expelled for rebellion against God, the gates guarded by an angel with a flaming sword. The Jewish vision settled on a temporal promised land, a nation under theocratic rule, lost, mourned, regained, lost and regained again, the theocratic vision mixing with more secular priorities. Christians look forward to paradise restored in the New Jerusalem, the heavenly city, and then only for the elect. Building an ideal state on Earth has seemed blasphemous for many— though the book from which the word *utopia* came "was written by [Thomas More], a man who died a martyr for his faith and bears the title of a saint."[2] The Christian ideal has always cut both ways: an otherworldly goal for the pilgrim's progress, but also a kingdom of God in the hearts of men, spreading in and influencing this world. The practical applications of this twofold idea have also been mixed: a history of benevolence and tragedy, Inquisitions and saints, confusion between the New Jerusalem and the old—yet unlike those of many of its critics, an ideal that supplied a moral context within which to judge its own missteps.

With Plato began the nuts and bolts of more humanistic utopia building, in his well-planned Republic. Government was to be handled exclusively by elite "philosopher-kings," whose control of society extended to the division of labor and child care. Thomas More, statesman, dreamer, and saint, wrote the book *Utopia*, recasting Plato's vision for late-medieval Englishmen. The Greek revival during the Renaissance fueled these classical utopian longings. With the concurrent rise of modern science and the machine, it seemed that at last had been found a workable means to accomplish humanity's impossible dreams. There was a boom in fictional and nonfictional utopias in the wake of the seventeenth-century Enlightenment, which helped unleash successive scientific and industrial revolutions. In 1893, Edward Bellamy eagerly anticipated the world of the twentieth century in his utopian novel *Looking Backward*. Bellamy's gushing conclusion: "Humanity has burst the chrysalis. The heavens are before it."[3]

Meanwhile, Karl Marx outlined his own blueprint for the ideal state, though he considered his utopian prophecies as definitely nonfictional. And now we see how one man's dream is another's nightmare: socialist utopias provoked a multitude of antisocialist fictional responses, probing unexamined assumptions and prophesying that centralized planning would end in slavery. Humanity's ever increasing ability to control nature sparked a debate on the nature of man: whether it could be changed; if so, in which direction; and whether freedom was a hindrance or a goal.[4]

But the best-sellers were the optimists, and the public thrilled to marvelous futures described in outlandish detail by its proliferating seers. The next-best thing to being there was the vicarious experience of utopia. With the rise of "scientific fiction" by authors like Jules Verne and H. G. Wells, the borders of a popular new narrative genre were first firmly sketched.

Yet the mistrust of rational planning expressed by the early naysayers trickled down to the masses as it became clear that centralization—along with science itself—unleashed a Pandora's box of troubles. The twentieth century brought not utopia but scientific horrors unimaginable to the optimistic Bellamy and friends, many springing from various utopian schemes. Confidence in the bright tomorrow was shaken. Growing disillusionment with science and worries about tomorrow were depicted in fictional dystopias, defined by Webster's as "an imaginary place which is depressingly wretched and whose people lead a fearful existence."

As I have indicated, this second branch of fictional futures grew up alongside that of utopian tradition. In our own troubled century, Aldous Huxley's *Brave New World* and George Orwell's *1984* are among the most famous examples of these pessimistic prophecies, most of which feature techno-totalitarianism, the collapse of civilization, and/or the de-evolution of humankind. "Cyberpunk" is one name under which this dark carnival flourishes today. Authors like William Gibson and films like *Blade Runner* portray a dreary dystopian future of social and personal chaos, where lines between humanity and technology increasingly blur.

In film history, even the most optimistic science fiction was powered by its evil twin. The genre was launched in a post-Hiroshima climate fraught with anxiety and paranoia, described by one critic as "the imagination of disaster."[5] Fifties science-fiction films are filled with giant monsters, shrinking men, mad scientists and world-destroying invasions from space.

The future for the fifties meant the nightmare of the sixties, marked by violence and growing techno-insecurity. In *2001: A Space Odyssey,* the ape-man throws his bone in the air where it dissolves into the advanced tool of a spaceship in orbit; yet in space, the tools turn on their makers; cool but crazy Hal is the beat and hippie version of the giant bugs who conquer the world.

And then, in the midst of this ever more dreary futurism—right in the nick of time, you might say—the classical outlines of the *U.S.S. Enterprise* broke through the dark clouds. *Star Trek* was out of sync with the general attitude of mainstream sixties science fiction; even the Cleaveresque Robinson family was lost in space. But while *Trek* creator Gene Roddenberry scorned fifties hokeyness, his vision of tomorrow was more in line with the optimistic futures of the past. And Roddenberry's combination of both realistic portrayal and optimism has proved to be unbeatable. Like many of its own stories, *Trek* was a last-second rescue for a genre and fandom on the brink of despair.

DEUS EX MACHINA

You're zipping along in your spaceship—just another day in Starfleet. Or is it? The communications officer reports a distress call from a freighter in space. Being good guys, you and your crew speed to the scene—and are horrified to find yourselves now in need of a rescue. For the distress call turns out to be a hoax, a decoy for an alien ambush. After a pitched but brief battle, your ship is blown to bits; the good guys are dead, the bad guys win. So much for the happy ending. Right?

Wait a second. The next moment reveals it is the viewers of this scene who've been hoaxed. For not only was the distress call phony, so was the subsequent action. As it turns out, all the fuss was merely a Starfleet computer simulation—the legendary Kobayashi Maru training exercise, in which space cadets face and test their mettle against the no-win scenario—the very place where Captain James T. Kirk launched his own personal legend by being the first and only cadet to defeat the no-win scenario: by hacking into and reprogramming the simulator, i.e., *by cheating*.

Thus, the thoughtful viewer's relief at this too timely rescue in the opening sequence of the film *Star Trek: The Wrath of Khan* will probably be tainted by the unpleasant feeling of being suckered. No doubt the producers hoped the rest of that film would wash away any disturbing questions their exciting teaser provoked; namely, What difference is there between the Kobayashi Maru and every other of *Trek*'s happy endings? Is it all just one big cheat?

There's no denying that many of *Trek*'s happy endings *are* cheats. Consider the typical story climax. Following classic narrative form, the darkest hour comes before the dawn. On *Trek*, this means that near the end of each episode and/or film, the story reaches the brink of disaster: the ship's shields are failing, the warp core has been breached, the *Enterprise (A–E), Voyager,* or *DS9* station is surrounded and outgunned by Klingons, Cardassians, Kazon, Borg, Romulans or Jem'Hadar. The fate of the ship/station, crew, time and/or space as we know it, is at stake: the future, far from optimistic, in fact never looked more grim.

Suddenly, somebody snaps his fingers and says, "Gee, why don't we

a. remodulate the main deflector dish?!"

b. realign the Heisenberg compensators?!"

c. reconfigure the lateral sensor array?!"

d. try inverse phasing?!"

e. decompile the pattern buffer?!"

And, not a moment too soon, the shields go back on line. The warp-core breach is contained. The transporter is operational. Disaster has once again been averted at the last moment, and we try to feel surprised; technology is the cavalry that comes to the rescue again. *Trek*'s techno-magicians, like forgetful wizards who suddenly remember the formula, have an embarrassing habit of hocus-pocussing their way out of plot predicaments and into happy endings, all thanks to *deus ex machina*, a "god in the machine."

Deus ex machina (pronounced day-uh-sek-*smock*-i-nuh) originates in ancient Greek theater, where the heroes of plays would likewise get themselves painted into desperate corners. At the darkest moment, when all looked lost, actors playing Zeus or Athena would be lowered from the "heavens" onto the stage using a wooden hoist. These gods could then produce a happy ending by simple command. Yet this all-too-convenient device was recognized even by the ancients as an unworthy solution to plot problems.

Such means of cheating one's way to a happy ending, in the narrative tradition, are not limited to literal machines.

On *Trek*, available gods-in-the-machine also include the occasional spontaneous recovery from amnesia, a timely intervention by the omnipotent Q, and even the old hackneyed standby, "It was all a dream," i.e., a "temporary temporal distortion" or a fatal no-win scenario that turns out to be only a training exercise.

Then there's that handy space-alien deus ex machina: a hitherto unknown physiological capacity that pulls them out of the fire. Spock staves off permanent blindness by a Vulcan "inner eyelid" ("Operation—Annihilate!" *TOS*). Worf is saved from paralysis by a handy Klingon "backup synaptic system" ("Ethics," *TNG*).

A variation on the god in the machine is what you might call "the devil in the machine," i.e., ever so timely breakdowns of gear. Hence, *Trek*'s stream of engine failures, computer bugs, and those pesky holodeck malfunctions. ("Scotty, we need those engines—now!" "Captain, I'm doin' the best I can. . . .") Likewise, Murphy's Cosmic Law ensures that the universe itself breaks down at the worst possible moment: various celestial anomalies, ion storms—which, luckily, are fixable at the last possible moment.

Among the flotsam of cyberspace one can find the *Star Trek: The Next Generation* Episode Generator. In this joke program, the user is offered a choice of bad guys from column A (Romulans, Klingons) and a choice of subplots from column B ("Meanwhile, Data falls off his chair"). Then, among a column of various plot solutions—like our "remodulate, realign, reconfigure" list above—is the choice to employ "the *Deus-Ex-Machina* Circuit" and save the day. Deus ex machina is an embarrassing *Trek* cliche.

To be fair, not all *Trek* episodes end with a god in the machine. In the best episodes, the solution to the plot problem comes from *within the action of the story*. This is in accordance with the most ancient rules of art. Kirk, for example, in an act of sheer will, prevents Dr. McCoy from saving a woman's life and so restores time as it was meant to be. Likewise, and rather self-consciously in the light of this discussion, the plot solution to the story which gave us the idea of Kobayashi Maru—cheating death—requires a regular character to save the ship and crew by choosing to sacrifice his own life.

We need to make some subtle distinctions about gods and machines. It would be easy, for example, to dismiss *Trek*'s multitudinous use of "technobabble" as mere deus ex machina—for obviously, what gets realigned, remodulated and/or reconfigured most by *Trek* engineers is *language*. With technobabble, realism depends less on real science than on the *appearance* of science. A string of scientific-sounding words is both an easy answer for lazy writers needing to keep the story moving and convincing enough for audiences worshipful but ignorant of real science.

On the other hand, without technobabble, the *Enterprise* would not fly. Astrophysicist Lawrence Krauss, in his 1995 book, *The Physics of Star Trek*, analyzed *Trek* technology and its use of scientific terms.[6] The bad news for Trekkers: most of *Trek*'s central technology turns out to be far more useful as an illustration of the limitations posed by the laws of physics than as a workable means for getting around those limitations. The unsolved (and usually ignored) problems include certain side effects to traveling at light speed and beyond (such as the fact that those in the starships will age at a different rate than those back on Starbase). And an even longer list of problems attends the use of that most central *Trek* technology, the transporter, the *Trek* teleportation device that makes possible ship-to-shore travel by the conversion of matter into energy and back again. Among Krauss's long and humorous list of problems of such conversion is keeping track of individual subatomic particles: but Heisenberg's famous uncertainty principle says it is *impossible* to keep track of individual particles. Thus, what *Trek*'s famous Heisenberg compensator compensates for is those annoying laws of physics.

When I was a kid, I debated with a friend the plausibility of the transporter. I took the affirmative side, of course, and to prove my point drew out a design. Beneath the transporter chamber floor, I began with an ordinary three-blade fan, pointed up—to keep the atoms in midair, I suppose, so we didn't lose anybody's particles down the drain. Below the fan, I drew a mysterious and scientific-looking box which I labeled "Matter-to-Energy Converter." Needless to say, I did not include a detailed schematic for the contents of my "black box."

Well, *Trek* techies work the same way. When they try to explain how their advanced thingamabobs work, the explanation is, basically, a fib to cover a fib. Q: How can you go faster than light when Einstein says that's impossible? A: Well, the ships don't really go faster than light; they create a "space warp" that causes space to literally warp around them. A: Really? Then why do you need "inertial dampers"? A: To keep passengers on the ships from getting smashed to bloody goo against the bulkhead when the starship accelerates from zero to light speed. Q: But I thought you didn't go light speed. Never mind. How exactly do the inertial dampers work? A: "Very well, thank you." (That last bit is an actual answer by a techie to this question.)

Such fudging about the particulars only proves, say some critics, that *Trek* is not true science fiction; that *Trek* needs to get a life. Fans of what is known as "hard SF" pride themselves on taking seriously the science part of science fiction. These purists usually have little or no patience with stories where the heroes are always remodulating themselves out of trouble.

Let me confess right off I speak not from voluminous fluency with hard SF, but rather from the perspective of one who views that subgenre as a recent variation of an old battle between realism and romanticism. The realism of "hard" fictionists like Zola and Dreiser was very much influenced by Darwinism and materialist presuppositions, and their prejudice that such a view was closer to "reality" was debated in their own time for similar reasons.

Likewise, say aficionados of hard SF (usually with some snobbery), the technology used in science-fiction stories must be "a reasonable extrapolation from known science." Author Robert Heinlein once proposed dividing all literature into "realism" and "fantasy," placing SF on the side of realism. That is, except for any

SF story that included technology the author couldn't reasonably explain. Such writers, said Heinlein, "cheated."[7]

And so the recent explosion of fantasy-like SF like *Trek* and *Star Wars*, along with the more overtly magical fiction that fills the fantasy section of bookstores, has served to heighten the old tensions in fandom. (Not least because more popular "soft" works are threatening to crowd "harder" works off bookstore shelves.)

This debate in science fiction goes all the way back to Verne (harder) and Wells (less so). I found myself in the thick of it once on a panel at an SF convention. Everybody was full of opinions, talking past each other at the top of their lungs. The one thing we all agreed on was that we hated stories which relied upon some unexpected, instant solution to plot difficulties. And the biggest offender in this category, the others agreed unanimously, was *Trek*. One panelist was a Hugo-award-winning author who'd turned down the chance to write a *Trek* novel—on principle. Another echoed the traditional hard SF complaint about those who wrote science fiction without any real understanding of science. Somebody else went on about how once they'd read an SF story that was going along great until it lurched off into magic. "And, boy, I bet that really broke the spell," I said, to some titters from the audience. Plainly, we needed to clarify our terms.

First, I conceded that *Trek* technology routinely breaks the laws of physics. But that shouldn't end the discussion. My fellow panelists, I suggested—diplomatically—had confused the distinction between implausible endings and the use of implausibilities in fiction. Traditionally, implausibilities of all kinds—magic, fairies, dragons, Heisenberg compensators, backup synaptic systems—have been considered legitimate in a work of fiction, especially fantasy, of course: *provided they don't appear suddenly at the last moment to rescue the characters from plot problems*. Thus, breaking the laws of physics is legitimate, as long as you don't also break the laws of drama.

In that sense, the narrative tradition has always recognized that certain kinds of "cheating" are okay. But while cheating the science in a story may be occasionally permitted, cheating the ending to a story, and the audience, is another thing altogether.

For that matter, those who suffer the most in a deus-ex-machina ending are the characters themselves, because instead of being able to make choices that matter—that is, to experience permanent consequences from their choices—the characters' free will and the meaningfulness of their choices is revoked at a pen stroke when some or another "god" intervenes and suddenly saves the day.

What really turns the tables in a discussion like this, though, is considering that all these notions of "cheating" are, within the materialist universe of hard science, the real deus ex machina.

There are plenty of hard SFers who treat their own preferences as if they were "reasonable extrapolations from known science." Yet what seems hardest of all for such folk is admitting that if "known science" is our *only* yardstick, nobody has any business saying there are any rules for art that can be cheated, or that cheating is *bad*—not unless somebody has come up with a *Trek*-like sensor device for measuring the Good, the Beautiful or the True.

In sum, the tensions within are a product of the tensions of the genre, is it science-fiction or science fantasy. And for *Trek*, the tensions are aggravated by the contradictions of its creator.

SCIENCE, FICTIONS, AND MAGIC

Gene Roddenberry liked to think he was his own man: he praised self-determination in and out of *Trek*, fought off interference, and made it clear he didn't accept the authority of others, god or man. Of course, if this were strictly true, the only rules we need discuss in connection with *Trek* would be Roddenberry's; any use of deus ex machina must be excused as examples of his revolt against the oppressive restrictions of so-called good drama.

But Roddenberry *was* concerned about the rules of good drama. He set out to make *Trek* "believable," he said, in a way he thought, say, *Flash Gordon* was not. Don't—he told prospective writers—try to sell me any story that gives a culture interstellar spaceflight capability and then has them engage their enemy with grappling hooks (something, in fact, one was very likely to see on old *Flash*). He urged his writers to test plot ideas and character responses in a non–science fiction setting—a Western, a navy story.[8] In addition to seeking to have *Trek* characters and cultures conform to the laws of common sense, Roddenberry also sought out technical advisors to help him ground *Trek*'s technology in real-world physics. Notions of warping space and matter-anti-matter drives, while not necessarily explainable, owe their origin to real physics theory.

At the same time, Roddenberry did not hesitate to bend or break the rules of physics for the sake of dramatic effect; he broke a lower law to obey a higher one, in this case the laws of drama. The producer insisted *Trek* was "about people, not technology" or abstract theory. Thus, space battles on *Trek* feature sounds of passing spaceships and shock waves from explosions in space, even though in real life the laws of physics would permit neither. Likewise, *Trek*, as noted, ignores various mind-boggling implications of Einstein's relativity theories which would make interstellar travel impossible or slow the action unacceptably.

Furthermore, "believable" to Roddenberry also meant some-times overruling scientific truth with what might be termed "human truth." As we will look into in detail, when pure science or, in *Trek*'s case, "logic" dictated one course of action, Roddenberry was clearly willing to side against "logic" on the side of what we might call human truths. The deciding factor for this sort of truth was obviously not a reasonable extrapolation from science but a reasonable extrapolation from Roddenberry's gut. In this way, the *Trek* creator served as an unconscious model for one more key tension of *Trek:* the objective measures of science and logic (represented by the logical Vulcan, Mr. Spock) versus the subjective intuition of human truths (seen in the impulsive Captain Kirk). Rare enough for a contemporary science-fiction writer, Roddenberry seemed to agree with Kirk on which mode of knowledge had priority. Yet, more like Spock, the producer was not always aware of, or at least willing to admit, this unresolved tension at the heart of himself and his work.

These unresolved contradictions in Roddenberry can be seen in his curiously negative attitude toward what he called fantasy. In giving priority to human values over scientific facts, Roddenberry admitted the limitations of hard science: that "scientific" facts about the universe were not enough, that sometimes one must go beyond science. Yet he shared the prejudices of hard-SF devotees when it came to his low opinion of fantasy, which he said was inferior to science fiction *because it was not based on science*. Furthermore, said Roddenberry, while science fiction observes strict obedience to its own internal rules, fantasy is arbitrary, giving characters "blink-of-an-eye" powers to get themselves out of trouble.[9]

The first complaint about fantasy is merely illogical; the second is a bit of stone throwing by somebody who lives in a glass house. We've already talked about *Trek* characters' capacity for getting themselves out of trouble by breaking rules of physics and drama, and even their own internal rules: how many times have we been told something is "impossible"—for example, using the transporter while deflector shields are up—and then seen an engineer snap his fingers, going "Unless . . . ," and offer a suggestion that included the words "remodulate" or "reconfigure"?

Well-made fantasy, however, like well-made science fiction—like all good fiction—rests on strict obedience to the established rules of an imaginary world, says someone who should know: J. R. R. Tolkien: such "believability," he said, is harder to achieve in fantasy than in realism, and thus might require more skill, not less.[10] Tolkien's friend C. S. Lewis, the author of *The Chronicles of Narnia,* agreed: "The logic of a fairy tale is as strict as that of a realistic novel, though different." [11] Indeed, fantasy is full of prohibitions and rules: be home by midnight or be turned into a pumpkin. None of this "unless we remodulate the glass slipper" or "reconfigure the magic coach."

Nonetheless, Roddenberry took pains to insist *Star Trek* was vastly superior to any fantasy, such as *Star Wars.*[12] He expended pages in the *TNG* writers guide sharply delineating the differences between fantasy and science fiction.[13]

Yet those less blinded by the science have found it much more difficult to distinguish between these two genres. *The Encyclopedia of Science Fiction* spends pages of tiny type in the attempt, surveying a wide range with pure forms on either end that blur in the middle, but finding no definite border between.

Thus, science fiction and fantasy are not evil twins, but rather fraternal twins.

There are magazines and publishers devoted to both genres. Both genres show up in same bookstores, at the same conventions. Both have many of the same fans, and many of the same authors. Science-fiction fans were among the first in the United States to discover Tolkien's *Lord of the Rings,* reading and discussing the work in their fanzines. And in an interview near the end of his life, Tolkien was asked what *he* liked to read: not much these days, he said, but popular SF; he mentioned Isaac Asimov by name. Tolkien and C. S. Lewis once agreed to each write a science-fiction story. They "tossed up," and Tolkien won time travel, while Lewis was to create an outer-space story. Only Lewis made good, eventually writing both an SF trilogy and a series of fantasy books about that fantasy land called Narnia.

Lewis admired the magazine *Fantasy and Science Fiction* for the same reason many hard SF fans might hate it: the publication included not just stories of space travel, but also tales of "gods, ghosts, ghouls, demons, fairies, and monsters."[14] The key to understanding the appeal of science fiction, said Lewis, is to realize that it is a modern re-dressing of an ancient human appetite. Hard SF critics criticize softer SF for using scientific jargon as a cloak for fantastic stories that have nothing to do with science. Lewis agrees, and joyfully. "The most superficial appearance of plausibility—the merest sop to our critical intellect—will do."[15] Lewis aims his disgust not at those sopping, but at those who complain about it. It's fun to talk about the physics of *Trek*, but only a truly misguided soul would let the violations ruin his appreciation for the show. One might as well insist on the plausibility of flying-carpet aerodynamics, the political structure of Oz, or the economy of Never Land.

A word that seems to bring together fantasy and science fiction in this context is *magic*. Yet that term has many meanings, some related, some not, all overlapping in confusing ways; making distinctions here is as difficult as dividing the genres themselves. What unites the usages of the term *magic* is a common connection to possibility and power; how these definitions differ is in the nature of one's relationship to that power.

The most pertinent definitions of the term *magic* might include:

Wonder. An emotional response to power, associated with childhood, a sense of humility in the presence of the strange and new.

Enchantment. To be under the control of power, falling under a spell (this includes the "willing suspension of disbelief," i.e., losing oneself in story—ranging from temporarily immersing oneself in the imaginary world of Narnia to the more permanent "spell" of a religious cult or belief—including "the cult of science").

Tricks. Illusions of power (stage and movie magic)—and willing a suspension of disbelief here can again provoke wonder—or the deception of a con man's sleight of hand.

Finally, there is *wizardry:* actually wielding power over the elements. In stories, a wizard is someone who manipulates nature—for good or for evil—and as such is a metaphor for anyone who wields power in real life, from the political leader who need only speak a word and armies march, to the storyteller who with his own brand of wizardry can put the reader under his spell. "Real-life" wizardry has to do with techniques which allegedly manipulate nature by supernatural forces. Some believers in this sort of magic say there is both a "black" and a "white" form.

Trek features an infinite diversity of magic. There can be no doubt the show produces, for many, the sense of wonder. One falls under the spell of *Trek*'s story: enchantment in this case, the "story" may be the plot of a given episode, but also the story of the entire *Trek* worldview). The special effects qualify as the magic-tricks sort of magic. And there are "wizards," those who wield enormous power over matter, time, and space.

We can see similarities between wizardry (good and evil) and applied science. Both vocations involve manipulation of the elements, the ability to point wand or phaser and "make it so." Arthur C. Clarke's dictum applies: "Any sufficiently advanced technology is indistinguishable from magic." There have been times the advanced technology of *Trek* has been mistaken by alien primitives for magic. And on other occasions, aliens with seemingly magical power have been debunked as frauds. But the science of *Trek* has been debunked by real scientists and shown to be the opposite fraud: not a phony magic that gets its powers from a machine, *Trek* is the apparent machine which gets its powers from magic. *Trek*'s control of the elements—the ability to manipulate particles of matter in time and space on command—is surely magic by another name: technobabble is so much pixie dust.

Ultimately, the "manipulation of the elements" aspect of magic is secondary to the magic of "wonder" in good science fiction or fantasy stories—which, by the way, is the difference between a "good" wizard in fiction and a "bad" one: one exercises power within proper boundaries; the other seeks to exercise power in such a way as to overcome all boundary making except the wizard's individual will.

Roddenberry would never have admitted *Trek*'s proximity to magic, but his successors seem to be a little more honest about the charade. This can be seen in an inside joke in the first of the film series made after Roddenberry's 1991 death, *Star Trek: Generations*. In one scene, Data is halted by a closed door; he "realigns his axial servo," waves his arm over the door, and commands, "Open sesame." And the elements do indeed obey. The *Trek* corollary to Clarke's dictum, admitted or not, has always been this: any bit of magic can be made to pass for science or technology if given a sufficiently scientific-sounding name.

Why go to all this trouble? Why do we need the illusion of science to experience what many go to fantasy for? Critic John Huntington says this is the exact question to ask: what is gained in any science-fiction story by the illusion of science?[16]

What is gained is the chance for sophisticated moderns to enjoy a reenchanted universe—to breathe air gone thin in a scientific age: that of Faerie. By Tolkien's famous definition, fairy stories need not include fairies, nor are they necessarily for children. Fairy stories are not about magical beings, per se, but a magical place. Most concern "the *adventures* of men in the Perilous realm or upon its shadowy marches."[17] By this measure, tales of Jason and the Argonauts, Ulysses, King Arthur, Sir Gawain, and Saint George are fairy stories, and—though Tolkien, who was fierce and exacting in guarding the integrity of Faerie, might disagree—I would venture to include such works as *The Wizard of Oz*, *The House of Wax*, *Star Wars*, and, by the same argument, *Trek*. The peculiar quality that makes Faerie so compelling, says Tolkien, involves the "satisfaction of certain primordial human desires. One of these desires is to survey the depths of space and time" (i.e., the final frontier). "Another is . . . to hold communion with other living things" (new life, new civilizations—contact). And the most important of these desires, said Tolkien, is "the consolation of the happy ending."

> A story may thus deal with the satisfaction of these desires, with or without the operation of either machine or magic, and in proportion as it succeeds it will approach the quality and have the flavour of a fairy story.[18]

Perhaps *Trek* falls short of the purist definition of Faerie; yet there can be no doubt that—however diluted with other elements—the sense of wonder blows from the same fantastic place.

On *Trek,* outer space is the Perilous Realm, "where no one has gone before"; it is Oz, Never Land, Middle-earth, and Narnia. In *The Voyage Home,* Kirk says "Welcome to Wonderland" to a twentieth-century woman who visits the spaceship in Earth's orbit; he calls the woman "Alice." In *The Undiscovered Country,* Kirk's final order as captain on the bridge of the *Enterprise* is to plot a course for "the second star to the right and straight on till morning." The *Trek* universe is teeming with ghosts, witches, goblins, elves, trolls, dragons, pirates, wizards, genies (the impish Q), princesses—all dressed up in space-alien clothes.

Thus, *Trek* viewers might accept pseudoscientific explanations for the same reason they put up with unlikely rescues, the notion of the whole galaxy speaking English and the explosions in space. Even plot, said C. S. Lewis, can be secondary for some readers (in this case "viewers"); for those whose most urgent priority is the desire to experience a particular atmosphere—"to breathe again the air of Narnia and hear the voices of the Narnian trees"[19]—for these, plot is just "a net to catch something else."[20]

The irony, in the case of *Trek*—and, one suspects, much of hard SF—is that science fiction is a net for catching "something" hard science seems to have chased from the universe.

And if that something could be said to be vital to the experience we know as "the happy ending"—if one accepts the conclusions of materialist science, the only way to reach such a happy ending is by cheating—deus ex machina.

Which brings us to another gain from the illusion of science: it provides a way to give science credit for those human values that are beyond the reach of science. Undiscerning viewers might become convinced that certain phenomena which are *not* "reasonable extrapolations from known science" (including the good, the beautiful, the true, human meaning, rights, dignity, mystery) might exist in a cosmos where nothing is "real" but the findings of materialist hard science.

What did Gene Roddenberry gain by the illusion of science? There's no question Roddenberry was under the spell of a particular scientific worldview: believing that *Trek* was superior to fantasy because it was based on science, yet discarding rules of science whenever his gut was inclined. What Roddenberry, and anyone else, might gain by an illusion of science is a so-called scientific legitimizing of their own personal preferences—a feeling of unassailable authority for what boils down to their own individual desires and will. Which brings us back to our original description of Roddenberry: a man who tended to accept no rules for behavior except his own.

All this discussion of rules and cheating (and even "getting a life") seems out of place in a society that has made much of abandoning moral norms. Yet *Trek* certainly presumes to offer a life to get, an ideal future—an *ought* for humankind. But since we are dealing here with an ought that relies so much on cheating, it should come then as no surprise if we propose next that *Trek* suffers from a chronic guilty conscience. This conscience manifests itself in periodic attempts at reform—remodulation—of *Trek* itself. Unfortunately for *Trek*, some of these remodulations are beginning to cause even worse problems.

2

Good Guys Versus Bad Guys
(And a Few Shades of Gray)

KICKING ALIEN BUTT
(IN A TOLERANT SORT OF WAY)

What makes for a happy ending? Usually this: the "good guys" win. The hero overcomes obstacles—often personified as "bad guys"—to obtain his or her heart's desire. Of course, there have been plenty of movies where the bad guys win by cheating all and sundry (including death) and get the girl. Not so satisfying, most people would say. Your happy ending, then, would seem to entail more than just survival and success. In the sort of happy ending demanded by most audiences, wrongs must be righted. The bad guys must get punished. *Virtue must triumph.*

Once upon a time, you could tell the good guys from the bad guys by the color of their hats. Nowadays, moral categories have become blurred. We are hesitant to divide the world into good guys and bad guys, sometimes because it seems impossible (consider the atrocities on both sides of the Balkan conflict) and most of the rest of the time because such simple divisions require demonizing one side (Them, of course) and baptizing the other (Us, obviously). The question of the age belongs to Rodney King: why can't we all just get along? Such agonized moral reflection may be profitable in many ways, and has produced its share of wonderful stories, but it's rather tough on genre or mythic story-telling, which still requires some manner of *good* good guys fighting it out with *evil* villains. The panic among action-film producers after the end of the cold war as they scrambled to locate new bad guys to replace the wicked KGB, which had suddenly and unexpectedly been defanged by history, has not yet been resolved.

Dave Barry, one of our most trenchant observers of the con-temporary scene, has mused over the difficulties of depicting evil in a media culture that celebrates tolerance:

> We're going to have to do something about children's televi-sion. Today's children watch shows like *Sesame Street*, which teaches them that the world is full of friendly interracial adults and cute puppets and letters that form recognizable patterns. This is, of course, a pack of lies. When I was a kid, in New York, my friends and I watched shows like *Captain Video*, which taught us that the world was full of evil forces trying to destroy the earth, which turns out to be absolutely correct.

Most of us smile because we realize there is something to this. While we understand that our traditional good guy/bad guy polarities have often been an oversimplification of moral realities, we can't shake the feeling that the mindless embrace of absolute tolerance is not much of an improvement. Instinct tells us that some actions are not just *different*, but evil. Actions such as intol-erance. This catch-22 presents a problem which is not quite as easily solved as some people like to think.

Star Trek has always been something of a weird amalgam of *Sesame Street* and *Captain Video*. The series features a spaceship full of friendly, interracial adults and the moral equivalent of cute puppets (for how far—really—is a Klingon from a Wookie, and both from the Cookie Monster, anyway?). At the same time, though, the *Trek* universe is clearly full of forces that are not just different, but evil, and bent on the destruction of our heroes— who aren't about to take it lying down.

The dirty little secret of the reputedly tolerant and enlightened *Trek*, then, is that it seeks to bring together people of all races, genders, sexual preferences, and even species, primarily so they can join as one to—in the words of the films *Independence Day* and *Space Jam*—"kick some alien butt." The Federation may make peace with the Klingons, but only so they can now work together to blow away those nasty Cardassians.

Let's face it. One can take this utopia thing too far. An action show requires action, i.e., conflict, i.e., some form of good guys versus bad guys. In a recent documentary about *Trek*, convention attendees interviewed talked about what they loved about Roddenberry's universe: tolerance, acceptance—the usual stuff. But they were all dressed like villains: Cardassians, Klingons, Romulans, Borg. (And I'd wager they'd have jumped at the chance to kick some Federation butt.)

Of course, this does not jibe so well with the public persona *Trek* likes to cultivate. The oft repeated party line is that *Trek*'s approach is "Difference isn't necessarily bad." The rock-like Horta in the *TOS* episode "Devil in the Dark" turns out to be just another mother protecting her child. The seemingly threatening Trelane in "The Squire of Gothos," *TOS*, is revealed in the end as just a child himself. The aggression of the nasty race of Gorn in "Arena," *TOS*, turns out to be only self-defense.

All we need do is understand the Other to embrace him. This central ideology of *Trek* was crafted by the party chairman, "the Great Bird of the Galaxy," as friends, coworkers and fans affectionately knew Gene Roddenberry: a self-described humanist, who in his latter years took to giving philosophical pronouncements like a guru on a mountain. Yet contradictions in his philosophy, and in his own life, are echoed in *Trek* itself.

First, let's talk about Gene. Unlike nearly any other television-show producer you could name (and how many *could* you name?), Roddenberry maintained an extremely high public profile. He was, for example, the first TV producer to get his own star on Hollywood's Walk of Fame. The Great Bird came to be closely identified—inseparably so—in the mind of his public with both *Trek* and the vision of a bright tomorrow represented by *Trek*. The Sci-Fi Channel dedicated its launch to the memories of two science-fiction pioneers: Isaac Asimov, and the Great Bird.

Born in 1921, Roddenberry was a World War II combat pilot, a commercial-airline pilot, and, like his own father, a Los Angeles cop. In the early fifties, he freelanced scripts to various TV action series, mostly cop shows and Westerns (including *Dragnet* and *Have Gun, Will Travel*). He began writing full-time, and in 1963 created and produced his own show, *The Lieutenant*, a marine drama. Three years later came *Star Trek*, and the rest is history.

Or mythology—depending on who you ask. The most highly documented facts about Roddenberry are probably the eyewitness accounts of his propensity for inflating his own deeds, taking credit for others' work, and generating his own personal myth. Original *Trek* executive producers Herb Solow and Bob Justman write, in their book *Inside Star Trek: The Real Story*, that

> if a good story or series point came from anyone . . . Gene Roddenberry appropriated it. This subtle "These are all my

ideas" syndrome would eventually affect Gene's relationship with many who worked on *Star Trek.* . . ."[1]

According to Solow and Justman, Roddenberry found a way to profit from every scrap of *Trek,* including adding lyrics to the opening theme (which were never used on the show), just so he could take half the profit from the music of composer Alexander Courage.

Every Trekker has heard the campfire tales of Roddenberry's battles with pigheaded and narrow TV executives and advertisers, beginning all the way back on *The Lieutenant.* The story goes that the ambitious young producer was forced to come up with a way to do intelligent television despite the sponsors or censors: and science fiction was to be the vehicle. (This approach had been pioneered by Rod Serling, who, unlike many of his writer contemporaries in the Golden Age of Television, found a way to remain in the ever more dumbed-down medium without compromising his integrity, using a vehicle he called *The Twilight Zone.*)

But while Roddenberry paints these battles as about moral principle, his former coworkers indicate that any fighting done by the Great Bird was really a matter of personal control. Such efforts to maintain and regain control of *Trek* continued during the entire original series run—and in later years during syndication. For as his post-*Trek* TV and film projects floundered, Roddenberry found himself hailed as a hero among the burgeoning *Trek* convention crowd, and cultivated a cult of personality as a rallying point in a campaign to resurrect *Trek.*

According to his not-so-sympathetic biographer, Joel Engel,

> when he felt it was necessary to the circumstances, Gene Roddenberry reinvented himself. He was the Mutable Man, defining and redefining his belief system and worldview to accommodate his own foibles. His unifying philosophy was that

his desires supported his actions, and his actions were supported by the facts. To remain unencumbered by self-doubt, he continually rationalized his behavior—and padded his resumé. [2]

After *Trek* itself was resurrected and reincarnated more than once, the series *Star Trek: Deep Space Nine* found Commander Benjamin Sisko hailed as "the Emissary"—a figure of embarrassing importance in the local planetary religion. Gene Roddenberry was the original Emissary, but not as reluctant as Sisko. To many religiously zealous *Trek* fans, the Great Bird became the personal embodiment of the show's utopian vision, an elder statesman and representative of a just and compassionate future. One is reminded of the space-alien species, the Organians, from the *TOS* episode "Errand of Mercy," who take on human appearance and endure our primitive ways with a weary, paternalistic nobility.

The reality, as the incredible number of kiss-and-tell *Trek* bios make clear, is much more complicated. Coworkers say Gene Roddenberry was creative, friendly, and charming—but most also speak freely about Roddenberry's darker side. We have mentioned the personal myth-making at the expense of others. There is also no shortage of stories of numerous affairs and adulteries (some thought he was sex-obsessed), a history of substance abuse, and personal conflicts featuring emotional manipulation and pettiness.

The contrast between the utopian *Trek* myth and the all-too-human Gene Roddenberry was striking. "My business dealings with him were always miserable," recalled actor Leonard Nimoy:

> Gene always had an agenda—his own. I didn't see him step up to bat and be the decent honorable humanist that he portrayed himself to be, and that always disappointed me. [3]

As we shall see, this conflict between myth and reality has manifested itself in ongoing inner conflicts on *Trek,* including a behind-the-scenes battle during the production of *The Next Generation.*

THE CONFLICT CONFLICT

Nearly two decades passed between the death of the original *Trek* series and its TV resurrection in *TNG.* In the intervening years, Gene Roddenberry seemed to have embraced his own myth of benevolent omniscience. He told Paramount producer Harve Bennett, who was brought on board to oversee the *Trek* films, that in the *Trek* future, humans have evolved beyond interpersonal conflicts. From a writer's perspective, being asked to make an action show without human conflict is about like being ordered (as the ancient Israelites were ordered by Pharaoh) to make bricks without straw. Bennett screened the original *Trek* episodes to see how Roddenberry had been able to accomplish this miracle: he discovered that he really hadn't. On the old *Trek,* Bennett found, all the human characters seemed every bit as prone to conflict and deadly sins as their twentieth-century ancestors.

And so Roddenberry was quickly marginalized in the production of *Trek* films. Henceforth, he would have to pursue his vision of a transformed humanity in a project made possible by the success of those films, a new TV series: *Star Trek: The Next Generation.*

The 1987 *TNG* debut, "Encounter at Farpoint," puts humanity on trial for a long list of crimes (which space prohibits listing here). To the judge, cosmic genie Q, this defense of a dubious species is made by the wise and moral Captain Jean-Luc Picard: "We've left behind our savage past." Like Clint Eastwood's reformed gunfighter in *Unforgiven,* humans "ain't like that anymore."

Sounds good. But this highly evolved consciousness on the screen was the source of some epochal human conflicts behind the scenes. The *TNG* writers' office could have used a revolving door that first season, amid rumors of what was evidently a very unhappy work environment for creating such a blissfully utopian scheme.

Among several ironies here is the echo of the Roddenberry myth—his constant frustration and battles with arbitrary authorities: networks, sponsors, even the marines (whom he had to make look good in *The Lieutenant* in order to use their facilities). Now it was Roddenberry who was the censor: "There was just no way [a *TNG* writer] could get away with suggesting that the Federation was anything less than a perfect government," says critic James Van Hise in his behind-the-scenes story of *TNG*.[4]

In short, the no-conflict rule drove the writers nuts. Indeed, insanity was the one acceptable means by which humans could be put into conflict with one another. Space madness was the human analog to the many technological bugs and breakdowns that made for *TNG* suspense, devils in the machine. So various forms of insanity spread on the new *Enterprise*, demonstrating, ironically, that for all the evolution, the dark side still lurked not that deeply within.

One episode featured another method for generating conflict without bending the new rules. An evil plot was discovered among Starfleet brass in "Conspiracy," *(TNG)*—originally seen by writer Tracy Torme as comment on the Iran/Contra scandal. The final rewrite of the script, however (and, going back to *TOS*, Roddenberry had irked many a writer by rewriting their scripts), put the blame for the conspiracy not on evil humans but on mind control by alien parasites: the devil made them do it.

Given these constraints, and the fact that you could only do so many space-madness episodes, the writers had no choice but to

make bad guys exclusively of nonhuman aliens. Thus the supposedly enlightened *Trek* was thrown back to the most primordial of
science-fiction conventions: Us against Them. In the *TOS*
episode "The Enemy Within" a transporter accident divides
Captain Kirk into a dark side and a light side; on *TNG*, it was as
if a galaxy-wide transporter malfunction split off the dark side of
humanity and distributed its many elements to Ferengi, Klingons,
Borg, Cardassians, Kazon, and less memorable species.

Continuing our theme of doubleness, we can find an upside
here. Scott McCloud, in his marvelous book *Understanding
Comics*, points out there are two ways of seeing: the realm of the
sensible, with textures and subtle shades, and the *conceptual*, i.e.,
stripped down—*iconic*. This duality of vision is played out in the
history of philosophy, theology, and art, with individuals and
schools picking one side (and usually attacking the other).
McCloud speaks of cartoons, but his ideas apply to myth, genre
films (contemporary myth), and generic television, like *Trek*.
Iconic forms amplify meaning through simplification: they are
less concrete, more abstract—"happy face" versus photograph;
iconic forms are also less particular and more universal. This is
why iconic forms like comics and myth are so popular: they are
more generally understandable, not requiring an understanding of
the particular codes involved in multitextured realistic art. The
plots of humankind's most classic tales can be explained in a sentence: the *Iliad, Beowulf, Frankenstein*, the Gospels. This isn't to
say *Trek* belongs in the same category as these, only that *Trek* is
popular because it plucks many of the same chords.

Since there are two ways of seeing, it would be a mistake to say
that one form—realistic or iconic—is inherently superior to the
other: realistic standards don't apply with iconic art. Characters
are often not real people but symbols of universal traits; stories,

the externalizing of inner conflicts or the literalizing of conceptual battles—a mythic recapitulation of classic human struggles:
generosity versus greed (i.e., the Ferengi), man versus machine
(the Borg). As Chesterton says of cardboard characters in a toy
theater: they may not be so well suited for psychological dramas,
but they're perfect to depict the Last Judgment. This is why
Chesterton could say he learned everything he needed to know
from fairy tales, and why fairy stories are recommended by certain
psychologists and educators: their simplicity makes clear the
nature of our inner struggles, the difference between good and
evil—who to cheer for, who to boo. Stark moral polarities also
satisfy a very human thirst for absolutes. How refreshing to label
something categorically wrong and rise above the murky, modern
quagmire of tainted good guys and criminals who are not really
responsible for their crimes.

Far better, too, to wage mythic struggles within the confines of
genuine myth, rather than mythologizing history—as in the trav-
esty of casting the tale of the American West as good cowboys
versus bad Indians (viz., "The only good Indian is a dead one").
Thus, Cardassians and Ferengi permit the return of *wicked* witches, *bad* wolves, *virtuous* heroes slaying *evil* dragons.

That said, we see an equally obvious downside to good/bad-
guy stories: stereotyping may be unfair and habit forming. Real
life is not always so neatly divided. Questions which should be
answered *both/and* might be made to seem as if they are merely
either/or, or *Us versus Them.* Some people tend to impose a black-
and-white mythic framework on real-life sociopolitical struggles,
absolutizing their own cause and demonizing their opponents.
Indeed, one writer has suggested certain similarities between the
acquisitive Ferengi and the worst of racial stereotypes associated
with the Jewish people. [5] It's one thing to rely on stereotype to

invoke classic moral battles; another to use a straw man, to stack the deck in moral debate. And how much of our "journalism" makes melodrama of current events: good guys versus bad guys, a happy or sad ending: a story.

Furthermore, in *Trek*'s case, identifying humans with "the good" engenders an air of moral superiority, paternalism, and even imperialism in their dealings with nonhuman aliens. Man becomes the measure of all things beyond his own planet as well. Humans are seen as the good guys of the galaxy, whose job it is to civilize the natives; "humanity" becomes a synonym for "moral." The Federation are the white male Europeans of space—a complaint the Klingons make with some force in the film *The Undiscovered Country*, though it goes curiously unanswered.

Meanwhile, as appealing as *TNG*'s utopian scenario seemed, it was impossible to maintain. For, despite claims to the contrary, humanity's dark side shows up constantly on *TNG:* petty ambition, greed, lies, anger, vengeance, madness, lust, jealousy, divorce, mutiny. The most egregious violations of Roddenberry's no-conflict protocol are reserved for nonregulars, including a long tradition of pigheaded and egotistical, even power-mad, guest Starfleet officers—all as required by plot. Picard has an ongoing conflict with his brother, Robert. Riker fights with his ex-captain and is estranged from his own father. So it goes.

The usual inevitable results of such negative emotions, however, are usually held in check on *TNG*, not by any convincingly explained changes in human nature, but by *deus ex Roddenberry*.

Among *Trek*'s most frequently redone plots is the visit to a seemingly utopian planet that turns out to be controlled by some tyrannical computer or semiomnipotent alien posing as God. (Among others: Landru and Vaal in *TOS*, the "god" in "Who Watches the Watchers" in *TNG*, the Caretaker in *Voyager*). These stories usually involve the overthrow of this god (the famous Federation noninterference directive be damned) and a speech to the natives to grow up and learn to get along without any such deus ex machina. Roddenberry hated authority, and especially religious authority; the intent here was obviously a condescending antireligious message. But the overthrown idols in these episodes could just as easily be metaphors for either humanism or Roddenberry's own authority. No doubt those who worked under the Great Bird on *TNG*, including his eventual successors, must have their own legends about battles with his authority, a controlling Vaal that eventually was overthrown.

MUTINY: THE POST- RODDENBERRY REMODULATION OF TREK

It becomes apparent, viewing the evolution of *TNG*, and in the light of the later *Trek* shows, that this strict dichotomy of good human/bad alien became increasingly limiting and uncomfortable to *Trek* writers. Nor can we discount simple guilty conscience from being a factor in what happened next. As a show with a moral agenda, an emphasis on choosing harsh realities over pleasant fantasies, *Trek* could hardly continue to do episodes that seemed to be telling overzealous fans and religious people to "get a life" if they were hiding from real life themselves.

Therefore, in true *Trek* fashion, and following the example of Captains Kirk and Picard facing their own no-win scenarios, the post-Roddenberry producers of *Trek* remodulated, realigned, and reconfigured. "After years of squeezing into Roddenberry's conceptual corset, something had to give. *Star Trek: Deep Space Nine*, the evil twin of the flagship show, provides a narrow escape valve for stories that don't fit the mold." [6]

The third (live-action) *Trek* television series, *Deep Space Nine*, was developed during Gene Roddenberry's last severe physical and mental decline, and premiered after the Great Bird died in 1991. The Creators of *DS9* were Roddenberry's *TNG* heir apparent Rick Berman (a Paramount executive who'd teamed with Gene in 1987) and coproducer Michael Piller. Both were determined to mix things up.

At first the duo took the easy way out, with an end run around Roddenberry's no-conflict rule. They relied again on The Enemy Without: "We decided that the conflict would come from within our characters—but not from the Starfleet humans," said Berman.

> So we brought along Odo, a grouchy security officer, and we brought along Quark, a shifty Ferengi. And we put all these people on Deep Space Nine, which is an inhospitable environment. That was a way of bending Gene's rule without breaking it. [7]

DS9 was to be less black-and-white—in the words of station commander Benjamin Sisko, it would feature "more shades of gray" ("Hippocratic Oath," *DS9*). The station (like the series itself, in a way) was designed by aliens, which in turn meant the new inhabitants would feel like aliens. The station's starship, *Defiant,* was configured for a war that was never fought. Everything was a bit out of whack. Even the coffee was lousy.

But the shades got grayer as this new chapter of *Trek* rolled on. Berman kept a bust of Gene Roddenberry on his desk, which he blindfolded during those discussions, he said, which the Great Bird might not have liked. [8] Indeed, the *DS9* episode "Homefront" was virtually a slap in Roddenberry's blindfolded face. The plot revolved around another conspiracy among Starfleet officers. This time, however, there were no parasites to blame. (The sequel episode, "Paradise Lost," should have been called "Parasites Lost"!) In the future, as we all knew, Earth has evolved into a perfect paradise. No crime, no disease—Gene Roddenberry's utopia. But now, and very quickly, a suspected invasion of shapeshifting aliens shatters all trust among human beings—à la *The Invasion of the Bodysnatchers*. "Homefront" sets human against human, the Federation against itself.

Suddenly made paranoid by the dangerous unreliability of appearances, the Federation begins blood-testing its own citizens to make sure those who *look* like good guys really *are* good guys. As it turns out in this story, the fears of a shape-shifter invasion are blown out of proportion to actual events. The episode's message seems to be a warning about the dangers of paranoia and mass manipulation. Nevertheless, by the episode's end, we see one doesn't have to be a shape-shifter to get on the wrong side of the Starfleet brass. An element of mistrust and intrigue more familiar in our own time has been reintroduced into the future. The possibility of changelings puts all the old certainties in question. Gene Roddenberry's paradise has been lost.

Indeed, despite the no-conflict rule, conflict within the Federation had been steadily building from the start. Kirk was always chafing under Starfleet rules and regulations. And any Starfleet guest star was likely to bring some kind of conflict with him or her on board. Prior to the *DS9* remodulations, these trends collided in the non-Roddenberry-produced film *The Search for Spock*, where the Federation is depicted as a bureaucratic establishment from whom Kirk and his band of good guys must steal a starship. (His opponent is a Federation captain who sports a Prussian riding crop!) Later, in *The Undiscovered Country* (under the Berman regime), a conspiracy among Starfleet officers to thwart peace talks with the Klingons is uncovered.

As Adam and Eve found, once you've bitten the apple and been ejected from paradise, things can only go from bad to worse.

The ongoing *DS9* plot thickened with the addition of a different sort of changelings. During the *TNG* series run, we learned of an old war between the Federation and the once-mighty Cardassian Empire. This subplot developed under Roddenberry's successors, and we learn that the end of hostilities resulted in redrawing of borders that left people on both sides of the conflict unhappy. Thus was introduced into *Trek*'s interplanetary politics an unstable and potentially violent political situation along the lines of Northern Ireland, the Balkans, Beirut, or Palestine. Under the terms of the treaty, certain Federation colonies end up on the Cardassian side of the border. Inevitably, this leads to violence. When the Federation is slow to endanger the treaty by intervening, the colonists are left hanging out to dry. They feel they have no choice but to take matters into their own hands. This puts Federation colonists in conflict with the United Federation itself, which now seems less United than was once supposed. The rebel group goes by the name of the Maquis (the French word for their anti-Nazi resistance in World War II!).

In the *DS9* two-parter "The Maquis," Commander Sisko learns of this in-house split from a sly Cardassian, Gul Dukat, after a mysterious bombing of a Cardassian spacecraft near the station.

SISKO: You know who's responsible?
DUKAT: I do. You are. Oh, not you personally, Commander. I know you to be an honorable man. You're not one to sneak around attaching imploding devices to impulse engines. But, believe it or not, there are those of your brethren who are willing to do such things. Morally superior human beings and other members of the Federation.

A fan-favorite episode of *Trek* was *TOS*'s "Mirror, Mirror," in which the crew encounters in an alternative universe their evil twins. The Maquis are a sort of "mirror" universe right within the Federation. Indeed, Thomas Riker, the double of Will Riker who had been created by a transporter accident in an episode of *TNG*, shows up here, years later, on *DS9* episode "Defiant." In an effort to carve out his own identity, Thomas has joined the Maquis.

Of course, the Maquis are not reflected opposites in the sense of being "bad" to Federation's "good." What makes it all so interesting is that the situation is much more complicated than that. For one thing, it's awful easy to sympathize with their grievances, if not always their methods. The Federation, too, begins to look less like a galactic happy family than an old-fashioned empire beginning to be spread too thin—"imperial overstretch" is the phrase coined by historian Paul Kennedy. Once above reproach, the Federation now finds itself making dubious treaties it can't defend, placing political and military expediency above what it once would have called "the right."

At least James T. Kirk didn't live long enough to see this. (Or was he part of the problem? Stay tuned.)

Meanwhile, perhaps wondering if the gray shades of *DS9* were too dark for some, Berman and Piller designed a fourth incarnation of *Trek* that, while still a part of this changed universe, sought to retain a bit of the black and white from the good old days.

Star Trek: Voyager begins with a series of accidents and coincidences that leave a mixed crew of Maquis and Federation regulars on the same ship, thousands of light years from home. Obviously, the premise is that they must put aside their differences and work together to get home. But in the meantime, they have a splendid opportunity to kick some alien butt. Er, I mean, to explore strange, new worlds in the far-off Delta Quadrant, where an alien being has hurled and so stranded their ship. Since they're so far from Starfleet, its regulations, its problems, not to mention Gene Roddenberry's blindfolded bust, they also have plenty of opportunity to explore differences among themselves.

However, just because the setting became more complex, that didn't necessarily mean the *Voyager* or *Deep Space Nine* stories were always plotted with equal sophistication. Often the baroque new world of *Trek* served as just so much noisy background for the same old deus-ex-machina solutions. *Voyager* especially, for its first few seasons, seemed lost in space in more ways than one, unable to withstand the temptation of cardboard plots and forced endings.

Still, the good guy/bad guy polarities of *Trek* seem to have been shattered—for good and for ill. We now see good and bad humans along with good and bad aliens: mixed together it makes for murky, but often very interesting indeed, shades of gray.

FUNDAMENTALIST TREK

Yet there was a discordant note in *Trek*'s new minor key. For while the two television series are exploring a grey new world, *The Next Generation* cast, now starring in cinematic *Trek*, seems stuck in the world of black and white. *DS9* has all but abandoned the self-righteous pretense of an evolved humanity, and *Voyager* gives it only occasional, if incongruous, lip service. Yet Jean-Luc Picard of the faithful *Enterprise* is the last true believer in Gene Roddenberry's "higher humanity," a faith he still preaches in the films with a starry-eyed, even fundamentalist, fervor.

The second *Next Generation* film, *Star Trek: First Contact*, flirted with some interesting questions put to Picard's character. We are astonished to see the usually low-key and tolerant Captain Picard uncharacteristically carried away with a lust for vengeance against the hated Borg. For a moment, it seemed as if Berman and company were going to carry their revisionism of *Trek* back in time (just like the Borg in the story!) to root up the unexamined assumptions of the last *Trek* for which the creator himself had been personally responsible.

But the boldly going stopped short. *First Contact* turned out to have the same plot as *Bill and Ted's Excellent Adventure*. In both films, a future utopia is threatened when the pivotal moment of the past which created the utopia is erased, and somebody's gotta go back in time to fix things. In Bill and Ted's case, they learn the forming of their garage band, the Wild Stallions, brings about world peace. In *Trek's* case, the Borg go back in time to prevent humanity from crossing that hitherto unidentified Rubicon which divided the barbaric past from Picard's "We're not like that anymore." In hindsight, *Trek* should have probably kept avoiding this particular issue, rather than making the most central moment of human history the centerpiece of their story.

For when the big moment finally comes, the moment that will put an end to millennia of human violence and barbarity and ignorance, we can't help but be disappointed at the dramatic revelation of How They Did It: *they didn't*. It was space aliens. Apparently, all humanity needed to bring about long-sought-after world peace was the knowledge that They Were Not Alone in the Galaxy. While this is a sacred tenet of faith among many devotees of the Search for Extraterrestrial Life, including the late Carl Sagan, anybody who has had much experience with human beings or knowledge of their sordid history is bound to find the idea wholly unconvincing.

The Europeans' discovery that *they* were not alone certainly didn't bring about world peace. On the contrary. They took advantage of their technical superiority and proceeded to provide history with the strongest argument in favor of *Trek's* Prime Directive—noninterference with newly discovered cultures.

In the film, humanity's first contact with aliens was almost a close encounter with the Borg, whose treatment of earth people would have made Cortez's treatment of the Incas seem downright enlightened. Even if humanity had survived such an encounter, the fact that they were Not Alone in the Galaxy would certainly have taken on new meaning. On the other hand, maybe if first contact *had* been the Borg, humanity *would* have pulled together (at least temporarily) for the first time. Our history shows us that nothing unites warring nations like a threat from somebody else. Like the Athenians and Spartans uniting to beat back the Persians, like the thirteen colonies uniting to beat back the British, all the nations of the planet Earth could have finally set aside their differences and, you guessed it: first contact would be with Borg backside.

Technically, *First Contact* doesn't suggest that aliens *save* humanity, but that, just by learning about the aliens' existence, humans were finally able to get it together and save themselves.

But that's not how the scene plays. As the mother ship descends, the people on the ground squint, shielding their eyes. The dust kicks up and becomes a low-hanging fog that swallows the glowing sphere. The crowd of people watch in breathless awe as the door of the ship smoothly—but relentlessly—folds open and becomes a long ramp thrust down into their midst. Bright light beams through the fog from within the vessel. Now a dark figure appears at the top of the ramp, backlit in the doorway, an imposing silhouette. After a brief hesitation, the figure descends—a robed figure, whose face is shadowed in a hood: which he now reaches up to lower! A light dawns in the faces of those watching as the figure is revealed to be—Gene Roddenberry!

Oops. Actually, *First Contact*'s literal god-in-the-machine answer to the central problems of human existence would have made Roddenberry apoplectic. A deus ex machina *anywhere but here*. Think of all the other films where we've watched this scene before, in general spirit if not all the details: *E.T., Close Encounters of the Third Kind,* and others. There's a name for this subgenre of sci-fi movies—the alien-messiah film.

Alien-messiah films combine religious emotions with the trappings of science fiction. There's no question its easy to mix the two up; scientists looking for life Out There do it all the time. Depending on which sort of messiah one looks for, the alien messiah can arrive in triumph, full of power and glory, or be vulnerable, an innocent, morally superior but misunderstood, usually killed by earth men and then resurrected. Perhaps it is the quintessential human act: killing the messiah. Here is one more reason *First Contact* rings false. The arrival of an alien messiah demands that the story move on to the next step: crucifixion.

Others have criticized alien-messiah films for being, despite the feel-good endings, profoundly pessimistic.[9] To long for beings from Out There to save us is to surrender to the notion that we can't solve our own problems—the essence of humanism. Hence, the irony of invoking the alien messiah on the reputedly humanistic *Trek*. Gene Roddenberry never realized it, but the high-water mark of humanism was over even as he embraced it. The Enlightenment idea that if we all had enough facts we'd act reasonably and everything would be okay was scuttled by the fact that, given enough *facts,* that notion proves to be pure hogwash.

It would be interesting to throw Roddenberry back into the current *Trek* mix, both to see how he'd deal with his rebellious progeny and to see if he'd ever admit that much of his vision of the future meant his characters had to live in a human past— philosophically speaking—that already seems outdated in our present. He did express some regret for making his universe so black and white. The Klingons, he once said, should have never been all evil. There's no such thing as a bad race.

Of course, this immediately raises the possibility that there's no such thing as an all-good race, either. If one is free to be good, one is free to be evil. The question remains: how can you make everybody be good without taking away their freedom?

Indeed, the solution to galactic peace offered in one of the most famous alien-messiah movies, *The Day the Earth Stood Still*, is a robotic police force. Klaatu warns the barbaric earthlings to mend their violent ways or the stellar fuzz will lock them up. (Actually, I think it was *blow* them up.) Crude but effective—if you don't mind adopting the tactics of the Borg: creating a peaceful society by robbing individuals of their free will.

An unsatisfactory solution, indeed. But not much more so than *Trek*'s own, which falls about as flat as the silly premise of one of H. G. Wells's worst novels, *In the Days of the Comet*, when a mysterious green gas from the tail of a comet brings about the dawn of a new age, magically causing lions to lie down with lambs.

G. K. Chesterton, both a friend and critic of Wells, wrote about him and his blueprints for utopia in a book called *Heretics:*

> The weakness of all Utopias is this, that they take the greatest difficulty of man and assume it to be overcome, and then give an elaborate account of the overcoming of the smaller ones. They first assume that no man will want more than his share, and then are very ingenious in explaining whether his share will be delivered by motor car or balloon. [10]

Or, in this case, by transporter, matter-antimatter drive, or replicator.

TRAGIC ENDING FOR TREK'S HAPPY ENDING?

Let's briefly sum up some of the things we've discussed in the last couple chapters as a foundation for where we're going next.

The official spin on the *Trek* perspective, the party line as laid down by producers and repeated by both fans and a media accustomed to parroting studio press releases, goes like this: *Trek* is a vision of the future where conflict is replaced by cooperation. One doesn't have to probe this future too deeply, though, to run across inner conflicts which undermine this view.

The public myth of *Trek*, along with the mythology that makes up the fictional *Trek* cosmos, can be traced (at least in part) to the myth-weaving abilities of that shrewd mythmaker, Gene Roddenberry. Like a figure of myth himself, the creator fell under the spell of his own creations. Finding himself the personal embodiment of many *Trek* fans' utopian longings, he accepted the role of emissary of the future. In the short run, this personalizing of *Trek* was key to resurrecting the series after it had been cancelled by NBC and was presumed dead. In the long run, though, the alien-messiah pose became a crippling burden to Roddenberry, affecting his judgment as a creative person. The fundamental need of an action show is action, i.e., conflict; the no-conflict rule stretched *Trek*'s credibility as a utopia to the limit. One also wonders if the pressure to live up to the godlike expectations of being an alien messiah took a personal toll on Roddenberry as well. According to "unofficial" biographer Joel Engel, the Great Bird battled substance abuse his entire career; Engel suggests such problems played a role in shortening his life.

Roddenberry designed his future with maximum freedom for the individual. Nevertheless, he built a superego into *Trek*'s psyche, a guilty conscience that haunts the show today. The moralistic bent of *Trek*, which makes it so attractive to many, means that this tolerant cosmos is intolerant of falsehood. The emphasis on choosing reality over comforting fantasies has helped shape the series, which in the years after the Great Bird's death remodulated itself to portray a more accurate representation of the "human truth" Roddenberry sought. An exception to this these changes, *TNG*, clings to the old black-and-white worldview, to making for a rather clunky effect. Spotlighting the moment of man's moral evolution in *First Contact* was a silly choice of plots, and the film is watchable only if the ending is ignored (just as we must ignore *Trek*'s other deus ex machinas, the fact that everybody in the entire galaxy seems to be able to speak English, and many other problems).

What cannot be ignored is the most undisputable fact in the human record, the negative reality that makes *Trek*'s optimism so compelling: that humans are in need of some kind of—shall we say—reconfiguring. Despite all our advanced technology and ever greater knowledge of the cosmos, people today continue to feel powerless and pessimistic in regard to humanity's ability to solve its own problems. They long for a messiah. Despite all the humanistic talk on *Trek* about faith in man, this very longing for a messiah was the chord *First Contact* sought to strike, and a role that humanist Gene Roddenberry was only too willing to play.

So there are some new Big Questions to consider: Do the flaws of *Trek*'s creator and creation subvert the vision? Does the reintroduction of human vice mean the end of *Trek*'s happy ending? Will the new shades of gray mean the end of *Trek*'s popularity?

Certainly the implications of having all that powerful technology in a cosmos populated by humans like ourselves should give us pause. Here was a problem the old worldview allowed *Trek* to sidestep. The feeling was that not only do humans survive, but they survive because they learn to control themselves and their dark side. If, however, humans in the future are pretty much like humans in the past, yet possess unsurpassed power in the form of advanced technology. . . . Following the implications of this pos-sibility, *Trek* might develop into a pessimistic show indeed.

On the other hand, adding a few shades of gray does not nec-essarily mean *Trek* can no longer be optimistic. As noted, human vice was always present; they just weren't always as honest about it. And there are still plenty of reasons to call *Trek*'s vision of tomor-row optimistic. That humankind survives so far into the future, however it happens, has got to be very optimistic. And for all the gray, there is still a strong element of good guys and bad guys. This notion of good guys defeating, and being morally superior to, bad guys is also optimistic. The idea that moral ideals exist which allow for cheating and guilty consciences seems optimistic, too.

Nevertheless, while the current group of *Trek* producers may not realize it, they have a tiger by the tail. Insisting on making *Trek* more "grown-up" risks raising grown-up questions— including the nature of *Trek* ethics, metaphysics, politics, and social structure. Maybe they'll answer those questions as they do questions of *Trek* physics: with technobabble of one sort or another. Maybe that's all viewers want anyway.

Then again, there have always been shades of gray: that is, *Trek* has never been quite as simple as advertised. There is the illogic of that Vulcan celebration of infinite diversity. And there is the notorious schizophrenia at the center of *Trek*, the inner con-flict that rages at the heart of its key character, Mr. Spock.

3

The Heart Has Its Reasons
(that Reason Thinks "Illogical")

THE IMPORTANCE OF BEING SPOCK

The single most important double on *Trek* is the half-breed science officer from the original series, Mr. Spock. The pointed-eared, green-blooded Spock has a human mother, Amanda; but his father, Sarek, is a native of the planet Vulcan. In *Trek* history, the Vulcans were once a highly emotional race, plagued by violent conflicts and wars, until their civilization nearly destroyed itself—just like Earth right before the happy ending of *Star Trek: First Contact*. Salvation for the Vulcans was not a visit from friendly space aliens, however. The Vulcans saved themselves by renouncing emotion in favor of a rigid, controlled logic: a desperate solution—essentially a castration of the psyche.

So Spock is a cool customer. Despite his human half, he is impatient with and intolerant of human emotion, which he considers "illogical." Yet, like all Vulcans, he must work to keep his

own buried emotions buried. And because of his human background, Spock finds this especially difficult; in fact, his buried
emotions surface from time to time in various ways. There are
moments of Vulcan ritual release, such as when the seven-year
mating instinct, Pon Farr, kicks in (and at such times Vulcans are
shown to be among the most dysfunctional species in the galaxy;
see "Amok Time," *TOS*). And then there is the ever popular space
madness ("The Naked Time," *TOS*), with a variation being alien
mind control phenomena (like the spores in "This Side of
Paradise," *TOS* which cause Spock to actually fall in love). Spock's
"human side" also emerges in less obvious ways, which we will
discuss later in this chapter. For now, let's just say that, to his credit, Spock's effort to suppress all but logical and empirical considerations is never completely successful.

We double-minded human viewers sympathize with Spock's
divided nature because it reminds us of ourselves. Likewise, we
sympathize with what is an all-too-familiar refusal to face the
truth about oneself. Spock's blindness to his lack is humorous,
often poignant. His agonized inner struggle is obviously the
source of his character's appeal; *Trek's* full-blooded Vulcans are
nowhere near as interesting. Tuvok, a *Voyager* crewman, seems a
kill-joy in his coldness and a hypocrite whenever he wavers in it—
not having the convenient excuse of being half human.

But while Spock's inner conflict is both fascinating and familiar, the thing that really makes it germane to our purposes here is
the particular nature of this inner struggle: the pitting of *logic*
against *human*. On reflection, it seems unfair to make *human* the
polar opposite of *logic*. Some of us like to think that being human
actually includes the occasional use of logic. The human Kirk, for
example, is not entirely without logic; we get a glimpse of what a
purely nonlogical Kirk, robbed of his reasoning power, might look

like in "The Enemy Within." Being fully human seems to involve a union of emotions and logic.

With its strict dichotomy of character traits, the Spock/Kirk battle over logic and emotion is reminiscent of the good-guy-versus-bad-guy conflicts we talked about last chapter. Once again, there are pluses and minuses to such clearly defined polarities. On the plus side, the logic/emotion conflict is both exciting and humorous, and it helps us see the different sides clearly in debate. But separating things into stark black and white also causes *Trek* to oversimplify and falsely stereotype some things that would be more truthfully portrayed with some shades of gray.

In this chapter we'll separate the twin concepts of logic and emotion into component parts to show how this particular good guy/bad guy conflict reflects a struggle central to the human condition—especially humans in an age of science—but also how such oversimplification can be both illusory and dangerous.

Let's begin with Spock's Vulcan "logic."

THE COLD EQUATIONS

First of all, the viewer needs to understand that what *Trek* calls logic, especially with reference to Vulcans, encompasses a much broader meaning than what is usually understood by that term.

According to the usual non-*Trek* definition, logic is not a way of life but a method of reasoning—less concerned with the content of an argument than its form. It's like a computer: if you put garbage in, you'll get garbage out. As Captain Janeway warns Tuvok: "You can use logic to justify almost anything. That's its power and its flaw" ("Prime Factors," *VOY*). Faulty data can lead to incorrect—and what some might call immoral, yet perfectly logical—conclusions. Spock sometimes claims—quite illogically—

that simply disposing of emotion will eliminate the need for violence ("Dagger of the Mind," *TOS*). Yet elsewhere, Spock admits that even Vulcans are quite capable of killing, so long as logic dictates the need ("Journey to Babel," *TOS*). Indeed, among the Maquis are Vulcans convinced of the logic of rebelling against the Federation. *TNG*'s two-parter "The Gambit" shows certain Vulcans using their logic to justify racism.

We've talked about rules and prime directives: of physics, of drama, and of a less definable, more "human" kind. The Prime Directive of logic is the law of noncontradiction, which can be stated as follows—more certainly than any law of science: Contradictions are never true. For example, we know (with absolute certainty) that the following statements can never be true:

1. Extraterrestrial life exists and extraterrestrial life
   does not exist.
2. A bachelor is a married man.

   Or, to put it another way, "A" cannot be equal to "non-A."

The logical corollary of this definition of logic is the positive expression of the law of noncontradiction, namely that the denial of contradictions is always true.

1. It is false that extraterrestrial life exists and that
   extraterrestrial life does not exist.
2. It is false that a bachelor is a married man.

What's so important about logical thinking is that cheating in this case, that is, permitting violations of the law of noncontradiction, would mean that truth and falsity no longer count for anything. And if nothing can be meaningfully asserted as true or false, there's no point in continuing our discussion about *Trek*— or anything else. The very possibility of communication depends on the truth of the law of noncontradiction.

In sum, logic is about checking arguments by this kind of rule to determine the validity of the argument. Logic is a tool, not a philosophy; it is no more a way of life than is a screwdriver.

On the other hand, what is known on *Trek* as Vulcan logic seems to be about more than just the form of an argument; Vulcan logic also seems to incorporate its own content, including certain foundational statements—presuppositions—which are, in fact, beyond the limited jurisdiction of the law of noncontradiction.

If we had to use the name *logical* to describe this particular perspective, we might say that it is *Trek*'s own version of a real-life school of philosophy, logical positivism. Strictly speaking, logical positivism is a linguistic thesis concerned not with identifying logical or illogical but rather meaningful or meaningless statements. This philosophical perspective is rooted in another, called empiricism, which has its own Prime Directive: the verification principle, which includes both a measure for form, like the law of noncontradiction, and a measure for content, which is tied to observation or theoretical terms summarizing observations. For example, while logic (that is, the tool for checking the validity of arguments) might be utilized to good purpose in a discussion about God, logical positivism would insist that any statement about God is meaningless, since He cannot be observed empirically—in other words, by conventional scientific measures; including quantification and predictability. Spock would probably render the same opinion in his Vulcan version of logical positivism by saying that statements about God are illogical.

On Earth, logical positivism has fallen out of favor among logical thinkers as they have realized that its foundational commitment to the priority of sense evidence is itself not provable by sense evidence. Likewise, empiricism, if extended into a worldview—what we might call hard empiricism, taking the prefix from our hard SF friends—is not a conclusion of logic, but rather a foundational proposition, a philosophical presupposition: All knowledge is gained through our senses. In other words, "Seeing is knowing," or, somewhat loosely, "Seeing is believing." This presupposition is very similar to the bias of those fans of hard SF who claim to accept only reasonable extrapolations from known science. But following such exclusive claims to their logical conclusions means dispensing with those human values which are not reasonable extrapolations from science, including human rights, dignity, meaning, and notions of right and wrong. In this way, says one critic of the genre, the hardness of hard SF risks repelling its own fans by becoming hard-heartedness.[1]

This may be seen in that classic example of hard SF, "The Cold Equations," by Tom Godwin. In this 1954 short story, a young stowaway on a spaceship upsets the ship's mathematically precise weight-fuel-deceleration balance. The only way the ship can complete its mission—delivering medicine to plague victims—is to jettison the stowaway into space. So far the predicament is like the one in the 1950 film *Destination Moon*, where the only solution seems to be to leave a crewman behind to die on the moon. In that film, however—at the last moment, of course—the spacemen on the moon come up with a way to solve the problem and get everyone home safely. Godwin's short story refuses to take the easy deus-ex-machina exit, and makes good on its premise. The cut-throat efficiency of "the cold equations" of physics is what kills the stowaway, "with neither hatred nor malice"—it's all so perfectly logical. While it may be refreshing to see someone face a problem that is not immediately solvable by technobabble for a change, the solution seems hardly satisfying—or human.

A *Trek* episode which uses the *Destination Moon*/"Cold Equations" idea is "Galileo Seven" *(TOS)*, wherein the logic-versus-human conflict is played at maximum volume. In this story, Spock—on his first command—is forced by circumstances to crash-land a shuttlecraft with a small crew on a hostile planet. Atmospheric conditions make it impossible for the orbiting *Enterprise* to locate the missing away team. Meanwhile, after some calculations, Spock is able to determine that the shuttle may be able to launch and reach orbit, but only if somebody is left behind to fend for themselves among giant ogre-type aliens. When a shocked crewman sarcastically suggests the crew draw lots to select this poor somebody, Spock insists the choice will be his alone, and "through logical means." This sort of logic seems cold indeed to the human crew. Behind Spock's back, the crewman suggests all is not right with Spock's head. "Not his head," replies Dr. McCoy, an old antagonist of Spock. "His heart."

And here's where the real battle rages: the war between head and heart, the tension between objective knowledge—"out-there," measurable-by-science knowledge—and subjective knowledge—"in-here" knowledge, intuition, gut feeling.

> SPOCK: Your illogical approach to chess does have its advantages at times.
> KIRK: I prefer to call it inspired. ("Charlie X," *TOS*)

Such ongoing repartee is the "Who's on First?" routine of *Trek:* Kirk saves the day with an impulsive action; Spock is left shaking his head. In the *TOS* episode "The Tholian Web," Kirk is presumed dead, and tells Spock in a prerecorded "last order" to "use every scrap of knowledge and logic to save the ship—but temper your judgment with intuitive insight." And if Spock can't find this in himself, says the message, he must seek it in McCoy.

Dr. McCoy, if anything, is even more illogical and emotional than Kirk. The good doctor really gets the sparks flying in debate with Spock.

> McCOY: Mr. Spock, you're the most cold-blooded man I've ever known.
> SPOCK: Why, thank you, Doctor. ("Court Martial," *TOS*)

In the climax to "Galileo Seven," McCoy is delighted when Spock relies on what seems to be gut feeling to save the day. Spock, of course, refuses to admit his action was anything but logical.

Yet McCoy—and the viewer—knows otherwise. We all know Spock "cheats" in his hard, cold positivism—just as surely as *Trek* cheats its happy endings (and, in case you're wondering, in "Galileo Seven" Spock is rescued from making any "Cold Equations"–type decision by another "lucky" turn of events.)

Likewise, any hard science fiction worth reading cheats at one level or another, when it introduces "illogical" human values—those things which cannot be extrapolated from science, stuff like the rules of good narrative and notions of ethical norms. Indeed, as we shall see, even Spock, in his later life, begins to be honest with himself about the limitations of his logic and opens himself to the possibility of a different kind of knowledge.

Nevertheless, *Trek* generally keeps the argument going. On *Voyager*, the shtick is rerun by the Talaxian Neelix and the Vulcan Tuvok.

> TUVOK: Your instincts were correct. However, one day your intuition will fail. And you will finally understand that logic is primary above all else. Instinct is simply another term for serendipity.
> NEELIX: And one day, Mr. Vulcan, I'll get you to trust your gut.
> TUVOK: That is doubtful. ("Rise," *VOY*)

Trek's unresolved conflict between (to put it another way) left brain and right brain, shows up not only between Vulcans and less logical species, but also in the double-minded approach *Trek* takes to science fiction. As noted last chapter, Gene Roddenberry shared both the hard SF fan's reverence for science and a scorn for what both defined (albeit somewhat differently) as fantasy. Yet Roddenberry understood that the most important elements of humanity don't reduce to cold equations. When somebody on *Trek* needs to sum up a significant moment or person, they don't reach for their pocket calculator—they quote Shakespeare. How often has James Kirk—and even more so Jean-Luc Picard, in that beautifully modulated voice of his—stood on the bridge of the *Enterprise* gazing into the stars on the ship's viewscreen upon the conclusion of an adventure, and offered up some fitting coda from out of the pages of *Hamlet* or another classic? An entire issue of the scholarly SF journal *Extrapolations* was devoted to *Trek*'s use of Shakespeare. The main thing we need to know about *Trek*'s use of the Bard is that Shakespeare is *Trek*'s poetic shorthand for "the best that has ever been said or thought," a metaphor for the humanities.

So *Trek* opposes the cold-equations way of seeing the world with an ideal they give the name *human*. Gene Roddenberry called himself a humanist. This term, like many thrown around carelessly on *Trek*, means different things to different people. In his case, though, what the Great Bird meant was that he had aligned himself with a loose consensus of ideas held by advocates of what has been called secular humanism. In the eyes of the secular humanists, their philosophy combined "the best that has ever been said or thought" with the conclusions of science. Secular humanism is a man-centered philosophy which views religion as regressive superstition and man's increasing mastery over nature (by means of science and technology) as the surest way to progress.

Gene Roddenberry's much-trumpeted emphasis on human values on *Trek* would seem to make his own show's frequent cheating via technobabble solutions to plot problems more than

just a violation of the conventional rules of drama: it is a betrayal
of his own highest ideals. In the worst examples, *Trek* conflict is
reduced to a war of technical abstractions, one bit of gibberish
counteracting another. By contrast, says author James Blish,

> A good SF story is a story with a human problem and a human
> solution, which would have not happened at all without its sci-
> ence content.[2]

This seems simple enough; but we shall examine later in this
chapter how secular humanism has of late begun to short-circuit
over its own internal illogic, that is to say, the not-so-self-evident
question of what makes any problem or solution "human."

But before we can do that, let's stay with Spock and give the
old logic-versus-human conflict further context in Earth history.

A BRIEF HISTORY OF MODERNITY

Trek fans know all about reruns, and sequels, and
episodes that are little more than rehashings of old episodes. Well,
the struggle that *Trek* plays as a tug-of-war between logic and
emotion is in many ways just a rerun of what has been perhaps the
central conflict of the history of Western philosophy. This conflict
goes all the way back to when Plato declared his famous war of the
philosophers (logic) against the poets (emotion).

Perhaps Gene Roddenberry had all that in mind when he sat
down to create the character of Spock. What is more likely,
though, is that he just wanted an alien on his starship—to remind
viewers they were watching a space show. "Probably half-martian"
is how the character of Spock was described in an early series proposal.[3] Rather than being cold and logical, the Spock of the pilot
and early episodes of *Trek* smiles and is generally high-strung.
The cool demeanor originally belonged to another character:

Number One, the ship's first officer, played by Majel Barrett (Gene Roddenberry's then mistress, later his wife). The story goes that when the network insisted on changes in the developing show, Roddenberry kept Spock by giving up Number One—and then passed her rigid personality on to the Vulcan. Leonard Nimoy, however, has said it wasn't until he was shooting the series' first regular episode, when a director advised him to say a particular expression—"Fascinating"—in an emotionally detached way, that he finally understood the character of Spock.

Over the years, Spock continued to evolve, often accidentally (dare we say it—intuitively?), but with increasing self-consciousness on the part of many thoughtful collaborators. Eventually, the character became something of an archetype, a symbol striking deep chords in our cultural memory. For TV audiences, Spock's stature nearly approaches that of an earlier exponent of pure logic, the great Sherlock Holmes. As with Holmes, the character of Spock transcended the insight or original intent of his creator to become a metaphor—not for a single trait, but of a characteristically schizophrenic age.

Indeed, the age just now ending, the modern age, is the most striking example from human history of this classic opposition of logic and emotion. The story of how that conflict emerged from an even earlier historical period which we know as the Enlightenment is also crucial to our understanding of Spock.

As we noted earlier, the history of planet Earth parallels that of the planet Vulcan. With the dissolution of medieval unity after the Reformation, Western Europe was the scene of bloody religious (and political-disguised-as-religious) wars. Battles raged over whose measure for human values was the true one.

The project of postmedieval Enlightenment thinkers was to find a new basis for political and social order, a way to ground all

knowledge—including ethics and other human values—in a neutral framework, something beyond debate. And what all people
have in common, some reasoned, was their humanity: the "neutral" framework for human society would be human experience.
Man was to be the measure of all things, and man's senses the
basis for divining reality—that is, Seeing is believing.

This is not to say that the shift to empiricism was solely
responsible for the scientific revolution which followed. (Actually,
as we'll note in the next chapter, some thinkers maintain Western
science arose only because of its particular religious context.)
Nevertheless, the empirical method, when applied to nature,
forced nature to give up many of her secrets. Natural phenomena,
hitherto shrouded in mystery and myth, were now observed and
understood—and utilized. The scientific method sparked an
explosion of discoveries and inventions.

At the same time, these practical successes distracted attention
from the fact that the Enlightenment's allegedly neutral philosophical framework, far from being unified, was a forked road: the
notion of man as measure was two-headed from the start. One
head, as you've already guessed, was the left brain: knowledge
equals arithmetic. All that really mattered, it was supposed, was
that which was quantifiable, measurable, logical. And, as we just
noted, this approach yielded tangible results. But an unintended
result was a growing conflict between man and mathematical
measure: things like human rights and human dignity cannot be
observed, predicted, quantified or weighed. Nearly everything
that makes our species human comes from a set of values beyond
the apprehension of science.

To be ruled by the scientific method alone was to invite the
dehumanization of man. To borrow a picture from culture critic
Francis Schaeffer, it was as if the Enlightenment had attempted

to erect the edifice of humanity as a two-story house, with the natural world at the bottom and human values on top. The problem was, if humanity was a part of nature anyway, how could any part of man's view of himself be held above nature? The floor gave way. Humanity crashed from its lofty position to the basement, sank back into nature, became just another cog in what Enlightenment thinkers described as one vast, cosmic machine.

Here is that central anxiety of science fiction: the fear of dehumanization, the fear of being an "I" reduced to a "thing" or an "it." Such fear isn't merely the animal fear of death; it is the sentient being's fear of erasure, of having one's individual identity wiped out, of being jettisoned by the cold equations, of being assimilated by the Borg. Along with other dualities, then, the duality of Spock embodies humanity's unresolved ambivalence regarding science and the scientific method. The question is still unresolved today: is science our savior or our destroyer?

The implications of such a logical view of man (as machine) were not lost on sensitive persons during and after the Enlightenment. The dehumanization of humanity was resisted by a philosophical Maquis, a counterrevolution called the Romantic Movement. Here, poets and philosophers joined together against the hard empiricists in defense of traditional human values: the value of the individual, the priority of the personal over the mechanical, all based on a second mode of knowledge—intuition, a means of grasping aspects of human reality that strict positivism overlooked.

What became an ongoing (and sometimes violent) seesaw between reason and romanticism formed the schizophrenia of modernity.

This tension is played out on *Trek* in any number of ways: Kirk versus Spock, Spock versus Spock, and Gene Roddenberry versus himself. The antireligious, pro-science Roddenberry placed himself in the humanist tradition—with its allegiance to reason and the scientific method—but he was also a hopeless romantic when it came to human values; he believed with Pascal that "the heart has its reasons that reason does not know." In this way, the Great Bird's "Spockian" split was no different than that of his fellow humanists, who had to become romantics of one sort or another in order to retain their humanity. And like Spock, neither Roddenberry nor his fellow humanists were always willing to admit the existence of their nonlogical halves.

Meanwhile, at the very moment Roddenberry was introducing the term *humanism* to a generation of television viewers, the battle raged at the university level between humanists and various other scholars who attacked the fundamental illogic of the humanist dual insistence on empiricism and a particular set of values. These antihumanists weren't antihuman, or even antihumanist in the sense of being against the long tradition of celebrating man's accomplishments and possibilities. What they were "anti" was "ism"—what they saw as a cult of humanism, which they said sought to replace one form of religious orthodoxy with another.

To understand the antihumanist side of the debate, we'll have to apply some more of the left brain to the right brain; that is, we will continue in our examination of what *Trek* means by opposing logic with emotion. A good place to pick up on that would be the film where Spock began to question the logic of his "logic."

HOW DO YOU SOLVE A PROBLEM LIKE SPOCK?

The movie *Star Trek: The Motion Picture* has been referred to as the Motionless Picture. And it is true; for various reasons we needn't get into here, this initial *Trek* film turned out to be much slower paced than *Trek*-starved fans were expecting. But despite the film's reputation for going nowhere, *TMP*, at least in one key way, went boldly where even *Trek* had not yet gone before. Back when they first decided to reconfigure *Trek* from a small- to a large-screen artform, Leonard Nimoy has said, the producers were determined to do something, well, large. And what could be larger for *Trek*, one wonders, than curing Mr. Spock?

TMP is about the head/heart split, and healing the breach.

The film was released ten years after the final episode of the TV *Trek* first aired. *The Motion Picture* was directed by Robert Wise, who also directed *The Sound of Music*, and both stories hinge on the same plot point: *TMP* opens with Spock on his home planet, having left Starfleet and human society to purge himself of all emotions in the barren wastelands of Vulcan. This is much the same thing Maria did when she ran away from the complicated challenges of the Von Trapp family and escaped to the austere simplicity of the abbey. But Spock, in the final stages of shedding his humanity, is told by his elders—just like Maria— to climb every mountain and ford every stream: that is to say, he is told his destiny was not here, but Out There.

Spock returns to the *Enterprise* just as his old starship and crew are chasing down a deadly space entity headed toward Earth. Spock puts on a rocketpack and goes out and "mind melds" with the creature, which almost destroys both his right and his left brain. Yet this encounter is a major turning point for Spock; for, in joining with V'Ger, he looks into a mirror at himself. "V'Ger," says Spock, on his return, "has knowledge which spans this universe." A state to be envied by most Vulcans, one would think. "And yet, with all its pure logic, V'Ger is barren, cold. . . ." (As in "Cold Equations"?) "No mystery. No beauty."

In other words, V'Ger has already achieved what Spock has been striving for his entire life. V'Ger is his "brother," Spock confesses. "As I was when I came aboard, so is V'Ger now. Empty. Incomplete. Searching." Spock draws a conclusion we never could have predicted: "Logic and knowledge are not enough."

SPOCK: No hope. No answers. It's asking questions.
KIRK: What questions?
SPOCK: Is this all that I am? Is there nothing more?

These are serious questions: the biggest anybody could ask. And how profound, and profoundly poignant, for the lifelong defender of logic to finally face his own incompleteness. Whatever its flaws, then, *TMP* asks the best and most honest questions of *Trek*.

In seeing himself in V'Ger, Spock experiences a life-changing breakthrough: V'Ger convinces him that the path of pure logic leads away from the wholeness he seeks; so he adjusts his course, surrendering to what he began the film rejecting: emotion. "I should have known," he says. Known what? asks Kirk. Spock grasps his friend with an unashamed, never-before-seen warmth and looks into his eyes. "Jim," he says. "This simple feeling"— friendship—"is beyond V'Ger's comprehension."

The climax of *TMP* involves a sexual-spiritual union between the machine V'Ger and organic emotional beings: V'Ger takes the form of a female crew member and then joins with a human male to create a new life-form. This unification would seem an appropriate conclusion to a story about the healing of the Spockian split—much as the union of Kirk's two halves in "The Enemy Within" healed his own split. The message is classic *Trek*: wholeness requires uniting abstract facts with human values.

So a film which began in the wasteland of logic ends in a warm glow of emotion. But lost in that effects-laden glow, however, is one particular "abstract fact" which, if noticed, might threaten to be the pooper of this party. That (apparently uninvited) fact is this: *Trek*'s marriage of right and left brain is actually a shotgun wedding. It is true that *TMP* features a unification of logic and emotion: but it is important to ask what kind of unity this is. In other words, while the message of *TMP* feels good, one still wonders if it is logical?

What if, for example, the abstract facts of the universe include the abstract fact that humanity is ultimately meaningless, and human values have no real basis except in the preferences of certain humans? And if we marry logic with nonlogic, do we lose the ability to discern the truth or falsity of what we believe?

Spock certainly seems to have lost his ability to explain what he believes. In a scene following his encounter with V'Ger, Spock does something we've never known him do before, at least not without being under the influence of some space madness: he weeps—for V'Ger, he says. Doctor McCoy, his old nemesis in all those logic/emotion debates, asks Spock if he's found the answer that V'Ger lacks. Spock says nothing in reply. Yet it is clear that something about what Spock believes has changed. This "crying" scene was not included in the release print of the film, nor in the novelization of *TMP* penned by Gene Roddenberry. Maybe the producers got cold feet about making such irrevocable changes. (The scene is, however, included in the video release.)

Yet even without the scene, it is clear something has changed. Because events of subsequent *Trek* films involve even more traumatic changes for Spock, this confrontation with his human side is lost somewhat in later events. Nevertheless, in the sixth *Trek* film, *Star Trek: The Undiscovered Country*, we have this intriguing moment when Spock lectures a Vulcan cadet:

SPOCK: You have to have faith that the universe will unfold as
it should.
VULCAN CADET: Is that logical?
SPOCK: Logic, logic, logic. Logic is the beginning of wisdom,
not the end.

Again, Spock doesn't elaborate on what comes next, after logic.
Perhaps this lack of an explanation is part of the point. There
comes a point when objective, propositional knowledge is not
enough: V'Ger went across the galaxy seeking not more facts, but
a personal relationship with his creator, an experience.

But where does that leave us in our effort to understand *Trek*?
Can we grope toward some kind of verbalization of where it is
that Spock goes when he goes beyond logic—of what he means
when he tells the cadet to have faith? Are these questions related
to the intuition Kirk (and Gene Roddenberry) is always drawing
upon to find those so-called human values? In pursuit of these
questions, we move into *Trek*'s real Undiscovered Country.

TO INFINITY AND BEYOND

The cold equations are easy to understand—hence
their appeal: they're cut, dried, systematized, and controlled. And
it's just as easy to understand the many complaints against the
cold equations: they're cut, dried, systematized, and controlled.

What is not so easy to fathom is the alternative to *logic*, what
Trek calls emotions. Logic, then, would dictate that our next order
of business is unpacking this term. For just as it is important to
know what *Trek* means by *logic*, we also need to know what *Trek*
is talking about when using the word *emotions*—especially since
that is another term with multiple meanings.

Emotion might be defined by some people as *feeling*. That
won't do us any good here; the words are interchangeable. Both

feelings and *emotions* can refer to the same multiplicity of definitions. Let's begin with *mood*—what we might call the "color" of
experience: psychological states we label with words like *happy,
sad, angry,* and *afraid.* These feelings are, according to a psychol-
ogist friend of mine, "biochemical responses to our beliefs about
events." And if *moods* was the only definition of *feelings* or
emotions, one could easily see why Vulcans would have no patience
with humans who are guided by them. It does seem foolish to
hold reason hostage to mood.

On the other hand, *feeling* refers to things besides mood.
There's that sense of doing an act "with feeling"—being personally involved as opposed to detached and dispassionate. This sort
of feeling doesn't seem intrinsically illogical: to make it so would
imply a foundational value of cool abstraction for its own sake.

People also tend to equate the notion of *to feel* with *to apprehend,*
or *to know*: a direct perception of truth which seems to involve the
head less than the heart or gut. Not just romantics, but humans in
all times have recognized (and fought about) this second mode of
knowledge: traditionally, its defenders would say this inner "sense"
is not irrational (against reason) but nonrational (a capacity that is
different than reason). As we have noted, it is impossible to
measure things like morality and beauty with mathematics or other
scientific means: we apprehend. Such knowledge includes a gut
feeling for practical choices ("I've got a bad feeling about this
place.") but also a sense for beauty and a sense for moral choices, an
understanding or knowledge of *ought* or *ought not.* In his book, *The
Metaphysics of Star Trek,* Richard Hanley makes a distinction
between what he calls higher and lower emotions. According to
Hanley, both the android Data and the Vulcan Spock—despite
what they may say about their own incapacity for emotion—
evidence higher emotions as a basis for thought and value.

For humans, the connection of all our emotions, even those we may call higher, to our physiological state makes all this business even more problematic. We "feel" hungry. We "feel" pain or pleasure. We "feel" attracted to someone. "Love" has come to be synonymous for both an emotional state and a physical act. As Vulcans would be very quick to point out, our feelings—whether knowledge, mood, or desire—are easily confused. Scrooge may be wrong in his initial dismissal of the ghost of Jacob Marley, but he is certainly right in his general suspicion that such emotional experiences might be attributed to indigestion.

Obviously, boiling down a multitude of meanings into a single term, whether *logic* or *emotion*, can lead to confusion. A good example of this is "Galileo Seven," with its oversimplified contrast of black (logic) against white (emotion). In this episode, *logic* refers to *a tool for reasoning* (that is, the law of noncontradiction), and also to *Trek*'s version of logical positivism, a belief in the supremacy of science. The term *logic* also seems to cover *a tendency toward ruthless efficiency*—which would only be a conclusion of true logic if the presupposition was, Living beings always matter less than accomplishing the task at hand (a presupposition, sadly, which many people seem to hold). Likewise, the term *emotion* is found to be working multiple duty: *emotion* refers to the whole gamut of meanings we discussed above: mood, a means of moral knowledge, compassion, and a "gut feeling" for knowing the best strategy.

Such confusion of terms makes it difficult for the viewer to understand what *Trek* has to say about either logic or emotion.

So we are left to wonder: Is the constant honoring of emotion evidence that *Trek* humans make choices based on their mood of the moment? Or do they utilize their emotions to apprehend moral realities which are real, but beyond the scope of positivism?

Likewise, when Spock admits the limitations of his logic in *TMP*, is he questioning the sufficiency of scientific positivism? If so, he need not necessarily dispense with logic—for, indeed, it is logic that should drive him to question the supremacy of positivism. Or is Spock's rejection of logic a rejection of the law of noncontradiction? In other words, is *TMP* about Spock's conversion from logic to existentialism?

Here we come to one more term that ties up a bundle of meanings, a term perhaps intimidating to those who don't fling it around at cocktail parties. Yet a general idea of what existentialism represents is key to understanding the questions *TMP* raises.

First of all, there is that sense in which the term existential might be universally applicable by all human beings in all ages: it suggests the idea of concrete experience of living versus abstract data, i.e., "cold equations." For example, if V'Ger collects only objective data about a person (height, weight, eye color), he can never realize the subjective experience of friendship. And so for Spock to likewise divest himself of all but his impersonal logic would mean he must forever give up personal relationships. This desire for personal contact is what draws humans into space, what impels V'Ger to seek its creator. This distinction here may be described as the difference between head knowledge and heart knowledge: Spock's dramatic encounter with V'Ger has taught him this, not just in his head (intellectually), but in his heart, i.e., existentially.

At the same time, there is another, more specific, understanding of the term *existentialism*, which has to do with the tragic predicament of post-Enlightenment man. Despite all the initial optimism born of absolute confidence in the scientific method, the road of scientific positivism has led to pessimism. For no scientific ground has been found for human meaning, value, dignity, rights, or the validity of love. Like V'Ger, the scientific quest for knowledge has not turned up any objective fact that would support any of these human values. Many who accept the conclusions of scientific materialism, yet can't live without human values, feel they have no choice but to discard rational thinking and make a nonrational "leap of faith."

Let me give you an example of what I mean.

In the fourth volume of C. S. Lewis's *Chronicles of Narnia* fantasy series, *The Silver Chair,* the evil queen of Underland works an enchantment on her captives in an effort to convince them that Underland is the whole of reality—that all their experiences in Narnia, the world above, were but a dream. But even as Puddleglum, that bold marsh-wiggle, falls under this spell, he steps forward and declares that what he has just been told by the witch is just a "made-up" world—the one with "trees and grass and sun and moon and stars"—is vastly superior to the dank, darkness of the "real" world in which they find themselves. Therefore, says Puddleglum, "I'm going to live as like a Narnian as I can even if there isn't any Narnia."

Along with the idea of concrete as opposed to abstract living, then, existentialism can also be the determination to "live like a Narnian," even if there is no Narnia. Existentialists seek to construct subjective meaning in a universe where science has found there is no objective meaning; they determine to live as a human being, as though that term still meant all the lofty and meaningful things it once did, even though logic and the conclusions of scientific positivism insists otherwise. Obviously, holding contradictory notions, Human beings have intrinsic value and meaning and Human beings do not have intrinsic value and meaning, is a violation of the law of noncontradiction. Yet the existentialist chooses to break this law in order to keep a "higher" one: they save humanity, by cheating: and at great cost: by discarding the idea of truth. Given the choice between knowledge and love, then, Spock chooses love; his only escape from the logic of positivism is by abandoning logic—trading science for fiction.

Many who have found themselves facing a similar no-win scenario have looked to existentialist philosophers like Karl Jaspers, who staked everything on a nonrational "final experience," which he said would give meaning to life. Such experiences, being existential, are said to be inherently impossible to explain. Perhaps Spock's cataclysmic encounter with V'Ger was his "final experience—an experience that, while it became for him a touchstone of meaning, was impossible for Spock to verbalize either to himself or others: this might account for Spock's failure to answer Dr. McCoy's question of whether he'd found his answer.

On the other hand, when Spock tells the Vulcan cadet to "have faith that the universe will unfold as it should," it sounds as if he has found some kind of explanation, one that seems to point to a belief in Ultimate Purpose, in turn suggesting a conviction of more than blind evolutionary forces at work in nature, of a sense of "fate" or "mind" behind cosmic processes. Given what we know of *Trek*, this seems unlikely. Rather, it would appear Spock speaks of a more existentialist faith, a blind leap, an absurd will to optimism: don't worry, says Spock; be happy.

In a later chapter we'll examine in detail the astonishing revival of faith and religion on *Trek* that occurred after Roddenberry's death. For now, let's just note that the sort of faith depicted in, for example, the *Voyager* episode "Sacred Ground" seems to be less a conventional religious faith, or even a faith that "the universe will unfold as it should," than it is a faith in faith. In that episode, the "logical" and "scientific" Captain Janeway encounters an alien religion and experiences her own sort of conversion experience; she learns, apparently, that salvation comes not merely by going beyond reason but by defying reason. A big problem for someone who's accepted this kind of faith is that there's no reasoning with them about it. On *Deep Space Nine,* Constable Odo points out contradictions between sense evidence and Major Kira's similar faith. She replies, "That is the thing about faith. If you don't have it, you can't explain it. And if you do, no explanation is necessary" ("Ascension," *DS9*).

The retreat from scientific explanations into quasi-religious talk seems an odd twist for a show founded on Enlightenment confidence in science. But, as we shall see, such a development represents only the logical unfolding of a universe that is premised on the priority of human values over the cold equations of physics. And for what is still regarded as a secular humanist show, *Trek* seems less and less shy of late about the religious overtones. Perhaps it comes with the cosmic setting: Carl Sagan's materialist *Cosmos* show featured organ music, churchlike sets, and an evangelistic delivery. And we've already noted the religious emotions surrounding the quest for extraterrestrial life in expectation of an alien messiah.

What we haven't mentioned yet is that the alien messiahs who provoke peace on Earth in *First Contact* turned out to be, of all species, Vulcans—an unexpected plot point in the apparently still-evolving *Trek* backstory. To learn now, after all these years, that it was mankind's "first contact" with the logical Vulcans which transformed Earth from dystopia into utopia was a surprise—and a disappointment: the alien messiah effect works best as a confrontation with the Ultimate Mystery, and our old familiar friends the Vulcans are no longer alien enough. And how disorienting to pin a feel-good ending on this emotionless race.

Perhaps in the same way science fiction provides a clandestine way for sophisticated moderns to breathe the air of Faerie, religious overtones and alien messiahs allow us to experience religious emotions under the cover of science as well. In any case, the feel-good fog certainly covers a multitude of contradictions.

Yet *Trek* needn't be so shy about covering contradictions. If *Trek* has rejected the law of noncontradiction and leaped beyond logic, how would anybody be able to identify a contradiction anymore anyway? This is certainly one way to solve the inner conflict between head and heart: eliminate one's ability to discern the split. Spock began *TMP* by trying to purge himself of heart; perhaps the moral of that story is that one must instead be purged of mind: i.e., "no brains, no headaches."

Most people can overlook a few contradictions here and there. In the *TNG* episode "Unification" there's a marvelous scene featuring, for the first and only time, both of *Trek*'s most popular half-humans. The Vulcan Spock and the android Data exchange perspectives on their differing aspirations: Spock's desire to rid himself of his humanity, Data's longing to be human. The odd thing is, although "Unification" aired within weeks of the release of *The Undiscovered Country*, a film in which Spock spoke almost scornfully of logic, this TV-*Trek* Spock acts as if the personal transformation begun in *The Motion Picture* and alluded to in *The Undiscovered Country* never happened; the Spock of *TNG*'s "Unification" is as anti-emotion as the ultralogical Spock of old. Such a contradiction shows that, despite the official story that this particular episode finally "united" *Trek*'s old and new casts, a wide disparity existed between the respective visions of the keepers of cinematic and TV *Treks*.

Before we dance on the broken-down wall between A and non-A, we may want to pause and consider certain consequences of too much unity. We'll examine this often sinister integration of logic and emotion later, coming back to the idea of emotion as "knowledge" from a different direction, and discover, perhaps, a certain redemptive logic to *Trek*'s occasional illogic.

In the meantime, let's touch on a more basic *Trek* conflict— that between the self and the Other, a.k.a. the individual and the community, and the difficulty of drawing the lines between.

4

Which Comes First: The Many or the One?

FREEDOM AND "THE CAGE"

Earlier we made note of some TV interviews with *Trek* convention attendees. What impressed me was not their praise for Gene Roddenberry's tolerant future but the fact that these guys were all dressed like Roddenberry's bad guys: Borg, Cardassians, Romulans—odd guests, you'd think, for a love feast. Once again we see that, even if humans do beat most of their swords into plowshares, there may still be a place for bat'telh.

For, along with tolerance, *Trek* conventions also specialize in Klingon cutlery: ceremonial knives that Klingons don't just use for ceremony, if you know what I mean. An imitation "Sword of Kahless" will set you back $135, and those two-handed, curved-blade batlettes come in either steel—$100—or aluminum—$125. At one *Trek* convention I attended, a pair of stage-fighting experts gave a demonstration of the bat'telh routine (using plastic batlettes). They admitted that a lot of the fancy stuff was just old-fashioned baton-twirler moves. I tried to imagine Klingons in skimpy spangled swimsuits marching in a parade. Somehow, I doubt we'll ever see that. For while *Trek* fans may long for utopia, they also love a good fight. Which means good bad guys—"good" in this case meaning "bad."

The list of our favorite outlaws is impressive: James Dean. Billy the Kid. Darth Vader. Al Capone. Pirates. Robin Hood. Prometheus. The Maquis. Our utopian longings, it seems, mix with other ancient itches: to be above the law, to be unencumbered by restraints, to be an individual—to be free.

The classic freedom song is "Freebird"; the classic expression of the age-old dream is, If I had wings, I'd fly. It's part of the American dream: to leave behind limitations and persecutions (political, economic, social, religious) and escape to open air—to space, for crying out loud—to reach the final frontier. Much has been written about the effect of the American frontier on the formation of the national character, and also the effect of its closing. The sudden experience of finitude for a culture formed in boundlessness seemed like being locked inside a cage.

The premiere *Trek* episode was called "The Cage," and featured "liberty or death" speeches from that pre-Kirk captain of the *Enterprise* Christopher Pike. In the likewise Roddenberry-penned episode "Omega Glory" *(TOS)*, we learn that among one particular oppressed alien species, freedom is a "worship word." And Captain Jean-Luc Picard brags to the Borg that human culture, unlike their own, "is based on freedom and self-determination."

Gene Roddenberry was a man as antiauthority, anti–organized religion, and anti–rules of any kind as you're liable to meet. Think of all the *Trek* episodes which climax in the overthrow of some tyrannical alien "god," and the inevitable speeches at the end of such stories to the newly freed inhabitants who must now take individual responsibility for themselves and their freedom.

The Prime Directive of *Trek* is noninterference—live and let live and "Who are we to judge?" The sacredness of the individual is the foundation for all interplanetary relations. The ostensible moral of the whole *Trek* story is to celebrate the infinite diversity of the cosmos—however "infinite" it may get.

The irony of all this, of course, is that the Prime Directive is a rule—a directive, one of Starfleet's commands. Furthermore, it is this very nonjudgmental absolute which often becomes a "cage" to escape from, a despot to be overthrown. This is especially true for James Kirk when he is driven to help some poor alien species overthrow their tyrannical "god."

We forgive Kirk his indiscretion—more than that, we applaud his indiscretion—because such law breaking seems noble, in the tradition of civil disobedience: an obedience to a higher law.

Of course, notions of higher laws suggest not just authority but transcendent authority, and absolute standards of justice. Yet if these existed, our capacity to approve of infinite diversity would surely be somewhat shackled. Worse, a transcendent law raises the specter of a lawgiver. And the only thing worse than a false god in Gene Roddenberry's universe would be a real God.

Here we find ourselves drawn into another Kobayashi Maru, the no-win scenario: damned if we do, damned if we don't. For Kirk is noble if he breaks the Prime Directive to obey a higher law—noble, but not free of any higher authority than his own self-determined preference. On the other hand, if there is no higher law, Kirk is absolutely free, but not so noble. He's merely following his personal tastes, and imposing these on weaker beings.

So it's another Spockian split. Beyond the tension between logic and emotion lie more conflicts swirling at the heart of *Trek:*

the struggle between freedom and order (especially moral order), and the ancient see-saw between individual and community.

We'll start with the second conflict, framing it in a traditional philosophical form as "the problem of the many and the one."

THE POLITICS OF UTOPIA

Why is it, one wonders, if humankind has achieved such a utopian sociopolitical setup in the twenty-third and twenty-fourth centuries, that Kirk finds constant cause to break rules? Is it perhaps because rule breaking is the fullest embodiment of infinite diversity? The opposite of rule breaking would seem to end in absolute conformity, which would abrogate the freedom of the individual. So no doubt rule breaking would be the logical end of a culture founded upon self-determination combined with absolute tolerance.

But it just doesn't seem like a very effective cultural glue.

Don't let them kid you: the Federation does interfere within their own allegedly self-determined culture. They're always chasing down some rogue Starfleet officer who's breaking the Prime Directive, lording it over the natives—like Mr. Kurtz in Joseph Conrad's *Heart of Darkness*. And while Starfleet never really nailed Kirk for his many infractions, Captain Picard was at least put on trial for breaking the Prime Directive in "The Drumhead," *(TNG)*. Yet, as happens many times on *Trek*, the really hard questions were avoided in that episode by sending the story off on a wild goose chase of a subplot, in this case another Starfleet conspiracy—another marvelous opportunity lost for discussing Federation politics in detail.

These are the hard questions *Trek* avoids: On what basis does the United Federation unite? Just how do they federate? And on what authority does Starfleet command? Set primarily within a military framework, with uniforms and hierarchical rank, *Trek* can usually get by with being vague on the structure of twenty-fourth-century civil authority. We do, of course, get a good look at all the bad examples of galactic government—the autocratic Romulans, Klingons, and Cardassians, whose political structures are simple: Might makes right. But—as with the nature of Kirk's intuition and the question of where, beyond logic, Spock goes—the political structure of the Federation remains another undiscovered country.

We do get bits and pieces. We know, for example, that nobody ever seems to vote on *Trek*. There's never really any water-cooler talk about current issues before any Federation ruling body, and if there is, there's no mention of how private citizens might participate in deciding matters. For all the infinite talk of infinite diversity, the Federation—until the rise of the Maquis, and except for occasional foiled conspiracies—appears a seamless political unity: too seamless, a Stepford society almost. Apparently, members of the self-determined Federation culture freely choose to agree on everything. It's the rationalist's dream come true: once everybody has all the facts, there's really only one logical choice in every matter.

Beginning with the *Trek* theatrical films, we see a Federation Council headquartered on Earth, in San Francisco. To make up for such anthropocentricity, which includes command of most starships, there is usually a token nonhuman alien at the head of the Federation Council (just as cop shows compensate for their lack of minority leads by making an African American the boss). *Trek* showcases plenty of interspecies intrigue, with various episodes involving interplanetary diplomacy and treaties. Yet prior to the death of Gene Roddenberry, we never heard of any differences of political opinion on planet Earth. One wonders, of all the squabbling cultures and systems which have risen and fallen on just Earth alone, which one of these finally won out?

In fact, it is Western civilization which seems to have triumphed in human history, judging from the Federation's emphasis on individual rights—the rationale for the Prime Directive, the cornerstone of Roddenberry's future ethics. This notion of the sacredness of the individual always seemed—for the Great Bird and the founders of the United States—to have been "self-evident." However, human rights have been far from self-evident on planet Earth. Such values have certainly not been shared by all the various non-Western traditions, where—as with the Borg—the collective has been more important than the individual.

In an article on China, for example, author Ian Buruma quotes local observers who note that " 'Asian Values' do not include the Western notion of human rights, let alone individual rights. Individual interests and rights, they say, must be sacrificed to the collective good."[1] Discussion of human rights by the West with China has been placed on the back burner as that nation has grown in economic and military power. What seems self-evident, then, is that any Earth-led Federation which holds the individual sacred must be postponed until such values are shared by every culture on Earth. And somebody's culture on Earth, it seems, is going to have to be interfered with, one way or another, to bring this about. So the luxury of absolute tolerance must wait until intolerance is no longer tolerated.

And so the seamlessness of Federation unity begins to look somewhat suspect. The appearance of the Maquis, the first organized dissent in the Federation, is reassuring. But while the presence of dissident opinion adds realism and richness to *Trek's* political landscape, it calls into question the cheerful, unexamined politics of earlier eras: the Federation now comes close to being recast as a new sort of cage. Stirring the ashes of old-style politics makes for a dramatic flickering of flames: the problem is, it shines a light on hitherto conveniently shadowed elements of Roddenberry's utopia.

As we've seen, the typical *Trek* approach to philosophical forks in the road is to speak with forked tongue. Accordingly, we'll see *Trek* has two solutions to the "problem of the many and one." The first solution: the many. And the second solution: the one.

EMBRACE THE OTHER?

Besides freedom, another *Trek* worship word is unification. Earlier we noted that unification is also the worship word for contemporary physics as well: many physicists' fondest hope is corralling the apparently contradictory laws which govern the diverse forces of nature into a grand unified theory.

Likewise, unification is a common goal in psychiatry, as it was for the ancient Greeks: uniting the warring elements of the human psyche in such a way as to achieve balance and harmony. This, we recall, was the lesson of "The Enemy Within," which reunited the warring sides of James Kirk. It's the lesson Mr. Spock so long refuses to learn, and the message of logical Spock's friendship with emotional Kirk. (Some people throw Doctor McCoy in there for a complete Platonic triad of the psyche: mind, emotion and will, making Kirk "will," presumably, to the doctor's "emotion.")

We've seen the central message of *Trek* formulated by one commentator as Embrace the Other (in sharp contrast to the message of earlier science fiction, Destroy the Other). *Trek* presents us with many races, genders, species on one starship, fulfilling one mission. They may be Japanese, Scots, or Klingon, but they're all wearing uniforms of the United Federation of Planets, traveling the universe on a United Space Ship, embracing Others via a universal translator, which would translate the Latin phrase *e pluribus unum*, "out of many, one."

It is an appealing vision, first broadcast to a world of iron curtains, Berlin Walls, segregations, hot and cold wars, and generation gaps. During the worst phase of the Vietnam War, *Trek* had both a Russian on the *Enterprise* bridge crew and episodes featuring Asian-looking Klingons with names like Kang and Koloth. The Klingon episodes usually featured a plot in which the warring sides were forced to make peace (see "Errand of Mercy" and "Day of the Dove"). Years later, on *TNG*, a Klingon has joined the bridge crew, after the Federation and the Klingons (stand-ins for the commies) have made peace, a foreshadowing of the real life end of the cold war and of a divided—"bipolar"—world.

In the *TNG* episode "Unification," which echoed the concurrent reunification of Germany, Spock seeks to unite the divided halves of his own race, the Vulcans and Romulans, as well as tear down a perceived wall between the original and successor *Trek* TV series.

On the other hand, we've also made note of the fact that unification is not necessarily always the way to a happy ending.

The *Voyager* episode "Tuvix" reverses the central gimmick of "The Enemy Within." In this plot, yet another transporter accident actually combines two members of the crew, Neelix and Tuvok, making a single individual—an unsettling *e pluribus unum*. Actually, it's not a bad deal. "Tuvix" embodies the best of both the other characters, and is actually a more pleasant individual than either. But as nice a guy as he is, Tuvix must be split into his component parts in order to give this story a happy ending.

One of the the happiest endings ever seen on television was the live video footage of people dancing on the newly broken-down Berlin Wall. But is it really a good idea to tear down every wall?, to embrace *every* Other? It's one thing for classic *Trek* to unite with *The Next Generation*. But what about uniting *TNG* with, say, *Laverne and Shirley*? It's fine to tear down the wall between East and West Berlin. But what about the "wall" between Germany and Czechoslovakia that Hitler breached?

Identity, which obsesses *Trek* in a thousand ways, is dependent upon walls: If Spock tears down the wall between his Vulcan and human halves, he's still Spock; but tearing down the wall between Neelix and Tuvok is a suffocating unity, indeed. At some point Embrace the Other becomes assimilation—the oneness of the Borg.

Trek knows this, and, despite its instinct to unify and reputation for embracing the Other, firmly resists assimilation.

In the *TNG* episode, "Up the Long Ladder," aliens in need of fresh genetic material want to clone Commander Will Riker, who refuses.

> RIKER: It's not a question of harm. One William Riker is unique, perhaps even special. But a hundred of him, a thousand of him—diminishes me in ways I can't even imagine.

When that blasted transporter acts up again in "Second Chances," *TNG*, Commander Riker's worst fear comes to pass: he is not split in two, but doubled, i.e., duplicated. Riker's twin—not a copy, but another original—goes off in the end to seek his own destiny. The double, who takes the name Thomas Riker, shows up again years later on the *DS9* episode "Defiant." As it turns out, Thomas Riker's struggle to carve out his own individual identity leads him to join the Maquis. *DS9*'s first officer, Major Kira, is an ex–resistance fighter, yet she tries to wave Thomas off this path:

> RIKER: Maybe that's what Will Riker would do. But it's not what I'm going to do. . . .

> KIRA: . . . This is about you, isn't it? You and that other Will
> Riker out there—the man with your face, your name, your career.
> You are looking for a way to set yourself apart. Some way to be
> different.

The need to distinguish oneself—sons from fathers, siblings (especially twins) from one another, the individual from mass society—is a powerful drive: in short, self-preservation.

> DATA: I have found that humans value their uniqueness—that
> sense that they are different from everyone else. The existence of
> a double would preclude that feeling. ("Second Chances")

According to William James, the test for the meaning or significance of anything depends on the answer to this question: What difference does it make?[2] The desire to "make a difference" is the very reason Captain Kirk gives for wanting to leave his comfortable (but illusory) retirement in the film *Star Trek: Generations*. To exist means "to stand out from."

Some seek to stand out by becoming "stars," aspiring to rise above the faceless mass, achieve immortality, "be somebody."

Yet fame, too, can be a cage. Actor Leonard Nimoy became so identified with the character of Spock that he felt not just his career, but his individuality was threatened. He tried to shed his alter ego, titling his first autobiography *I Am Not Spock*. But like William Shatner and the Great Bird himself, Nimoy made his peace with *Trek*, reconciling with the side of his psyche he'd tried to repress. Nimoy's second autobiography, penned long after Spock had become a cultural icon, was titled *I Am Spock*.

Of course, some would argue that this sort of fame, in the long run, and in the larger context of galactic history, doesn't really make that much difference. It's merely a comforting illusion—and perhaps, as we have discussed in the case of our irrational human values, therapeutic illusion is a necessity.

Mention of illusion in this context brings us to the Eastern, as opposed to the Western, solution to the problem of the many and the one—that there is no many, only One. Diversity is an illusion, maya. Intellect is a villain, dividing One into many. We must go beyond logic to realize our oneness with all things. Brahman is dreaming and has forgotten. Salvation, the happy ending, comes only by recognizing the dream for what it is, surrendering individualism, and merging with the impersonal One.

On *DS9* the shape-shifter, Odo, is another sort of half-human; he maintains humanoid form as best he can so he might live among that species. But in the episode "Broken Link," Odo inexplicably loses his ability to maintain any shape. He must return to the home planet of his race, where he seeks answers in the Great Link—an ocean of liquefied changelings. There, Odo is told he must leave behind all his dealings with "solids"—i.e., non-changelings—and remain in the Great Link, a drop in the sea.

Odo admits the attraction of oneness: as a half-human, he has always felt like an outsider, alien-ated, personally fragmented. The lure of any promise of wholeness is tempting. But this sort of unification, as it was in the case of Tuvix, is too costly: Odo must give up his individuality, his self, his identity. As Chesterton says, the East does not command us to love our neighbor, but to be our neighbor. Indeed, love would seem to be predicated upon Otherness. Living as an individual among other individuals, Odo has learned the joys of Otherness. He rejects the Great Link, and prefers to live with alienation—and love.

There are additional flirtations with Eastern thought on *Trek*, for the same reason Odo was momentarily attracted by the idea of a Great Link. In a fictional cosmos riven by inner conflicts, the promise of wholeness would seem to be the very answer to *Trek*'s central quest. But when push comes to shove, *Trek*, like Odo, chooses the Western "one" (sacredness of the individual) over the Eastern "One" (denial of the individual).

Despite all the vaunted openness to other cultures, then, *Trek* is decidedly Western—in this attitude, but also a few more.

Against the Eastern urge to surrender to nothingness, for example, *Trek* follows the Western tendency to seek explanations: to push against emptiness in search of edges, foundations, prime directives, absolutes. The taste for unity and wholeness manifests itself in an effort to break down the phenomena of existence into ever smaller categories and so to understand. And only where there is a conviction of an order of things can science thrive, insisted philosopher Alfred North Whitehead, who attributed the rise of Western science to Christianity.

The oneness of the East, on the other hand, blurs distinctions: even between good and evil, sickness and health. Hinduism sees disease as maya (illusion) and has no tradition of humanitarian service. A trip to India shook up even that guru of oneness, Joseph Campbell, whose views of myth inspired George Lucas's "force."[3] Campbell was "so appalled by the caste system and the lack of respect for the individual that he returned a confirmed Westerner, celebrating the uniqueness of the person."[4]

The danger in the West is in becoming too unique, too distinguished, too individual: one risks being a freak, an outsider, an alien.

> DATA: I have learned difference sometimes scares people. . . .
> LAL: I do not want to be different. ("The Offspring," *TNG*)

As we've already seen, the Western approach to the one and the many is reduction to ever more diversity, atomization, with no sense of cohesiveness: there turns out to be no "reasonable extrapolation" from Western science of a basis for love or community.

No doubt the characteristic alienation of Westerners makes the family feeling of *Trek* especially appealing.

Yet the future human society depicted in *Trek* offers no real solution to the problem of the many or the one either: as usual, *Trek* merely oscillates between available extremes. "The needs of the many outweigh the needs of the one," explains Spock to Kirk in *The Wrath of Khan*, when he sacrifices his life for his friends: a perfectly logical explanation—though logic fails to explain why earlier Spock would throw away his own career to help his ex-captain, Pike ("The Menagerie," *TOS*). Perhaps in that earlier instance Spock was giving in to his human side. His human friends certainly use a contrary sort of logic to explain their own sacrifices for Spock. "The needs of the one outweigh the needs of the many," rationalizes Kirk in *The Search for Spock*.

Again: the classic *Trek* approach to double trouble is double-talk.

Of course, the complex *Trek* is not above taking a simple, and even more classic, science fiction approach to dealing with a repressed Other: the hard questions about *Trek* politics raised by the Maquis are mercifully snuffed when the Maquis rebellion is suddenly wiped out by the Cardassians ("Blaze of Glory," *DS9*).

Yet the brief existence of the dissident Maquis shows that the keepers of *Trek* are at least still trying to boldly go. The Maquis are evidence of both *Trek's* vigorous guilty conscience, and something Gene Roddenberry probably didn't count on—the fact that even "the future" continues to "unfold," as Spock tells us.

To continue in this vein of linear progression: we're going to talk about a particular unfolding subplot as a picture of *Trek's* approach to the many and the one. First, though, we'll breeze through some film theory so as to have a frame for our picture.

THOSE IRRESISTIBLE BORG

In what follows, we'll view *Trek* as its own separate film genre (or rather, a subgenre of the science-fiction film).

Films can be classified by type: Western, screwball comedy, science fiction, etc.; by categories that include particular conventions: typical action, characters, etc.; and by iconography: typical images. These distinctive genre features change over time, affected by external factors (the end of the cold war, or changing attitudes toward minorities, for example) and internal factors, including (as in *Trek*'s case) the death of the original visionary and succession by producers who began to reexamine the established conventions. Film scholars speak of four stages in the evolution of a genre as conventions change.

First, there is the experimental stage, in which conventions are first isolated and established, and the task at hand is pretty much just straightforward storytelling. Then there is the classical stage, in which the conventions reach stability; both the audience and the artists understand the code. The genre mostly reaffirms what the audience already believes about that genre. Third, there is a period of refinement, in which conventions are fine-tuned, and even subverted and parodied.

Trek passed through the first two stages on *TOS;* the conventions seemed to have been established by the middle of the first season. *TNG* took a step back with a bit of an experimental interlude, then continued the classical tradition for much of the series' run. Eventually on *TNG,* and then especially with the advent of *DS9,* we see refinement: self-conscious play with the established conventions: *Trek* begins to draw attention to some of its own internal contradictions, including its moral self-confidence and its cheery utopianism.

Finally, with *DS9* (and even on *Voyager,* which seemed to have begun as an unintentional parody of classic *Trek*), we've gone through refinement all the way to the fourth stage of evolution: the self-reflexive stage, in which the genre and its own conventions become the very content of the story. After drifting about in the Delta Quadrant rehashing old ideas, *Voyager* seems to be finding itself as the most self-reflexive *Trek*. The plots are often knowing confrontations with established *Trek* conventions, sometimes to question, sometimes to subvert. "Tuvix" is an example of taking up unfinished thematic business, and other episodes reexamine *Trek*'s take on issues like fantasy, death, religion, and science—providing, perhaps, not the last word on the subjects at hand, but at least another, fresh, word.

The *Voyager* episode "Unity" is another example of this. In the episode, a few unasked questions about the many and the one are finally asked in a subversion of the usual Borg encounter.

But "Unity" came at the end of a long, developing Borg subplot, beginning back on *TNG*, which it is instructive here to review.

The Borg are the Great Link on legs: a fully assimilated, faceless mass, bent on assimilation of all cultures. Their motto: "Resistance is futile," echoing Jacques Ellul's warning about the unstoppability of technique in *Technological Society*. Each Borg is an anonymous cog in the machine: not an "I," but only "we." The half-machine yet also half-organic-being element of Borgishness, of course, raises all the expected questions about humanity versus technology whenever the Borg show up. But it is their collective element we discuss here, a model of the confrontation between many and one.

The exception among Borg stories was the episode in which the species was introduced: "Q-Who?" *(TNG)*, a nonstory which exists only to scare the Federation crew in their close encounter with a new species, then whisk them from harm's way via deus-ex-Q.

The next encounter was infinitely better, the two-parter "The Best of Both Worlds," acclaimed as *TNG*'s finest hours. Here, Captain Picard is kidnapped and assimilated by the Borg, complete with bio-implants and DNA rewrites. Picard is saved by a twist on the god in the machine: the machine part of Data interfaces with the Borg-ified Picard, finding a still-human element within the captain strong enough to retain a sense of individuality. Picard reminds Data that the evil robots' Achilles' heel is their collective nature: put one to sleep, he suggests, you've put them all to sleep. Data, who represents the best of both worlds—technology under control of humanity, a "god" within a machine—puts the Borg to sleep, and so the good guys win.

The next episode in the sequence is significantly titled "I, Borg." An *Enterprise* away team finds a lone Borg on a planet, brings him aboard their ship, and begins to nurture within him a sense of self, of individuality. They give him a name, and "Hugh" goes home referring to himself as "I." This is a subversive move indeed, with potential to transform Borg society.

Indeed, in the episode "Descent, Part 1," the crew encounter a group of Borg who exhibit symptoms of individuality: they each have their own names and pursue goals beyond efficient assimilation of their neighbors—goals such as vengeance. In part 2, Hugh returns and explains that up until his previous encounter with humans the Borg were "a single-minded collective":

> HUGH: The voices in our heads were smooth and flowing. But after I returned, those voices began to change. They became uneven. Discordant. For the first time, individual Borg had differing ideas on how to proceed. We couldn't function. Some Borg fought each other. Other Borg simply shut themselves down. Many starved to death.

In human history, the discord and anarchy following the French Revolution and within Weimar Germany were similarly terrifying, and the frightened masses of those countries turned to strong leaders to restore order—Napoleon and Hitler. The strong leader the now un-collected Borg turn to is the android Lore, Data's evil twin. Lore molds the Borg back into a unified fighting force to help him fulfill his own evil plans. Hugh explains:

> HUGH: You probably can't imagine what it is like to be so lost and frightened that you will listen to any voice which promises change.
> WORF: Even if that voice insists on controlling you?
> HUGH: That's what we wanted. Someone to show us a way out of confusion. Lore promised clarity and purpose.

Later in this story, Hugh leads a new revolt against the rogue Borg, and the evil Lore is eventually offed by brother Data.

Which brings us to the self-reflexive "Unity," which examines some of the assumptions of the earlier good guy/bad guy Borg stories. In this episode, the crew of the starship *Voyager* find an abandoned Borg ship drifting near a planet populated by diverse creatures from across the galaxy: humans, Romulans, Cardassians, and others—all former Borg. A malfunction in the Borg ship has restored to these once assimilated beings their individual person-alities, and reintroduced that age-old problem: interpersonal con-flict. The mere knowledge that Somebody Is Out There doesn't help these creatures to put aside their differences. The only com-mon enemy they might rally together to fight is any unreformed Borg, but apparently none of these are still around. Finally, the diverse and squabbling former Borg on the planet don't have a strong leader like Lore to step into the power vacuum. So a few of them come up with a new solution to their renewed problem of many versus one: they decide they need to restore their collective by reinstituting the Borg mind link.

> EX-BORG: When we were linked we had no ethnic conflict. There was no crime, no hunger, no health problems. We lived as one harmonious family. . . . All we want to do is to take the one good thing that existed in the midst of that horror—our unique ability to cooperate and problem-solve—and use it to create a safe and productive community.

When Captain Janeway refuses to reactivate the orbiting Borg ship's neurotransponder to restore the collective, some of the ex-Borg are able to create a smaller mind link—including in it *Voyager*'s first officer, against his will. They force him to help them restart the transponder, and the story ends with the newly reunited Borg speaking in the eerie, collective "we."

> BORG: We are the new cooperative . . . We regret that we forced Commander Chakotay to assist us. But it was necessary to our survival. His link with the cooperative has now been severed. Our lasting gratitude. . .

Chakotay wonders how long these new Borg will be able to maintain their nonaggressive ideals in face of such power. (It seemed to me they surrendered their ideals as soon as they forced a mind link on their fellow citizens.) The question this episode raises, but doesn't really answer, concerns the possibility of any middle ground between individual conflict and mass mind. Earlier in the story, an ex-Borg notes of their conflict-ridden world, "It's not exactly a United Federation around here—if you know what I mean." But we don't. Again: how does the Federation unite? A little more self-reflection is in order.

Just maybe, there's a glimmer of an answer to that question in the *Trek* film *First Contact*. Here the Borg collective (unaffected by the individualism of Hugh) is again the villain. Since they have been unable to lick humans armed with Federation technology, the Borg (just like a bully) go back in time to an era when humans are weaker. The *Enterprise* heads them off at the past. Once again, the machine Data is the key. When the android is captured by the Borg, he is tempted with his heart's desire—they offer to give him real flesh if he'll betray his friends. Picard appears and offers to surrender himself to the Borg if they'll spare Data. But Data proves that humanity is more than just skin deep. He out-humans Picard: withstanding temptation and overpowering the Borg, Data saves humanity (again).

The moral of this story is a little confusing. Are they saying it will take a machine to save humanity from the machine (the message of the second *Terminator* movie)? *First Contact's* message gets even more clogged, as we've already discussed, when the alien messiah (a logical, machinelike Vulcan!) arrives at the end of the film. Nevertheless, buried among the red herrings of the story was this suggestion: that between radical individualism and the mass mind of collectivism, one finds the self-determined sacrifice of self.

THE MOST "HUMAN" HUMAN

When it comes to self-evident truths, one of these seems to be that the self must surrender some freedom upon accepting the bonds of community. Again, being a member of a culture, living within cultural boundaries, requires accepting limits on self-determination. Whatever civilization humans have achieved has been based not on not self-determination but on self-restraint: not merely choice, but voluntary renunciation of certain choices.

Vulcans, knowing a little something of self-restraint, would be quick to agree. Earlier, however, we suggested that the Vulcan brand of restraint tends toward the extreme. And so we recall Freud's insistence that, if not given other avenues of escape, repression can damage the psyche, with repressed drives eventually emerging in harmful ways. This belief seems vindicated in the case of the Vulcans, with their maniacal *pon far* and similar rituals—and also for that other extremely rational being, Sherlock Holmes, who took the occasional vacation from a logical lifestyle with cocaine. Freud (who shared this latter habit) thought the goal of a healthy psyche was rational control of the unconscious drives—though certain of his disciples went farther, insisting that any denial of one's impulses can cripple the psyche: so if it feels good, do it.

The *Trek* episodes which most praise freedom and damn repressive authority are played out against what some might still call Freudian backdrops. In "Who Watches the Watchers?" *(TNG)*, and "Looking for Parmach in All the Wrong Places" *(DS9)*, the settings are galactic pleasure planets—sexual theme parks: no commitments, no jealousies; just good, clean fun. In both stories, such simple joys are contrasted against a repressive (and neurotic) authority figure to be overthrown.

Gene Roddenberry seemed to view authority figures primarily as sexual censors. God, said *Trek's* creator, is "the guy who knows you masturbate."[5] The greatest limitation of working in television, said he of the legendary battles with pigheaded networks, was that "you could not have visible nipples."[6] The original *Trek* may feature women on the bridge crew, but note they're all wearing miniskirts. The bikini-clad bimbos on *Voyager's* holodeck show that the latest *Trek* is still not above appealing to Roddenberry's utopia—a juvenile sex fantasy, with absolute freedom from the consequences of one's actions. (Funny how few of those Hollywood freedom lovers have little to say about being imprisoned in the "cage" of their sex drives.)

It's important to remember that one might repress many things: not just drives and emotions, but also conscience, guilt, and logic.

And for all *Trek*'s talk of freedom and self-determination, the highest Federation values depend upon some measure of self-restraint. Humans obviously don't follow the drastic Vulcan solution. But, despite the casual sex of the pleasure planet Risa, certain human desires are still held firmly in check.

Otherwise there would be no inhibitions to overcome in such scandalous fashion in all those space-disease stories. Indeed, after the shipboard chaos caused by the alien infections of these literal "psychotic episodes"—the violence, the lust run free—comes the happy ending, shown as dependent upon putting the id-genie back into the bottle. There are no speeches about liberty and death here, but gratitude for at least one sort of cage.

Humans also restrain themselves by showing mercy, in their characteristic refusal (at least on *Trek*) to kill enemies in their power. It's almost embarrassing to keep hearing some alien who shows similar restraint in killing accused by his peers of hanging around humans too long. (How nice to imagine a future time when "mercy" and "humanity" make for an automatic connection!)

Finally, there is *Trek*'s highest ideal, self-sacrifice—self-determined, yes, but a choice, not for self-preservation but self-surrender. Spock sacrifices his career to help his ex-captain, Pike, whose own injuries were caused when he laid down his life to save his crew ("The Menagerie," *TOS*). Spock follows this example, saving his own crew in *TWOK* at the cost of his life. Kirk lays down his career to resurrect Spock from the dead in *TSFS*. But Spock should have expected this; when he faced identical Kirks— one real, one a shape-shifter—in "Whom Gods Destroy" *(TOS)*, he identified the changeling because he knew only the real Kirk would be willing to sacrifice himself. Indeed, Kirk exits the blissful unreality of the Nexus in *Generations* not just to die, but to sacrifice his life—one last time—for the galaxy. His successor, Picard, is continually offering himself to die for others, and when his turn finally comes, you can bet it will be so others may live. In the *TNG* finale, "All Good Things . . . ," Picard passes "judge" Q's test by sacrificing his life for humanity in three different time periods!

Such an obviously central motif on *Trek* points beyond the simple external freedoms of flaunting traditions and authorities to a higher freedom, an inner freedom: from the tyrannical demands of the self for preservation, from the frantic need for identity, from clamoring lusts and ambitions, to a supreme confidence in one's identity that allows utilization of precious self-determination not to preserve or fulfill, but to relinquish, self.

This is behind the calm, knowing look of Obi Wan Kenobi as he deliberately relaxes his guard and submits to the light saber of the evil Darth Vader; we know who is the real winner of that fight. (And with that blow also dies the facade of *Star Wars*' Eastern pretensions, the idea that good and evil are two sides of one reality. Self-sacrifice is robbed of all its nobility if the distinctions between good and evil, me and not-me, are not real.)

"Greater love has no man than he lay down his life for a friend," says Christ in the greatest story ever told, a conviction echoed in lesser stories. Kirk, in one of *Trek*'s most poignant moments—Spock's funeral in *TWOK*—eulogizes, "Of all the souls I have encountered, his was the most human." This rings true and so we are moved—to the strains of Scotty's bagpipe rendition of "Amazing Grace." Spock is "the most human" because his self-sacrifice seems to touch the core of what humans ought to be. Data may be a machine, but he is far from the ruthlessly efficient Borg; sacrifice of his one chance at humanity to save his friends is paradoxically his most human act. The viewer recognizes this, not because of any appeal to logic but because that famous gut feeling of Kirk's is also at work in us: telling us that the highest freedom is to be able to do as one ought. (Hold your objections to my use of that last word until we get to the next chapter, where I assure you we'll unpack it in detail.)

Let's review some of the things we've talked about in this chapter. A key theme of the ever divided *Trek* is the grasping after unity, the impulse to embrace the Other. This longing has expressed itself in occasional flirtation with Eastern monism and its promise of oneness. Yet *Trek* is held back from the Great Link by another central value: the sacredness of the individual. The unresolved, often unrecognized, tension between the individual and community, freedom and order, keeps *Trek* lively, true to life, and also confused. Despite all the bluster about self-determination, *Trek* no more has a solution to the problem of the many or the one, an alternative to either monism or alienation, than they have a solution to Heisenberg's uncertainty principle. In either case, technobabble gets the job done.

What is somewhat disturbing about *Trek*'s confused patriotism is a frequent stacking of the deck in an oversimplified good guy/bad guy presentation of this unresolved tension, which leads to an uncritical championing of a "freedom" freed of any real content.

One can rise above all limitations and restraints—depose both pope and king, shake off the bonds of community, overthrow the tyranny of logic, break the chains of nature, shed the straightjacket of humanity, escape even the handcuffs of freedom—and so finally, be truly a rebel without a cause: we behold the glamour of the ultimate outlaw, the (to paraphrase Chesterton) slobbering madman with a sign over his final, inescapable cage: "He achieved complete self-determination." Free at last, finally, from meaning itself; for indeed, meaning requires a "cage," a frame, a context, without which one is as shapeless as poor Odo liquefied on the floor. Escape the shark cage and you're free to be eaten—and a starship is a sort of cage: demand liberty or death on the *Enterprise* and you'll get both, floating free in nothingness. We recall William James's test of meaning: What difference does it make? That is, Free to what end?

Talk of the purpose of freedom, as well as of "context" and "order" and "ought," is bound to be making some readers uneasy—and so they should be. For if we must have borders for self-identity, one wonders where they are drawn and who draws them. And if we open that Pandora's box, other hard questions are free to fly out: Whence comes this idea of the sacredness of the individual? Why ought your right to freedom limit mine? It's one thing to search the galaxy asking what it means to be human; it's another thing when somebody claims to know the answer.

The Prime Directive would suggest that our discussion ought to stop here and leave the reader to his or her own uninterrupted development. But then there is that noble tradition of breaking that particular restriction, in obedience to a higher law. . . .

5

No Golden Rules Except for This One

WE'RE NOT LIKE THAT ANYMORE: MULTICULTURALISM

In chapter 3, we recalled that in the *TNG* premiere episode, "Encounter at Farpoint," humanity was put on trial for its many crimes by that impish space genie, Q. We'll ignore the question of Q's authority to be our judge (as does *Trek*) and admit the obvious: the case against allowing human beings to spread into space, if it actually made it to trial, would be formidable. Our species' well-documented record in dealing with the Other is redundant and clear. No dominant culture on Earth has not at some point beheaded, burned, lynched, gassed, Gulaged or otherwise abused outsiders and/or their own dissenters.

Any space aliens monitoring humanity from afar, taking note of our fanatic desire for contact—along with our inflated expectations for contact and our bad record of dealings with the aliens in our own midst—would be wise to lie low; making human history may not be in their best interest. If past is precedent, the future is easy to predict: first contact of humans with weaker aliens, says

C. S. Lewis, will end in ways the black man or the red man could detail. And if the space aliens are the stronger, our own species' ambassadors will be "very properly, destroyed." [1] In Lewis's own science-fiction stories, Earth is under galactic quarantine, known among its neighbors as "the silent planet." Confronted with his species' dismal record, a human representative before some cosmic court would do his species at least some credit by being rendered silent (or, at the very least, pleading the Fifth).

Jean-Luc Picard, on the other hand, argues before Judge Q with the noisy conviction of Scrooge on Christmas morning. Humanity, he insists, has learned from its mistakes. We're not like that anymore. In fact, humanity has learned the very lessons of *Trek:* difference isn't bad, diversity isn't to be feared, and absolute freedom of individual choice is sacred above all things.

Don't you wonder if the Great Bird of the Galaxy saw himself as Q, that playful but ultimately benevolent space deity who tests humanity, patiently teaching them the joys of celebrating infinite diversity? If man is to survive, said Roddenberry,

> he will have learned to take a delight in the essential differences between men and between cultures. He will learn that differences in ideas and attitudes are a delight, part of life's exciting variety, not something to fear. [2]

Once again, recall the context. *Trek* premiered in the mid-sixties, when institutionalized racism was more deeply entrenched. Yet the *Enterprise* launched fully integrated—with a white male European captain, yes, but the crew included African Americans, a Russian, an Asian, women—even Vulcans. The everyday reality of the twenty-third century became a source of hope for minorities in the twentieth century, an unenlightened and savage age.

Nichelle Nichols, tired of Hollywood racism and having her

role reduced to "hailing frequencies open," was ready to quit. At an NAACP dinner, somebody asked to meet her: it was Martin Luther King Jr., and he encouraged Nichols to hang in there. At a time when there were virtually no blacks on television, he said, Nichols's weekly presence on the bridge of the *Enterprise* as an equal to whites among a multiracial crew was a radical source of hope. Ms. Nichols hung in there. Years later, black women from *TNG*'s Whoopie Goldberg to Mae Jameson, the first African American female astronaut, cited Lieutenant Uhura as a personal inspiration.[3]

Whatever his personal faults, Roddenberry must be credited with shedding his own self-admitted racist upbringing to visualize this future society where equal opportunity is the status quo.

And here again, the Great Bird was ahead of his time. For what began perhaps on his part as a vague moral instinct grew in the next thirty years into a much articulated, if still contested, way of thinking. *Multiculturalism* has now gained center stage in both the academy and the general culture. The moral fervor of multiculturalists derives from a desire to right wrongs committed against previously excluded minorities. At the same time, assertions of the inherent oppressive tendencies of all majority rules has called into question the superiority of any set of values.

"Judge not," then, has become the foundation for postmodern ethics. One could almost say nonjudgmentalism has become our culture's Prime Directive. (Thus, the contemporary climate we describe as PC—Politically Correct—might also be described as PD—Prime Directive.) As with the character of Spock, the ideas behind the Prime Directive have evolved over time, affected by internal and external factors. We've been talking about the PD all along; now we'll stop to examine it.

THE PRIME DIRECTIVE: THOU SHALT NOT JUDGE

According to the standard *Trek* encyclopedia definition, "General Order Number One" prohibits Federation crews
from "interfering" in the "normal development" of any alien culture they encounter.[4]

In theory, the PD protects aliens from the tragedies which mar
the cultural development of Earth (which may or may not be
"normal"—in which case, is noninterference actually interference?
But I get ahead of myself). No doubt history would contain fewer
of the bad examples on Q's list if certain Europeans, for example,
had observed the PD in their encounters with Native Americans.
The PD conveys respect for self-determination of cultures, and
humility with regard to norms.

In practice, the PD is problematic. There are (as I have just
suggested) inherent problems of definition: the PD is based on
the unexamined assumption that there exists such a thing as the
"normal development" of a culture; and it keeps somewhat vague,
depending on episode needs, just what constitutes interference.

Since any social exchange requires some order of interference,
the PD is invoked in its most pristine form in cases involving non-
spacegoing cultures; here is a fairly clear-cut matter of honoring
galactic "virginity" by abstaining from contact. (Though, as with
most abstinence, this is easier said than done.)

For cultures who have had contact with beings from other
worlds, there is more selective definition and observance of the
PD, as per individual script needs. The definitions are often quite
arbitrary: in one episode, rescuing a crewman from primitive
natives who want to sacrifice him to their god is breaking the PD,
but beaming one of those natives to the *Enterprise* to see their
robotic "god" in orbit around their planet is not. Go figure.

The PD exists primarily as a source of narrative tension: it functions at times in the same away as a fairy tale's essential prohibition, i.e., Be home by midnight, or else. The existence of the PD makes simple situations hard, hard situations impossible.

One can readily see the practical advantages of the PD. *Trek* history is strewn with examples of somebody breaking the PD, followed by the negative consequences of interference. There are accidental breaches, as in "A Piece of the Action" *(TOS),* when a book left behind by a Federation landing party alters the course of a planet's entire history. Less excusable, but equally tragic, are the intentional violations. Like Kurtz in *Heart of Darkness,* various Federation officers have abandoned their duties to seek power over some backward culture, as in "Patterns of Force," "Bread and Circuses," and "Omega Glory" *(*all *TOS).*

And clearly, once the PD is broken, the contamination is difficult to contain: it usually involves compounding the problem. In "Who Watches the Watchers?" *(TNG),* secret Federation observers are seen by primitives who mistake them for gods. Solving that problem requires more intervention to make it clear they are not gods. In "A Private Little War" *(TOS),* the Klingons break the PD, giving weapons to one side in a planetary conflict. Kirk decides his only choice is to give weapons to the opposing side, but ends up washing his hands of the affair in frustration and splitting.

So we begin to see the theoretical difficulties with the PD. The notion that other races might not observe our PD brings up the question of whether enforcing noninterference on one culture requires some measure of interfering with another. Yet such inherent difficulties (and they've only just begun) only serve to make noninterference even more appealing from a superficial standpoint. For the simplest solution does seem to be just not getting involved, and then making such uninvolvement seem noble.

But it's just not that simple. While it's an easy matter to defend noninterference when the intervention seems clearly destructive, the question gets thornier when a little bit of intervention might help. It's the classic ethics-class question: Would you trespass on somebody else's property to save a neighbor who was drowning? The issue in the *TNG* episode "Pen-Pals" is similar: a planet faces a particular doom which the *Enterprise* is in a position to prevent. There follows a fascinating debate among the crew over that ethical quandary, though it is cheapened by a deus-ex-machina ending: they decide to intervene, then find a convenient way to magically avoid the negative consequences.

None of this was ever very difficult for James T. Kirk. He broke the PD with little hesitation and minimal doubletalk. Kirk destroys the computer-god-enslaved societies in "The Apple," "Return of the Archons" and "A Taste of Armageddon," and transforms an unjust social structure in "The Cloud Minders," *(TOS)*. If he needs an excuse, it's usually "self-defense." (Hey, it's been good enough for many an invading army.) But, of course, "self-defense" doesn't work in the episode "Mirror, Mirror" when Kirk risks the lives of his own crew to save the race his evil twin was ordered to destroy. Furthermore, Kirk has no excuse later for altering that alternative universe by trying to talk the "evil" Spock into doing what Kirk thinks is right.

The excuse Kirk uses when breaking the PD in "Return of the Archons" should raise some eyebrows: the noninterference rule, he implies, only refers to a "living, growing culture"—and, in Captain Kirk's opinion, the culture on the planet in question is most definitely not. This opens up a PD loophole about an astronomical unit wide. Such reasoning suggests, first, that cultural "health" is an absolute, transcultural standard; second, that imposing said health, even against a particular culture's will, is morally good; and third, that James T. Kirk is qualified to, on his own, diagnose and then cure the unhealthy cultures.

In *TOS*, only Spock worries much about the unexamined assumptions of transcultural norms like *health*, or the morality of imposing them on others. In "The Apple," the landing party runs into yet another computer-enslaved race which trades their services to their "god" in return for a blissful social order. Spock admires what he sees as "a splendid example of reciprocity." Doctor McCoy, the most knee-jerk of humans, retorts that only a "computerized Vulcan mind" like Spock's would say such a thing.

> SPOCK: You insist on applying human standards to nonhuman cultures. I remind you that humans are only a tiny minority in this galaxy.
> McCOY: There are certain absolutes, Mr. Spock. And one of them is the right of humanoids to a free and unchained environment. The right to have conditions which permit growth.
> SPOCK: Another is their right to choose a system which works for them.

Notice the "rights" Spock conjures out of someplace besides the "cold equations" of positivistic science. Accordingly, Spock continues to draw upon resources we know not of and comes around to the humans' view on the issue, though not without reservations.

> SPOCK: If we do what it seems we must, in my opinion, we will be in direct violation of the Noninterference Directive.
> KIRK: Those people are not robots. . . . They should have freedom of choice. We owe it to them to interfere.

Pause and consider, for a moment, that last sentence. The line supplies the title for an article on Prime Directive problems in the academic journal, *Extrapolations*. Author Mark Lagon echos common criticisms of Kirk's style, joining those who suggest that the captain's confidence in his own righteousness recalls many a paternalistic empire's "civilizing" mission in barbaric colonial countries. The often barbaric results of that approach are the reason the PD was invented in the first place.

Of course, Kirk himself is an anachronism, a captive of his era—which turns out to be less the twenty-third century than the mid-sixties, or even the fifties. The case has been made that Kirk was merely an old-fashioned cold warrior, zealous to spread America's way of life—even if that meant interference. By this reading, and despite *Trek*'s liberal reputation, *TOS*—aired at the height of the Vietnam War—is seen to be rather conservative. In "A Private Little War," we have an evil empire behind a third-party conflict, with Kirk doing the dirty but necessary job of supporting the other side. In "A Piece of Action," Kirk's solution to the PD violation is accomplished by coercing a new civic order into existence with the threat of Federation force. Even *Trek*'s much-loved episode "City on the Edge of Forever" features a pacifist who must die so a just war might be fought. Critics have accused the *Trek* of the sixties of parroting then-U.S. foreign policy: lip service to national sovereignty, and use of any pretext for intervention to defend American interests.[5]

In the forward to one of his *Trek* novelizations, James Blish tells the story of a real "Captain Kirk" in the U.S. Army in the jungles of Vietnam, who held off a Viet Cong attack by bluffing over his radio that he was going to have his orbiting starship fire phasers on the enemy position. Gene Roddenberry, who was once a cop and speech writer for an archconservative police chief, lived in Los Angeles during the Watts riots— Roddenberry wrote of those riots, "We simply cannot allow that sort of thing,"[6] sounding very much like a man willing to violate the Prime Directive.

As the years passed after *Trek*'s premiere, the culture changed and so did Roddenberry; he continued to weave the *Trek* (and his own personal) mythos, becoming more sensitive to the issues involved in what was soon to be called multiculturalism.

Thus, on *The Next Generation* (a more enlightened *Trek*), the PD was observed more strictly. That is to say, it was given more sophisticated lip service. Yes, Captain Jean-Luc Picard will break the PD, as he does in the episode "Devil's Due"—but not without soul-searching and hand-wringing. In theory, Picard is ready to let his own crewmen die rather than break the PD. In the *TNG* episode "Justice," Picard seeks a way to rescue young Wesley Crusher, who has somehow violated the local laws of yet another totalitarian techno-god. But instead of blowing the god out of sky, as Kirk might have done (and freeing the society in the process of self-defense) Picard talks the god into letting Wesley go, using an argument longer on rhetoric than logic—but it works, one god in a machine done in by another. (The moral of "Justice" is, Where laws are absolute, there can be no justice, a credo that on *Trek* also seems to apply to the laws of drama.)

And yet, as a show with a conscience, *Trek* has a guilty one in this case. Cheating death is to be expected of an action show; cheating moral quandaries can leave a bad taste in one's mouth.

The *TNG* episode "Pen Pals" can almost be seen as an attempt to exorcise the accumulated PD angst. Here, Data makes unauthorized contact with an alien child on a world soon to be destroyed by natural causes. Picard orders the android to stop. There follows that terrific debate over the prime directive: Worf, the Klingon, is strictly pro-PD. The very human Dr. Pulaski denounces the PD as rigid and cold—so many "cold equations."

The logical place for such a debate to form would be around the PD's built-in flaw: that it is a norm regarding "norm-al" cultures outlawing norms. The questions, as noted above, should have been, Who defines "normal" and, What constitutes "interference?"

Instead, the debate in "Pen Pals" ignores this Gordian knot and drifts off into wispy metaphysical speculation. Picard worries about messing around with the planet's destiny—he might as well have said "karma." Geordi wonders, in effect, if the fates have decreed that everyone on the planet die. "Who are we to change whatever cosmic plans may exist?" questions Riker. Troi notes that any cosmic plan may actually include intervention.

So, just as the *Enterprise* has eluded pursuers by losing itself in clouds of cosmic gas, the PD discussion in "Pen Pals" loses the real point in a mystic fog. One commentator compares the debate in that episode to a religious sect making argument that medical intervention would be a violation of God's will.[7]

Most satisfyingly, it is Commander Data (the android!), with a passion beyond his programming, who clears the fog: at issue, he says, are sentient beings, not philosophical abstractions. Picard patronizingly notes that the PD exists to "protect us from our emotions"—in other words, there are times one needs cold equations.

In American history, discussion over federal intervention in the South during the Civil Rights movement was shaken from a similar paralysis of abstraction by TV footage of police dogs attacking men, women, and children in Mississippi. Likewise, the issues in "Pen Pals" are made painfully concrete when Data "accidently" hits a volume control and those around the table hear the desperate voice of a small child calling into space. Picard is human enough to break the PD, bringing the girl on board ship, and eventually allowing the crew to save her planet.

And we applaud. Our deepest human instincts have been confirmed. But now, with the PD broken, Picard and company must face all the consequences, right? Well, no. After the planet is saved from destruction, Dr. Pulaski "wipes" the little girl's memories of having been on the ship, unbreaking the PD, and sends her home. For all the gut-wrenching agony over messing with somebody's cosmic destiny, let alone the belief in the sacredness of the individual which is the rationale for the PD, nobody has any second thoughts about the morality of erasing someone's memory, a questionable tactic that surfaces again to solve other plot problems in later *Trek* episodes.

The Prime Directive is a striking example of why it's not always possible to divide problems into "good guys versus bad guys." And, though they still rely too often on simple solutions and gods in the machine when it comes to PD problems, *Trek* is at least cognizant of the difficulties, and increasingly so.

The issues raised by the PD might also serve to illuminate those most thorny of theological problems, concerning suffering and individual freedom. Why would a loving, all-powerful God not interfere to prevent pain? "It has something to do with free will," says the Supreme Being in the film *Time Bandits*—perhaps a logical answer in a theological debate, but still difficult to accept when the issues are less abstract. Nevertheless, nonintervention seems to be God's protection of free will as well.

Certainly it is providential that the alien messiahs in *First Contact* didn't have a Prime Directive—especially when one considers the times humans saved the galaxy later. (Just think of that the next time Picard is willing to let some civilization destroy itself rather than interfere with their "normal" development!)

For, whatever those *First Contact* aliens did, they somehow caused humanity not just to solve the problem of "the many and the one," but also to master the trick of doing justice in a nonjudgmental society. And don't you wish somebody from the twenty-fourth century would break the Prime Directive and explain to all of us stuck in the late twentieth century (and still dodging bullets from various culture wars) the way to a promised land that is both tolerant and just?

In sum, noninterference seems—if not always admirable—at least somewhat workable: yet on *Trek* it works by avoiding the problem of cultural clash altogether. Obviously, as we discussed earlier, the PD cannot form the basis of social cohesion within the Federation itself. For no society can be founded upon the refusal to make judgments. Nor can it form a basis for the moral choices of *Trek*'s heroes. Behind the love of diversity must be an unspoken, unexamined unity, the moral foundations of *Trek*.

THE TAO OF STAR TREK

In chapter 3 we talked about *Trek*'s different meanings for *emotion* or *intuition* as opposed to *logic* (or what may be loosely considered *Trek*'s version of logical or scientific positivism). One of these meanings of *emotion* was *knowledge*, the celebrated intuition which is the source of human values.

Yet, if the problem is logic (the belief that only those statements which do not violate the law of noncontradiction are meaningful, combined with the notion that only scientifically verifiable sense-data is an acceptable basis for making statements), then intuition as a cure is often worse than the disease. Science may be too rigid and limited a guide, but intuition is too vague. Unlike the cold equations, there are no universally agreed-upon criteria to judge anyone's gut feeling. Beauty, morals, human meaning, and purpose seem to be in the eye of beholder. The authority of romantic and other nonscientific ideals always boiled down to "your intuition and what army?" Counterrevolutions against reason have led to counter-counterrevolutions, one after another—competing ideologies, violence, and oppression (which Vulcans so abhor).

Nevertheless—and, paradoxically, this is a big "nevertheless"—one of the most humanizing influences on our species has been an ancient tradition of moral education which is not simply a list of rules, but a training of the sentiments—the emotions—to incline them towards virtue, i.e., that which has always been taken for granted as a universal moral order. Using stories and examples, children are taught to like that which *ought* to be approved by all humans, and dislike that which ought *not* be approved. C. S. Lewis wrote of this universal moral pattern, once recognized by all cultures, as the Tao (pronounced "dow").

There is a long list of recent popular books whose titles begin with *The Tao of* . . . including *The Tao of Coaching, Architecture, Dying, Leadership, Sex, Motherhood, Physics, Philosophy, Kite Flying, Golf, Baseball, Pooh* (as in "Winnie the"), and *Muhammad Ali.* Such books are an attempt to construct the entire skeleton of eternal wisdom from a single tooth—much like the similar pile of *All I Need to Know I Learned from* . . . books (of course, there's a *Star Trek* one, but in that particular case I thought the author might have learned more from kindergarten.)

The Tao is a religious concept originating in China, though the idea is similar to those found in many oriental religions.[8] In general, *the Tao* means *the way,* and is used to represent behavior that is in harmony with the structure and rhythm of the universe—though asking Chinese philosophers to describe "the way" is like asking directions from a Zen gas station attendant whose orienteering is similar to the sound of one hand clapping.

Whether tao was the best word for what Lewis had in mind may be debatable, but his definition had to do with a universal moral order which could be discovered—and explained. While all cultures have not in any way agreed on the particulars of this alleged objective moral order, or tao, they have over the centuries admitted both its existence and its authority. Take the example of marriage: men may have disagreed about whether it was lawful to have several wives or only one, but they have always agreed that a man mustn't have any woman any time he wants. And in most cultures it is wrong to steal, or murder, or dishonor one's parents. Certain strictures seem universal—this begins to explain Lewis's meaning of tao.

In this way, and despite the opinion of Spock and his Vulcan brethren, seeking to live one's life according to the dictates of the tao would not be intrinsically illogical. For if there is an objective moral order in the universe, would it not seem highly logical to seek and conform to such an order? Indeed, the ancient Greeks believed in an ordering principle in the cosmos similar to the tao: the Logos (which means *word, measure, proportion, pattern,* and *rational faculty*), from which we get our words ending in *logy:* biology, geology, theology—that is, *knowledge of.* Logos is also the root word of logic.

Thus, what is illogical is the idea that disbelief in the tao is the automatic conclusion of logic. This may be the conclusion of positivism, yes, but as noted, that would be philosophical presupposition, not scientifically proven fact. Far from being illogical, the existence of the tao would provide the only logical basis for all those human values that reason alone can't support. It is in the context of the tao that Captain Kirk's continual breaking of the Prime Directive to rescue some poor species from itself appears to be noble and moral. The particular *Trek* episodes where this happens would not have happy endings if Kirk obeyed the cold equations of the Prime Directive and left the aliens as he found them, enslaved or oppressed (at least not in the eyes of those viewers— and they are many—who operate within the framework of the same tao). Lawbreaking, in the sense of civil disobedience, as in the case of Rosa Parks, means breaking a lower law to remain faithful to a higher one; Kirk and the audience seem constantly pulled by a prime-*er* directive. When Martin Luther King dreamed of a time when people weren't judged by color, but character, the issue was not judging per se, but right judging, judging from within the framework of the tao.

Constable Odo, the lawman on *DS9*, is a firm believer in the tao, a universal morality. That's a bad joke, of course, because Odo is a shape-shifter—a changeling in search of an absolute. As Data longs to be human, Odo longs to find a justice which transcends cultures ("Things Past," *DS9*). In the episode "Destiny," Odo is accused by a fellow shape-shifter of seeking not justice but order—which she assures him he'll find in the Great Link. But order is the last thing anybody will find in the oneness of the Great Link, which literally liquifies the problem of making distinctions. Whatever his motivations, Odo would never be happy in the Great Link. He's much too fond of moral categories. He has, for example, no trouble making judgments about Ferengi. "You're disgusting," he tells Quark. (To which the latter replies, "It's a living.")

Trek's other chronic rule breaker, Major Kira, is a source of constant frustration for Constable Odo: "Cardassian rules. Bajoran rules. Federation rules. They're all meaningless to you," he tells her. "Because you have a personal code that's always mattered more" ("The Circle," *DS9*). As a classic example of the cynic who, down deep, still believes, Odo rejects the shape-shifting of personal codes in search of a transcendent ought.

On the other hand, Gene Roddenberry, prophet of the all-tolerant, multicultural future, made it clear that he rejected any transcendent, transcultural standards or oughts, which would include the tao. His celebration of infinite diversity amounts to cultural relativism: different strokes for different folks. "I believe," said Roddenberry, "that all peoples, customs, rituals and all that sort of thing are equal."[9] What humans call nobility—exemplified by showing mercy to victims—is scorned as weakness by Klingons; and who are we to judge?

In recent years, espousal of cultural relativism has become the new norm of Western culture. (That's another bad joke, but if you didn't get it this time, don't worry; I'll get more mileage out of it before I trade it in.) Traditional notions of any universal moral orders have been attacked on all sides as being so many masks for the personal preferences of power elites.

To complicate things further, some philosophers have been telling us all along that, while there's really no such thing as the tao, we shouldn't let that stop us from living our lives as if there were one. The thing to do is invent your own moral order, but without pretending that it is universal; i.e., live and let live: Tao plus Prime Directive. This approach is illogical, admittedly so, but some would willingly embrace illogic, as we noted in our discussion of Spock and V'Ger, rather than surrender humanity.

So, again, given the notion of therapeutic self-delusion, it's difficult to know what *Trek* means when it refers moral judgments to intuition. Do they mean that Kirk's civil disobedience of the Prime Directive is not about conforming to a larger pattern of "the good," but that his own personal whims happen to match exactly what some people once called "the good" (and what the majority of viewers believe intuitively to be "the good")?

To be honest, it is hard to believe Jim Kirk is deep enough to be able to play any such sort of existentialist mind games with himself. Surely he does what he does because it seems to him like the right thing to do. It has been suggested that men of action like Kirk can act so decisively because they don't think things through—at least not to the level of philosophical paralysis which often manages to gum up the works of smarter guys.

The fact that Kirk's personal whims match the majority of his audience's expectations for universal standards of justice may make for a happy ending. But it doesn't necessarily prove the existence of the tao, say critics; it only proves that certain cultural conventions are so ingrained that we assume they are reflections of an absolute moral order. The mass audience, in this way, is culturally programmed to respond in certain ways.

The task of a cynical writer or producer would seem to be to identify the audience's expectations, and give the customers what they want: *good* guys. It may be that *Trek* writers are that cynical, but one can't help thinking that, like Kirk, there are some true believers. Gene Roddenberry was often confused about what he believed, but his faith in his own values seemed real.

Nevertheless, one can use logic to justify anything—including cultural relativism. To its credit, though, *Trek* rarely takes its relativism to the logical end. Instead, *Trek* relies on those unexamined Kirkish assumptions that, while all cultures are equal, some are more equal than others. Consider the probable *Trek* attitudes toward the customs, rituals, and values of the Ku Klux Klan, the drug cartels, the Mafia, or child pornographers.

Educator William Kirk Kilpatrick has written about these difficulties of doing justice in a nonjudgmental society

> The notion that all ideas are to be respected is a fairly recent one—and not an easy notion to defend. . . . Wife beating is considered a minor matter in India and in some Latin societies. Child prostitution is not uncommon in some parts of the world. Slavery reportedly still exists in Mauritania and the Sudan. Infanticide is practiced in parts of China. In dozens of societies, civil rights and free speech are only words.[10]

Different strokes? Such practices are less likely to provoke Roddenberry's delight in "life's exciting variety" than they are to be listed among those barbarities Q seeks to restrain.

Despite the PC mumbo jumbo, *Trek* heroes constantly make moral judgments, from the arguably less enlightened classic *Trek* days right on down to the present. *DS9*'s Benjamin Sisko, an African American, seems especially prejudiced. "There's a limit how far I'll go to accommodate cultural diversity on this station—and you just reached it," he explodes to Worf, who has just engaged in a Klingon cultural practice—ritual murder ("Sons of Mogh"). And when aliens who breed sentient creatures to use as hunting game pass through the station, Sisko can't help expressing his disgust. "I can't judge what is right and wrong for your world. But on this station . . ." ("Captive Pursuit").

Even *Trek*'s most self-consciously (self-righteously, some might say) values-neutral incarnation, *TNG*, casts its entire series' run as a trial. This more enlightened *Trek* opens and closes with episodes featuring Q presiding over the trial of humanity, book-ending seven seasons' worth of episodes with this central question: has humanity progressed from barbarism or not?

The charge of barbarism assumes a standard: one presumably must be able to measure progress from barbarism to something "better." As C. S. Lewis said, "A man does not call a line crooked unless he has some idea of a straight line."[11] Likewise, Picard's defense of his species ("We're not like that anymore") admits to an absolute standard—of which humans have fallen short, but have lately repented of their sins and mended their ways.

In the *TNG* finale, "All Good Things . . ," the "moral" of the entire *Next Generation* series is delivered by Judge Q from his bench. We lean forward, expecting finally to understand the source of his moral authority, and by extension, the moral basis of *Trek:*

We wanted to see if you had the ability to expand your mind and your horizons and for one brief moment you did. . . . For that one fraction of a second you were open to options you had never considered. That is the exploration that awaits you. Not mapping stars and studying nebulae but charting the unknown possibilities.

Talk about a disappointing verdict! After a seven-year trial, a weekly accumulation of evidence to prove humanity has really left behind barbarity, Q pulls the rug out from beneath us: there is no such thing as barbarity. Deus ex machina. It was all a dream. The judge's standard turns out to be "open-mindedness."

A better lawyer than Picard should have been able to throw the case out of Q's court before the end of the first *TNG* episode! Why should humans be made to feel defensive about their barbarous past? For what is infinite diversity if we all must share the same standards of civilization and barbarity? What are Hitler, Stalin, Pol Pot, Idi Amin, the KKK, ad nauseum, if not diverse?

Such sleight of hand is also called bait and switch: *Trek* characters behave as if their actions correspond to a real and universal moral pattern. But by the time we get a closer look, they've replaced it with "open open-mindedness." *Trek*'s morality turns out to be a shell game: and we just lost track of the pea.

Then again, maybe *Trek*'s rejected-but-still-assumed universal notions of right and wrong depend upon some advanced piece of technology we know nothing about. Such a device wouldn't be without precedent. For example, the entire galaxy speaks English via a rarely talked about, never explained, tool the "universal translator," which automatically translates speakers' words into the languages of listeners (like the Babel fish in the *Hitchhiker* books which, dropped in one's ear, eats spoken foreign languages, excreting the words, in the host's language, into his brain).

We can see the possibility for such a device in the *TNG* episode "Descent," Part 2. Here, Commander Data has been kidnapped and reprogrammed by his evil twin, Lore, and so has gone "bad." Captain Picard tries to talk his android officer out of doing the wrong thing, not on the basis of either logic or emotion, nor by any appeal to the Prime Directive, but with reference to something, as the Pythons used to say, "completely different:"

> PICARD: Isn't good and bad, right and wrong, a function of your ethical program?
> DATA: That is correct.
> PICARD: What does that function tell you about what you and Lore are doing to the Borg? It tells you that these things are wrong, doesn't it, Data? ("Descent," Part 2, *TNG*)

Could it be that not just androids, but certain nonandroids of the future, namely the *Trek* humans, utilize some sort of "ethical program" as well? A bioimplant, perhaps? A universal moral translator which automatically translates everyone's individual choices into the common good, a "subjecto-objecto-harmonizor" which mediates self and Other, moment by moment, behind the scenes?

A deus ex machina by any other name . . .

PAY NO ATTENTION TO THAT MAN BEHIND THE CURTAIN

Is there no justice? Imagine. You've accomplished everything the powerful superbeing demanded of you—after he terrorized and threatened you and promised bad things would happen if you didn't. You've proven yourself. Then you find that it was not enough. Fortunately, somebody rips aside the curtain and you see that all the smoke and fire is just a cover for a bunch of humbug.

Of course, the difference between the finales of *TNG* and *The*

Wizard of Oz is that the superbeing Q is a faster thinker than the debunked Oz: Q rips aside his own curtain before little Toto has a chance to debunk him, and with some fast talking (technobabble? ethic-babble?), he snatches away the one weapon that could have destroyed him—critical judgment—sending the humans off feeling pleased about their great luck and potential.

Lots of luck. A less nonjudgmental judge wouldn't have let humanity off the hook so easily. And, thanks to Q, they are now more dangerous to the galaxy than ever. For what they "ain't like anymore" is a species with a clear sense of right and wrong, and they're too nonjudgmental to see their own moral confusion.

If Q didn't think to include this moral confusion as another bit of evidence against humanity, it's because Q suffers from the same confusion. As does the series in general: *Trek* claims to celebrate cultural relativism, but as a vision of a "better, more humane" future, it presents regular moral oughts. *Trek* claims to be about noninterference, but is not shy about interfering with viewer beliefs in presenting these oughts, the goal being that viewers change and think more like *Trek*.

Trek is so nonjudgmental it fails to notice the slip and slide of its own definitions—of logic and emotion; nor its simultaneous intuition of moral standards and questioning of all standards; its easy adoption of the authority of science, and all the absolute confidence that entails; its frequent recourse to religious overtones, even as it denounces religion.

In Q's case the situation is even worse: Q uses force to teach tolerance; an example the *Trek* humans at times seem only too eager to follow. Perhaps this is the natural end of combining moral fervor, a refusal to judge, and incredible personal power.

Later *Treks*—beginning with *TNG*—seem more conversant with the problems of cultural relativism and free choice. Yet

McCoy's argument about "absolutes" is roughly the same used by Captain Janeway defending her actions in the *Voyager* episode "The Gift," when she decides—much like a cult "deprogrammer"—to hold the former Borg, Seven of Nine, against her will and force her to leave the Borg collective and become an individual.

> JANEWAY: You lost the capacity to make a rational choice the moment you were assimilated. They took that from you. And until I'm convinced you've gotten it back, I'm making the choice for you. You're staying here.
> SEVEN: Then you are no different than the Borg.

The contradictions and blindnesses of *Trek* are no different than those of secular humanism, and philosophers of late have begun to pay more attention to the men behind this particular curtain. They ask how far judgments about cultural health can be from the sinister psychiatry of Soviet psychiatrists, who regularly diagnosed dissenters of the regime as insane, prescribing a hellish sort of "treatment"—which included drugs and prison.

Contemporary philosophy likes to think of itself as being well into the self-reflexive stage, busily questioning hitherto unexamined assumptions like *normal* and *abnormal*. What they say does seem obvious (in hindsight at least): that the power to define *normal* automatically carries with it the power to define *abnormal*, and so to exclude abnormal beliefs and behaviors. And it does seem a suspicious coincidence that the control of these definitions has traditionally been in the hands of the most powerful segments of society. But then again, we've always suspected these things to some degree: Might makes right. History is written by victors. Whoever has the gold makes rules.

Yet there is loose in our society today a new skepticism—concerning all history, all rules, all claims of right.

ODO: It's been my experience that all humanoids have an agenda of some sort. And that their agendas can influence them without their even realizing it. (*DS9*, "Destiny")

Values once deemed normal, or natural, or universal have been attacked by deconstructionists as so much technobabble—artificial constructs, personal preferences of the ruling class, tools for social control. When *Trek* first aired, for example, it was not necessarily normal to have women in a position of authority, or blacks treated as whites, equals. When *Trek* questioned those dominant norms, it participated in such deconstruction.

This debunking of accepted norms has meant liberation from the restrictive categories of modernism and marked the start of a new era, which has been dubbed postmodernism. This revolution in thought has been greeted with joy by those groups who were formally marginalized by the dominance of old ideas of *normal*.

Yet the acids of postmodernity just keep eating away. Our traditional confidence in norms like progress and truth seem ever more quaint as the years go by. The overconfident *Trek* heroes begin to seem like so many Don Quixotes, romantic fools, country boys in the big city. On *DS9*, Worf is put on trial for murder (a common plot). His defense attorney is Commander Sisko, who says he believes the trial will be about finding the truth. His opponent, a Klingon prosecutor, laughs in Sisko's face; the trial is not about truth, it is about power. Sounding very postmodern, the Klingon believes truth is not something to be found; rather, "Truth must be won" ("Rules of Engagement,"*DS9*).

In the next chapter, we'll see that the postmodern solution to humanity's age-old conflict between the norm and the Other is not doing away with the Other but doing away with the norm.

For now, we'll pause to review *Trek*'s ambivalence over making "normal" judgments, and how this confusion stems from *Trek*'s conflicted—or unexamined—or ignored—assumptions.

Appropriately for a science-fiction series, the actions of *Trek* heroes seem to require a theory of quantum ethics. Measured in one way, *Trek* is nonjudgmental, inclusive, and tolerant. Measured another way, however, *Trek* is exclusive and full of judgments—some might say to its infinite credit. While *Trek* preaches cultural relativism, it practices as if there were a universal moral pattern. *Trek*'s repressed Other is the tao.

For *Trek*'s patented moral fervor loses all credibility if what they say *ought* to be is the abdication of all moral standards, an openmindedness which means having no convictions whatsoever.

Modernity's attempts to define humanity according to materialist or romantic criteria resulted in tormented half-humans; postmodernity gives up on the task of definition. The divided Spock, as a symbol of modernity, gives way to a new symbol, for postmodernity: the anguished shapelessness of Odo ("How much longer before I totally lose my ability to remain solid?" ["Broken Link," *DS9*]). After telling us for so long that emotion is what makes us human, *Trek* shies away from digging too deeply into the implications of emotional knowledge, letting the moral intuition of Kirk fade into the touchy-feely counsel of *TNG*'s ship shrink, Deanna Troi.

As a seeker for justice, Constable Odo would be able to tell you that tolerance—as it is now commonly expressed—cannot hope to create a just society; such tolerance is actually the elimination of all possibility of justice. Instead of making moral judgments about vices humans have always identified as evil, we must reject such "prejudices." Instead of calling greed and violence bad, such judgments must be seen as bigoted and backward; greed and violence become merely additional diversity to celebrate. The irony of abandoning all judgment, however, is that, in the end, we can no longer say that bigotry is bad, or that justice is good. Luckily for *Trek*, if "cheating" is the only away around this no-win scenario, it is abandoning any yardstick which might say cheating is morally wrong.

And if the post-Roddenberry remodulation of *Trek*, i.e., the introduction of shades of gray, continues to echo changes in the surrounding culture, there won't merely be a mixing up of good and bad guys, but a mixing up of good and bad. For if there is no tao, there can no longer be any *good* guys. Whether *Trek*'s happy ending can survive such changes remains to be seen.

Meanwhile, in impulsive, Kirkean fashion, *Trek* continues to ignore the logic of its stated positions to draw from the best of human prejudices. (We note that, so far, no Federation vessel includes any Klansman or neo-Nazi on its bridge crew.)

There is some evidence, though, that *Trek* is beginning to see that its own humanism is another form of bigotry to be shed.

6

"We've Got to Save Humanity"

AN EMBARRASSING SORT OF PROBLEM

You find yourself walking the corridor of—yes, it's your old high school. But something's not quite right. Not only is your vision blurred at the edges as if someone has smeared vaseline on the rim of your eyes, but you're walking around in your underwear. Yet nobody seems to notice this problem except you. You hurry to your locker, knowing that if you can just get it open, everything will be all right. But its been twenty years since you were in high school, and you don't remember the combination! Then, in the nick of time—deus ex machina—you wake up. Thank God, it was all just a dream—a classic stress dream—but also a picture of humanity in the school of nature. For, of all the creatures in the jungle, only we humans seem to be—metaphysically speaking—locked out in our underwear.

You'll thank me for changing the metaphor: of all the pageant of creation, only humans seem chronically unsure of their lines, stumbling through their performance. For example, observes

Chesterton, if we want to get a man to say no to his tenth whiskey, we slap him on the back and tell him, "Be a man." And yet, "No one who wished to dissuade a crocodile from eating his tenth explorer would slap it on the back and say, 'Be a crocodile.'" Why not? Because unlike humans, crocodiles don't seem to have any trouble fulfilling their responsibilities as crocodiles. Humans, on the other hand, are haunted by the both the idea of an ideal pattern for humanity and the unshakable conviction that they have fallen short of it. Unlike humans, crocodiles "have no notion of a perfect crocodile," says Chesterton, and whales "no allegory of a whale expelled from a whaley Eden."[1]

Humans alone are self-conscious. Humans alone sense a chasm between *ought* and *is*. Humans alone dream of utopias. Whether or not you believe in any "fall" of man, it seems clear that something drastic separates humanity from the rest of nature. Are butterflies or tigers alienated? No, they're inside nature in a way humans are not. Humans are the outsiders—the aliens.

Does that tell us that feeling alienated is what it means to be human? If so, why does everything within us say this ought not to be? And what, exactly, "ought" humans to be anyway?

That last is among the most-asked questions of science fiction. It surely was among the personal obsessions of SF writer Philip K. Dick, whose bizarre tales were turned into the films *Total Recall* and *Blade Runner*. Dick's "Phildickian" agonizing over such questions was sparked, he said, by something he'd read while researching a story, a line from an SS officer's diary: "We are kept awake at night by the cries of starving children." This particular grain of sand irritated Dick's soul forever after:

> "There was obviously something wrong with the man who wrote that," he recounted. "I later realized that, with the Nazis, what we were essentially dealing with was a defective group mind, a mind

so emotionally defective that the word 'human' could not be applied to them." [2]

But how can a human do anything inhumane? Can humans really be dehumanized? Again, could a crocodile ever be de-crocodilized? The question of *Blade Runner* is, How can one distinguish a replicant (evil twin) from the original? But what if there is no original, only replicants? Do evil twins stop being evil?

These questions of human identity and meaning are central to *Trek* because they're the questions raised by space and technology. The cosmic insignificance of one particular species in an endless void demands some kind of explanation for the sort of importance we place on our own moral choices and our history. The infinite possibilities of science for reshaping humanity call into question how far we can go before we lose something "essential."

This question of what it means to be human lies behind the agonizing of all those half-human characters; in fact, it is the unspoken question in virtually every alien encounter on *Trek*—for "alien" automatically suggests "norm." And how can you find your position without a fixed reference? Moreover, how can man be the measure of all things, if there is no measure for man?

THE MEASURE OF A MAN

As with many of the terms on *Trek, human* can refer to different, sometimes contradictory, meanings—often with no indication the user is aware of the conflicting definitions. In other words, you gotta watch the shells to keep track of the pea.

Richard Hanley, in *The Metaphysics of Star Trek*, distills *Trek's* use of *human* into three categories: biological, psychological, and moral—paralleling the classical divisions of body, mind and soul. [3] I divide *Trek's* use of the term much less neatly:

1. a member of a particular species, *Homo sapiens,* in contrast to chimpanzees, Cardassians, or androids;

2. a member of any intelligent, biological, sentient species, i.e., a humanoid; this use of *human* is rare, usually used only when a *Homo sapien* observes that the android Data is not human, which is a bit chauvinistic; more properly, one should say Data is "not a humanoid";

3. an attitude of compassion; warm and sympathetic, as opposed to cold, unfeeling, mechanical: humane;

4. prone to particular frailties and limitations, as seen in the sayings, To err is human, and, I'm only human;

We pause here to recall that the range of human "frailties" stretches from forgetfulness to genocide. Bearing that in mind, notice how the previous definition is contradicted by the next:

5. exhibiting ideal behavior, i.e., the qualities summed up in the inspirational appeal to "the human spirit."

Once again, such confusion of terms is used on *Trek* to humorous advantage. Kirk thinks he's paying Spock a compliment by telling him, "I suspect you're becoming more and more human all the time." Greatly offended, Spock responds, "Captain, I see no reason to stand here and be insulted" ("The Tholian Web," *TOS*). Kirk is thinking, of course, of definition number 3 ("warm and sympathetic") and Spock of number 4, (the classic human frailties, i.e., those displayed in their traditional form by the "alternative" *Enterprise* crew in the episode "Mirror, Mirror." Spock describes those humans in this way: "They were brutal, savage, unprincipled, uncivilized, treacherous. In every way, a splendid example of *Homo sapiens*. The very flower of humanity.")

Acquiring these less-than-ideal traits is clearly not the goal of those characters on *Trek* whose fondest wish is to become more human, like Commander Data: the poignant longing of this android is not merely "to err," but to develop emotions and embody ideal values. In Data's ongoing "character arc," he learns both the advantages and disadvantage of being human as he pursues his quest. In the same way, Odo aspires to embody what he admires as humanity's firm sense of justice.

From this notion of connecting a particular species with a particular set of values comes the positive expression, "to humanize," which is the final challenge of Alvin Toffler's book *Future Shock* — to "reach out and humanize distant tomorrows."

We talked earlier about Gene Roddenberry's self-described humanism, a philosophical framework with its own set of ideal human values—another strand of the evolution of that term.

To the Greeks, humanism had to do with a particular balance in life. Later, the term came to refer to the study of Greek and Latin classics, the humanities. Today, humanism has become a catchall phrase used by different humans in different ways.

A specific meaning attached to this term during the last century is allegiance to that bundle of ideas we identified earlier as secular humanism. Among these ideas are the centrality of man; respect for human reason and its proudest achievements, science and technology; and rejection of the supernatural and religious beliefs as a hindrance to human progress. Such ideals are embodied in documents called *Humanist Manifesto*s *I* and *II* (1933 & 1973), which were signed by various twentieth-century thinkers.

Gene Roddenberry was knowingly aligning himself with this particular set of humanists when he took that name and made it clear that humanism was the guiding philosophy of *Trek*. The Great Bird joined the American Humanist Association in 1986, and was awarded the group's Humanist Arts Award in 1991. He also sat on the board of advisors for *The Humanist* magazine.[4]

This humanist perspective is manifested on *Trek* in various ways: the insistence on the naturalistic origins of life, the idea that human nature is basically good and getting better, and the idea that human destiny is in humanity's hands alone. At the same time, though, this brand of humanism has also traditionally taken credit for a number of ideas it borrowed from the Western religious tradition, including many of its moral values and—especially important for *Trek*—its high view of the individual. This value, as we mentioned earlier, has not been shared by all cultures on Earth, but finds its origin in the Judeo-Christian notion of *imago Dei*—man created in the image of God. In his excellent book, Richard Hanley is concerned with discovering the criteria by which *Trek* awards "human rights" to nonhuman species. Left unexamined, though, is the basis for human rights and dignity, which secular humanism has always been at a loss to account for (given its naturalistic presuppositions) and has simply assumed something similar to the Judeo-Christian belief in imago Dei— without the Dei, of course, just a deus ex machina.

As we discovered last chapter, despite the emphasis on cultural relativism, *Trek* stories are full of oughts, i.e., moral judgments of behaviors. Compassion, creativity, honesty, and tolerance are good. Lying, greed, aggression, and violence are bad. Roddenberry's future society mixes oughts with the libertarian ethical ideal: do whatsoever thou wilt, as long as it doesn't hurt anybody else or interfere with their own freedom.

Even the enemies of humanity on *Trek* (usually definition number 2 above) recognize the high ethical ideals of humanity (definitions 2 and 4). Thus, along with the Kirk-Spock running gag about being human, there is another regular *Trek* punchline connected with humanity: whenever a member of a notoriously violent species refuses to kill a prisoner, he's told scornfully,

"You've been around humans too long." One example: when Goran'Agar, a soldier of the Jem'Hadar, orders his men to bring back the escaped prisoner O'Brien alive, an underling accuses him of being like a human—"weak, soft, inferior" ("Hippocratic Oath," *DS9*). And in the *TNG* episode "Mind's Eye," a Klingon says to Captain Picard, "Your modesty is very human, Captain. I'll excuse it." And later, the same episode and Klingon: "Who cares for motives? Humans perhaps."

In our own time, of course, if we were to run across space aliens who gun down strangers at fast-food joints, or lure victims into their apartments to kill and eat or have sex with the corpses, we might fairly accuse them of "being around humans too long"! Thankfully, though, on *Trek*, humans aren't like that anymore. *Human* becomes synonymous with the tao—definitions 3 and 5 combined into a new, specific meaning for the term:

5) A particular set of moral values, including self-sacrifice, mercy, compassion, loyalty, and justice.

Here we find the center which holds everything else in the *Trek* cosmos in place. And most viewers would agree: in this sense, humocentricity is a good prejudice. Spock may be insulted when Kirk tells him "everybody's human." Klingons may complain the Federation is "a humans-only club" *(TUC)*. But it seems clear that most of the aliens on *Trek* could use a little humanizing. In fact, the worst bad guys on *Trek* are the most de-humanized: the Borg (the cold equation incarnate) and a long parade of villains of similar bent, embodying varying degrees of coldness.

It is true that this idealizing of humanity can encourage self-deluded superiority or imperialism. But when you realize this use of *human* is just *Trek*'s way of smuggling in humankind's ideal values (while still claiming to be nonjudgmental and open-minded), you can let the occasional self-righteousness slide.

For there are worse alternatives. In fact, *Trek* itself of late seems intent on charting a new course: for a place where—along with racism, sexism, and ageism—even humanism must be labeled bigotry. It would be bad enough if this were due to getting the definitions mixed up (an old habit for *Trek*). But this new tendency seems a deliberate shift on the part of producers who are either intoxicated by *Trek*'s righteousness or bent toward the logical ends of its premises. In the *DS9* episode "Sword of Kahless," Commander Sisko, as might be expected, passes a negative moral judgment on a Klingon ritual murder. Lieutenant Dax, however, usually portrayed as the more enlightened (PC!) character, suggests Sisko is being bigoted and intolerant.

The greedy Ferengi, Quark, makes the accusation more clearly: "You Federation heads are all alike. You talk about tolerance and understanding. But you only practice it towards people who remind you of yourselves. Because you disapprove of Ferengi values, you scorn us, distrust us, insult us, every chance you get" ("The Jem'Hadar," *DS9*). To this accusation, Picard might sputter in tolerant confusion, but Sisko (and Odo!) would have no trouble calling Federation values superior to Ferengi values.

Nevertheless, there's some confusion as to which side of this debate the producers of *Trek* would take; the keepers of the official perspective of *Trek*, with its (confused) guilty conscience, may well have begun feeling guilty for their long-stated bias in favor of humanistic values; the center may no longer be holding.

Trek's alien values have often functioned as stand-ins for values humans have traditionally judged as reprehensible or evil. If *Trek* forgets this, the next Other viewers will be urged by *Trek* to embrace will include behavior that, in more unenlightened times, might have been branded as inhuman. But who's going to notice? Discarding moral norms makes it impossible to call anything wrong, and abandoning the norm *human* means we can be dehumanized without even knowing what we've lost.

WE'RE NOT LIKE THAT ANYMORE, PART 2

Let's talk about Gene Roddenberry's particular brand of secular humanism and also what happened to humanism in general in the years since the creator (and his creation) first embraced it.

This is, of course, the same secular humanism which has long been a boogeyman to religious critics. There is some truth in the characterization of *Trek* as a humanist Trojan Horse, but *Trek*'s philosophy has never been as coherent as critics claim.

For one thing, preaching a coherent philosophy is the least of a myriad of factors considered when a gigantic corporation like Paramount or Viacom puts up money for a television or film series. Far more than philosophy, film and TV production of this kind are affected first and last by economics. Entangled with this priority and affecting it are ratings, censors, studio politics, and a multiplicity of writers, directors, and actors. Another factor to consider is the catch-as-catch-can way this particular studio asset was batted from hand to hand. Gene Roddenberry walked away from the original *Trek* in its third season, came back after his later career went nowhere, and lost control of the *Trek* films to others whose vision was even less coherent than his, before finally— before his death in 1991—passing *Trek* to a new producer who keeps his bust of the creator blindfolded because he tends to break Roddenberry's "rules."

Apparently fed up with hearing *Trek* lauded as the Gandhi of television, a pair of the show's original producers added to the flood of *Trek* books in an attempt to regain some perspective:

It's important to understand that first and foremost *Star Trek* was not created or developed as a critical study of truth, life's fundamental principles or concepts of reasoned doctrines. We just wanted a hit series.[5]

No wonder, then, our brief analysis in the previous chapters shows *Trek*'s "unified philosophy" rambling all over the map.

This is even less a surprise if one examines Gene Roddenberry's statements regarding his brand of humanism. As *Trek* did, in fact, assume a cultlike stature in pop culture, the creator took seriously his role as guru. Yet whenever the Great Bird was quoted in interviews on subjects like religion, morals, politics, or metaphysics, one strained to hear much more than self-important gobbledygook.[6] Even if *Trek* had been a unified presentation of Roddenberry's views, it still wouldn't have been very coherent.

Nor is secular humanism, as represented by its most intelligent and articulate exponents, all that internally coherent. All the contradictions and unexamined assumptions at the bottom of *Trek*'s moral philosophy and its basis for individual rights, which we found in the last two chapters, afflict secular humanism as well.

Indeed, among most thinkers, secular humanism had already been declared obsolete and rejected when Gene Roddenberry embraced it.

For many, the optimistic humanism of the *Manifesto* variety cited above was dealt a mortal blow by the horrifying events of the twentieth century (you know the list, I won't mention them here). These thinkers interpreted the "death of God"—the nineteenth-century collapse of religious belief—much differently: it meant not blissful freedom, but the death of human values, of man himself. The optimists thought they could retain Judeo-Christian ethics and values apart from God; Nietzsche scoffed that this idea was impossible, and over the next hundred years, more and more philosophers are coming around to Nietzsche's way of thinking.

The sixties, when *Trek* was first aired, marked the final breakdown of modernity and Enlightenment optimism. People saw science not merely as a positive tool for progress, but as a destroyer—creating terrible weapons, despoiling the environment, and robbing humanity of its significance. Likewise, the notion that there was a goal to "progress" toward depended upon the values of whoever was using that word, and the vast skepticism of authority which now pervades the cultural air we breathe began to spread. Sartre identified this "striptease of humanism" for the youthful protesters of an establishment they saw as blind, complacent, and armed with both a dangerous technology and a smug but baseless confidence in its own infallibility.

Like most of his generation, Gene Roddenberry didn't seem to really get what was going on in the sixties. The episodes of the original *Trek* which have aged the worst are those which attempted to connect most directly with their times—such as the notorious "space hippies" in the episode "The Way to Eden" *(TOS)*. True, in many ways, the sixties was about a tragic search for a mythical Eden, but no more so than modernity itself, or even *Trek*.

The counterculture's tragic failure to provide an alternative to the society they were protesting meant that their demands for freedom and rights must degenerate into a culture of self-indulgence: former protest songs are now the soundtrack for Boomer consumerism; since the effort to change the world failed, the final, final frontier to be conquered is self-fulfillment.

In the years between the original *Trek* series and *TNG*, these changes in attitudes filtered throughout the culture. Though *TNG* was in many ways a throwback—and let's face it, nostalgia was a very powerful factor in the resurrection of *Trek*—the successor series was affected by these cultural changes. As the logic of Spock was passed on to Data the android, Captain Kirk's intuitive sense of universal morality was replaced by the self-oriented therapeutic sensibilities of Counselor Troi. The emphasis seemed to have become less on finding the "right" thing to do than on clarifying how one felt about a course of action.

Despite all the nonjudgmentalism and tolerance, *TNG* heroes continued to act as if both morality and humanity corresponded, in some sense, to some objective pattern (and often they were made synonymous, as we've just seen). Captain Picard, in the *TNG* finale "All Good Things . . . ," assumes some kind of unified norm, saying, "We've got to save humanity!"

And as has been the case with other bits of thematic unfinished business, unexamined assumptions, or cheating, *Trek* of late seems to have become guiltily cognizant of their very un-PC practice of referring to humanity as if it referred to an absolute pattern which all "humans" should seek to follow.

In the *DS9* episode "Looking for Parmach in All the Wrong Places," we run into another manifestation of the burgeoning political diversity within the Federation. Here, a radical group called the Essentialists stage a protest on the pleasure planet Risa over their fears that dependence upon technology has made the Federation soft and so open to enemy attack. This is an old and legitimate worry of science fiction. H. G. Wells projected a future that included lazy and ineffectual Eloi, a split-off from humanity who had indeed gone soft because of their extreme dependence upon technology. As someone who has at times been impatient waiting thirty seconds for his coffee to warm, I do wonder what the effect of food replicators, holodecks, and transporters would be on society and individuals.

Yet instead of taking the charges of the Essentialists seriously, the episode simply changes the subject. The protest group
becomes merely stand-ins for a favorite *Trek* target—religious or
political conservatives. Serious discussion about what human
"essentials" might actually be is tabled by the portrayal of those
raising the questions as pigheaded fundies.

On *Voyager*, in the two-episode "Basics," the crew is stranded
on a barren planet without a single piece of technology—a marvelous opportunity to confront life without those magical
machines. I waited all summer for part 2, then was utterly disappointed. Any discussion about what the "basics" of being human
might be was, again, ignored as the story chased after some dumb
subplot involving cavemen and dinosaurs. The *DS9* episode
"Paradise" was what "Basics" might have been—a Starfleet crew
stranded on a planet for years—yet they, too, missed their chance.
Once again, consideration of the venerable SF theme of technology versus nature was avoided in favor of a cartoonish cult society
plot, making freedom the punchline once more.

At first it seemed very odd to me that *Trek* writers would raise
the issues of human basics and essentials but then back away so
cowardly from the discussion. Isn't that what *Trek* has always been
about? Trying to identify what it means to be human? Likewise,
it seemed strange that *Trek*, which has traditionally valued intuition over logic, would shy from contrasting technology with a
classic back-to-nature plot, as in *Logan's Run* or the original theatrical release of *Blade Runner*.

Then I realized what many in the SF community have already
concluded: if we make technology the bad guy and nature the
good guy, we risk suggesting that there is a *human nature*, a
universal pattern, against which certain artificial values are unnat-
ural. Women were once told it was *natural* to be mothers instead

of getting an education, making a career. Thus, goes this argument, the label of "natural" becomes a tool for oppression. Ergo, commitment to absolute freedom and self-determination means that nature has become the last refuge of a scoundrel.

In philosophy, the "essentialist" position is opposed by the "existentialist." The first group would say there is a universal human nature to which all individual humans ought to aspire. The second group argues that there is no fixed pattern; we just make it up as we go. Existentialists rejected the idea of any fixed human essence when the conclusions of materialist science made it clear that the essence of humanity was "to be entirely without significance"—much as Spock, in *Star Trek: The Motion Picture*, when forced to choose between logic and meaning, chose meaning. The existentialist solution to the problem of meaninglessness: free the individual from any fixed destiny and he is thus able to create his own meaning. The price of this solution: the end of any universal notion of being human.

So along with progress and truth, one of the many formerly unquestioned norms which have crumbled under the disillusionments of the twentieth century and the relentless questioning of the deconstructionists is the norm of "humanity." The possibility of being oppressed by somebody's personal notion of what it means to be human has been forestalled by the abolition of man. The logic of postmodernity, with its rejection of all norms, including "human," has lead to what an increasing number of people are calling—without irony—posthumanism.

HOW I LEARNED TO STOP WORRYING AND LOVE THE BORG

We've shown that the traditional problem of science fiction has been confronting the Other and that the traditional solution has been to neutralize, assimilate, or destroy the Other. And we've also discussed how, in science fiction, "the Other" can be made to stand for various phenomena—from the human unconscious to different ethnic groups to technology. Indeed, the machine, along with *things*, and *its*, and the fear of being reduced to a thing or an it, are among the central anxieties driving traditional SF. In the typical happy ending, good triumphs over evil; in the usual SF happy ending, humanity reigns supreme over technology.

We've also discussed how *Trek* presumes to subvert the traditional mission of science fiction, i.e., pursuing a new goal of "embracing the Other," yet nonetheless continues to make make judgments of the Other and maintain segregations.

In the case of the Other that is technology, *Trek* has taken a traditional approach: Kirk's human values overrule Spock's cold equations; technobabble makes the *Enterprise* fly, but Shakespeare has the last word; the archenemy is the Borg, an organic being which, unlike our heroes, has been subsumed into system: dehumanized. The cyborg—half human, half machine (either figuratively or literally) remains the testing ground of what it means to be human. On *Voyager* a former Borg, Seven of Nine, joins the crew and takes her place in the tradition of *Trek* characters struggling with identity, trying to become more human.

Even the *Trek*'s entirely mechanical character, Commander Data, is—like Robby the Robot in *Forbidden Planet*—a reassuring, domesticated machine, a "humanizing" of technology. Data is rendered nonthreatening (unlike the Borg) by his gentle ways, the fact that he wants to become more human, and the fact that he is the only one of his kind: after they made Data, his creator pretty much "broke the mold" (except, of course for his evil twin, Lore). The robot, says one critic, is "the single most important" image in science fiction:[7] humanity's evil twin, the ghost haunting technological progress, our own alien double.

Yet, as with other symbols on *Trek*, the character of Data can be invested with various meanings. Like Spock, Data can also function as the Outsider Who Wants to Belong, or the Oppressed Minority Who Deserves Rights and Dignity. And if we don't keep track of the pea being shifted between walnut shells, we'll find ourselves rooting for the rights and dignity of the cold equations.

In the *TNG* episode "Measure of a Man," Starfleet wants to disassemble Data to figure out what makes him tick, so the android is put on trial to determine his rights. As he once defended humanity, Jean-Luc Picard now defends the machine; the captain argues for the inherent rights and dignity of all sentient beings: Data is not an *it* but an *I*. Picard's argument consciously echos the historical case for the rights of African Americans, once also considered by some to be *its* or *things*.

But watch carefully: in another episode, the pea will subtly switch walnut shells. In "Datalore" *(TNG)*, we go from machine as metaphor for humanity to humanity as metaphor for machine:

> PICARD: If it feels awkward to be reminded that Data is a machine, just remember we [human beings] are merely a different variety of machine. In our case, electrochemical in nature."

Here it seems the case for bestowing human rights upon a machine was based not on elevating the machine to the status of humanity, but on devaluing humanity to the status of machine. No doubt the task of humanizing machines becomes much easier if humans are already machines. This perspective has always been challenged by those who argued the case for the soul, or at least a human essence.

But as we noted in the previous section, human essence seems doomed to the same extinction as the human soul. The species formerly known as human almost unanimously now views itself as a machine—electrochemical or socio-organic: an *it*. And how illogical to fear becoming an *it* or a *thing* if we've never been anything else. "We Are (Already) Borg"[8] is the title of a *Wired* magazine article by Donna Haraway, author of the famous *Cyborg Manifesto* (1985). Haraway, a professor of "the history of consciousness," argues for a positive rereading of the cyborg metaphor. No longer a symbol of mindless automation, the cyborg now becomes a symbol for autonomy: freedom from the cage of humanity opens a vast, virgin frontier of self-determination.

The word cybernetics was coined back in 1948 by MIT math whiz Norbert Weiner after he observed similarities between various phenomena in nature, technology, and society; all of these, he asserted, were based on information exchange. Thus, humans have always been networked with other networks, those of nature and society. If the line between "natural" and "artifical" has always been blurred, it follows that humans can be "artificially" reconstructed without making much difference. And so the robot or cyborg goes from being a bad guy to being a symbol of liberation.

Haraway and other procyborg thinkers argue that the line between organic and machine blurred long ago with our assimilation of technology from language to tennis shoes. This artificial reconstruction of humanity, i.e., "maximum choice," is threatening only to those bigots who believe in fixed human essence; an ought for humanity: belief in the existence of humanity becomes a highly charged political assertion, part of some essentialist or fundamentalist agenda, indeed, a religious commitment. Technophobia is as politically incorrect as homophobia.[9]

All this obviously calls for a careful rethinking of both our traditional perspective on "the machine" and on "man."

Human identity has certainly taken a beating since the heady days of the Enlightenment. Today our species, having long abandoned the once static pattern of being made in the image of God, would seem to stand on the threshold of a new step forward in evolution—though "forward" suggests a direction and "our species" must be rejected as an oppressive notion. In any case, "evolution" has always taken it for granted that a human was a work in progress anyway—though, again, one can hardly speak of progress, since that makes it seem as if there is a goal: let's just say we have no idea where we're going, but thanks to the explosion of old boundaries and new technologies, we can get there faster than ever. (And when I say "we," I don't mean to suppose you're coming with me, but you get the idea, I hope.)

With the advent of bioengineering and genetic manipulation, some hope to take a rational hand in molding their identity—in the words of the prologue to the *Six Million Dollar Man*, "We have the technology. We can rebuild him. Make him better than he was." A slogan used both by feminists and homosexuals ("Biology is not destiny") is now a rallying cry for posthumanists. What began with pacemakers and hearing aids, these say, must now continue with bioimplants, the integration of the human brain with computers: not even the sky is the limit.

Indeed, the promise of transcending traditional human limits and limitations by "postbiological man" seems attractive: we might finally cure our diseases, heal our species' chronic defects. The recent advances in cloning of animals have brought to public attention the breathtaking new technologies we've just begun to exploit: these include the manipulation of human biological structure at the intracellular level. We can go beyond merely healing to actual improvement, overcoming traditional human frailties and improving our lifespan, intelligence, and strength.

The notion of eugenics (rationally interfering with the processes of reproduction to improve human stock) is an old idea, developing along with Darwinism, but losing favor for many years due to revelations of horrifying experiments by Nazi eugenicists. Yet what some people call genocide, other people call a day's work—and logic can justify anything. So there has been a recent resurgence of interest (and increasing public approval) of the possibility of manipulating the human condition at the DNA level. Some argue that the ultimate potential—maybe even salvation—of the human race lies in our rational evolution to a higher life-form, one with augmented abilities. Perhaps we can actually repair some of our species' characteristic defects, some would say, which have produced so much bad history. (Though who decides which are the "defects" and what constitutes "repair" would take us back into that circular discussion of normalizing normlessness.)

Meanwhile, some warn of possible negative consequences of genetic manipulation: among these are the division of our species into biological "haves" and "have-nots," or, more worrisome, the division of our species into divergent strains. The Infinite Diversity in Infinite Combinations of *Trek*'s galaxy may one day be found on planet Earth alone; we may manufacture new aliens.

One very prescient element of *Trek*'s backstory, which first appeared back in the sixties on *TOS*, was the revelation that human history in the late twentieth century featured experiments in eugenics, the breeding of "supermen," which ultimately led to a series of what became known as the Eugenics Wars ("Space Seed," *TOS*, see also *TWOK*). These wars were not merely between the eugenicists and their creations, but between those who wanted to improve human stock and the "Normals"—a precursor to the Essentialists, one presumes—who wanted to keep humanity as it was, warts and all. (The prediction was a little ahead of schedule, however, since in "Space Seed" we learned that the eugenically bred supermen took over Earth in the mid-1990s!)

Another concern of those critical of new biotechnology is the old science fiction (and real-life) worry over an increased ability by a government to monitor and control its citizens. Bioimplants and computers promise a totalitarian efficiency that George Orwell in *1984* (likewise somewhat ahead of his time) and the old Soviet monolith only could dream about. On *Trek*, the Jem'Hadar are a race of creatures who have been genetically modified to require a particular chemical substance—"the White"—from their masters, the Founders, and so are kept entirely under control.

Without sounding too alarmist, though perhaps that is the proper tone here after all, this would seem to be the place to make mention of the notorious willingness of secular humanists to

> justify and recommend abortion, infanticide, euthanasia, and the sterilizing or killing of the physically handicapped and mentally limited, as the Nazis did. . . . [This is] clear evidence of the direction in which their basic attitude takes them. . . . After all, when their philosophy starts with permissiveness and aims at a perfectly happy community here on earth, there is no other way for their thoughts to go.[10]

The authors of the book *Christianity: The True Humanism* accuse their secular counterparts of being foxes who seek to be put in charge of the henhouse:

> Those who start by echoing the second *Humanist Manifesto* [1973]—"the preciousness and dignity of the individual person is a central humanist value"—end up as social engineers devaluing all individuals who do not measure up to their ideal.[11]

This much is true: the first *Humanist Manifesto* is shy in the use of word the *ought*—though it is full of *wills* and *musts*; the sequel manifesto, however, is even less guarded.

With the arrogance of scientific certainty, those who begin with freedom and individual dignity too soon speak of using "rational" methods to achieve progress, conforming the world to a standard of "good" identified by an elite. "What we call Man's power over Nature," says C.S. Lewis, "turns out to be a power exercised by some men over other men with Nature as its instrument."[12] The centerpiece to Lewis's book *That Hideous Strength* is a scientific body called the National Institute for Co-ordinated Experiments, or N.I.C.E., a hive of humanistic programmers.

Question: Which is the greater danger, scientific illiteracy among the uneducated masses, or a scientifically literate elite? "No other species does science as much or as well as we," says Carl Sagan. "How then can science be 'dehumanizing?' "[13] And by this logic, how can anything science does be called inhumane?

Be all this as it may, the self-described posthumanists welcome the impending brave new world of genetic manipulation and other "improvements," and are busily posting their own manifestos on the Internet—not realizing that manifesto making would seem to be a retrograde, "modern" phenomenon. In the postmodern, posthuman future, no one group will speak for all, or presume to draw the borders: there will be infinite diversity, indeed.

Among the extreme procyborg, it is often suggested that the time has come for carbon-based biological life to surrender the field to the more superior silicon-based life forms. This suggestion has been made on *Trek* more than once, but never by the "good guys" (see "The Ultimate Computer" and "The Changeling" *(TOS), and Star Trek: The Motion Picture*—which in many ways was a remake of "The Changeling"). Yet consider the merits of the argument: hardware (the machine) is without question more durable and efficient than "wetware" (organic life). Certainly, intelligent machines would be a much more logical mode for exploring the galaxy. If there is anybody out there, its more likely they, too, have evolved into intelligent machines, some say. The notion that any "Borg" are necessarily aggressive and seek to assimilate organic life, says one writer,[14] is a needless projection of our own species' violent and intolerant tendencies onto another. Evolution to "the next step," insist posthumanists, will feature tolerance—even of those who do not choose to join in evolving[15] (and even if tolerance is intrinsically incompatible with evolution, apparently).

On the other hand, those efforts by human "essentialists" to restrict evolution—the attempts to hold back progress, restrict cloning and genetic research—are backward and must be stopped. Resistance, posthumanists make clear, is futile.

GUESS WHO'S COMING TO DINNER

If there were no *Trek*, my access to the Internet would surely be three or four times faster. That is to say, you can't swing a cybercat without hitting a *Trek* discussion group. Such groups do for *Trek* what the old Baker Street Irregulars pioneered for Sherlock Holmes: bridge gaps in stories, weave theories to explain contradictions, follow the implications of plot developments backward and forward, debate character motivations. Some groups are general; others specialize in particular *Trek* shows, characters, species, or some other angle of interest. Physicists, for example, hash through extremely technical discussions of *Trek* technology, speculating on how devices work, theorizing over contradictions or violations of known science.

There's even a Jewish *Trek* E-mail discussion group, where I spent some time "lurking." At issue when I joined was whether or not the android Data could convert to Judaism. The discussion soon became as highly technical as the physics debates—but much more personal: the question provoked a hairsplitting, flamethrowing fracas involving the minutia of Jewish Law, rabbinical opinion, and talmudic analogies. Did Data have a soul? How about a foreskin? Would keeping kosher require a weekly shutdown, the argument being that he runs on electricity, and electricity qualifies as fire, which Orthodox Jews are not allowed to light on the Sabbath.

The debate over Data swiftly became a debate over conversion, i.e., what exactly was involved in becoming and in being a Jew?

Presented under the subject line "Who Are We?" the discussion moved to whether or not Jewishness was a matter of physical descent from a particular people. . . . Of course not—or else how could anybody convert? Then it's a religious thing. Well, not necessarily—there are plenty of nonreligious Jews. Oh, yeah? Reformed Jews may think they're Jewish, but unless they observe the Law—like we Orthodox do—then they're not true Jews. Say, fella, that's not very nice. Who are you to say who's a real Jew or not? It's not what I say, pal, it's the Torah, the rabbis, etc. (Then some misguided peacemaker tried to inject a little *Trek* tolerance:) Please, everybody. We accept all Jewish denominations in this discussion; nobody is qualified to judge anybody else. (This really drove some people nuts.) Are you out of your mind? If we accept everybody without judging, why would anybody need to convert from one religion to another anyway?!

In sum, the Jewish discussion of *Trek* was overshadowed by the same identity crisis which now racks contemporary Judaism as a whole—especially the Jews of Israel. Are Jews a race, like Vulcans? or a religion, to which even a Vulcan might convert?

It all may seem irrelevant, perhaps even humorous, to a non-Jew. But nobody will be allowed the safety of simply "lurking" on this debate for much longer. The same controversy is being played out, and will be increasingly so as time goes on, over a much more ecumenical issue: what does it mean to be human? Is being human a matter of common origin? Physicality? Limitations? Common beliefs—that even an android could hold? Who are we?

Like Jewishness, *humanity* can no longer be defined in such a way a to please everybody. Indeed, in the face of utter self-determination, maximum individual choice, the term loses meaning. And while some mourn this abolition of man, others welcome dehumanization as a liberation: one more celebration of freedom from oppressive limitations, a new dance atop another broken wall.

Yet with this end of "man," *Trek* faces a crossroads: its original mission would seem also to be at an end, with no "humanity" either to find or to save. Likewise, with no "humanity" to function as moral yardstick, *Trek* seems forced to relinquish its patented sense of idealism, its universal moral pattern, its *ought*.

Of course, *Trek* may treat this fork in the road like all the rest, speaking with forked tongue, taking both directions at once. In truth, *Trek* has always been torn by an internal debate over this particular split: is the creed behind *Trek* essentialist or existentialist? Is there an ideal pattern for morality, for humanity, or is there absolute freedom from all human patterns?

Despite its progressive philosophy and advanced technology, *Trek* has always shown remarkable restraint with regard to overcoming the traditional limitations of "humanity" (a point that we'll discuss in greater detail in the next chapter). Thomas

Richards, who pointed out *Trek*'s fixation with barriers in his book *The Meaning of Star Trek*, argues that keeping intact this "great divide between man and machine" is the basis for *Trek*'s optimistic vision.[16] Yet given *Trek*'s celebration of diversity and individual freedom, along with their godlike technological powers, such sentimental clinging to human frailties seems a flimsy barrier to keep them from venturing across the posthuman frontier. Indeed, Richard Hanley argues that such prejudices defy "common sense," and that *Trek* fans should become more open-minded about exciting new possibilities for human survival, including interfaces with robots or computers.[17]

One can understand the hesitation some would have at the idea of surrendering humanity's essence. After all, this root value—whether it came from being made in the image of God, or from some secular mask for the same idea—has always been what has separated man from beast, a separation most human beings have traditionally welcomed. Our human essence has been the source of our intrinsic dignity and value here in the West, imago Dei by any other name. Richard Hanley seeks in his book to discern how *Trek* determines moral consideration among species. He says the fact that nonhuman aliens and sentient machines on *Trek* are given the same moral consideration—the status of "personhood"—calls into question any notion of special status for *Homo sapiens*. Perhaps it's no great leap to concede that one might be a "person" without being human (i.e., an alien or an android), but for Hanley, the converse also holds true: that one can be a human without being a "person"[18]—that is, a member of the human species may, if it falls short of someone's criteria for personhood, be declared a nonperson—something we have seen in our history before. This casts a rather dark shadow over all this magnanimity of widening "personhood" to include aliens.

Ironically, in the *TNG* finale "All Good Things . . . ," it is Captain Jean-Luc Picard himself who threatens to destroy humanity. But if *Trek* (and humanity) follows the inhuman logic of tolerance, and is so done in by its own wild virtues, we have a ready-made excuse: we were only human. A fine epitaph, indeed.

In some ways, the abolition of man is an almost admirable strategy. The problem of injustice is solved by the elimination of any standard of justice. The problem of the Other is solved by getting rid of the norm. And the problem of man's inhumanity to man is solved by dispensing with "humanity" altogether. "We're not like that anymore" takes on a rather different meaning.

Then again, for a show set in outer space, this seems a matter of phasering oneself in the foot. For if you get rid of the norm, you necessarily lose the alien. As Flannery O'Connor says (and if you've ever read her, you realize she should know): "In order to recognize a freak, you have to have a conception of the whole man." I wonder. Without any aliens, what happens to wonder?

In any case, humanity itself seems to be in the position of the Talosians, who rescued a young human girl from a space wreck— saving her life, but making of her a misshapen mess. "They had no guide for putting me back together," says Vina. Luckily, the Talosians could give Vina the illusory appearance of humanity.

We'll talk more about illusions in chapter 8. First comes chapter 7, where we'll continue the discussion of defining humanity in connection with the flesh—and beyond. The question to examine will be this: Under which category do we file the duality of body and soul—"half-humans" or "evil twins"?

7

Spirits, Bodies, and Other Alien Beings

OF OTHER WORLDS

C. S. Lewis knew what it meant to live a divided existence. Like Spock, Lewis was rigorously schooled in reason. But while Spock's inner conflict involved his logical and human sides, Lewis struggled to reconcile his logic with a powerful imagination: he loved myth, fantasies, and romantic poetry. As you might guess, Lewis was out of step with his age when it came to his literary tastes. One modern he appreciated, though, was William Butler Yeats, a poet both modern and romantic, who seemed to have bridged the gap between fairyland and the scientific age. Gradually, it dawned on Lewis what made Yeats tick: the man *really* believed. When as a young man Lewis had a chance to meet Yeats, the poet babbled on about "magic and ghosts and mysteries."[1] At the time, Lewis had reluctantly made his peace with materialism, having given up any hope of connecting that "real world" with the "other worlds" of his imagination. The encounter with Yeats, an obviously intelligent man who rejected the monopoly of material reality, was quite unsettling for Lewis.

Yeats, in his latter years, devoted his attentions to what he said was the central revelation of his life, *A Vision,* a long and complicated dissertation born of automatic writing. But if this be romanticism, Yeats was not the last of that line. For science-fiction author Philip K. Dick, in his final days, poured his energies into a two-million-word handwritten scrawl of philosophical ramblings and metaphysical diagrams. Dick's *Exegesis* was also, he said, the result of a supernatural vision.

This bridge between romance—including that branch discussed here, fantasy/science fiction—and the supernatural turns out to be very well traveled. The Heaven's Gate religious cult couched their suicide gospel in the language of *Star Trek.* Japan's Aum "Supreme Truth" cult drew its apocalyptic theology from Isaac Asimov's SF classic *Foundation* series, a story that features a group of quasi-monks who guide society through the cataclysmic fall of civilization. The gospel of Scientology, founded by SF author L. Ron Hubbard, is big on electronic devices and extraterrestrials. Faithful Mormons (males) are promised their own planet to rule in the afterlife. Devotees of New Age physics connect the bizarrities of quantum theory to Eastern mysticism. And UFO cultists speak of the imminent coming of space aliens in tones once reserved strictly for messianic hopes.

We spoke earlier about connections and boundary blurring between fantasy and science fiction. Clearly, similar connections and fuzzy borders exist between both of these genres and one more "world": that of the spirit—the occult, sorcery, supernatural beings, and visions of a reality beyond the natural world—which has found a seemingly natural place in the world of science fiction.

In the middle of that frenzied panel discussion at the science-fiction convention I spoke of earlier, as we squabbled over the border between hard SF and fantasy, we were interrupted by a fellow standing in the back of the room, wearing a tuxedo and leaning on a cane. He joined the fray with a quote from Aleister Crowley, the infamous practitioner of black magic and self-described Satanist. "Magic," said the man, "has rules as strict as those of science, and these are set forth in the works of magicians going back centuries." The fellow obviously wasn't talking about stage magic in this case, and his assertion set off a torrent of disagreement from the panel. The hard-SF defenders, who I'd nearly reconciled to the validity of fantasy as a story genre, weren't about to admit the validity of sorcery.

Like that confident young materialist C. S. Lewis, many of us will find the connection between science fiction and sorcery both confusing and disturbing. For science would seem to be about debunking the spirit world, which hard-SF fans dismiss as groundless superstition. Nevertheless, one finds science fiction and fantasy shelved with books on the occult and the paranormal—not just at used bookstores, but in the dealers' rooms at SF conventions. The same folks who watch *Trek* are liable to be fans of the *X-Files*. The science and religion come together in that poster of a UFO hanging in Agent Mulder's office that says, "I want to believe."

For *Trek*, this "other world" of the spirit is one more toward which it shows two faces. And while there has been an evolution of *Trek*'s view of the supernatural versus strict materialism, as with everything else, *Trek* still seeks to have things both ways.

VERY SUPERSTITIOUS

The traditional *Trek* view of spirituality—at least, of organized religion—is single-minded: implacable hostility. We should not be surprised, says *Wonder* editor Rod Bennett, if we run across, in one of those future timelines that fill various *Trek* encyclopedia, this momentous date: "Final Extinction of Christianity, Judaism, Islam, etc." There would certainly be nothing in most of *Trek* to contradict this idea. True, there's that *TOS* episode on a parallel "Rome" planet where what are thought to be sun worshipers turn out to be Son worshipers, i.e., the Son of God. But that's just a dramatic punchline for a particular episode rather than a statement of the overall *Trek* point of view of religion, which is, as just mentioned, is invariably "treated as a dupe or a con."[2] Indeed, religion seems to be lumped along with all those things humanity has left behind—sickness, crime, poverty, and racism. The irony: though *Trek* requires a deus ex machina to solve practically all its problems, humanity, it seems, must get by without assistance by any god.

The name for this view is *materialism* (also known as *naturalism*): the idea that everything that exists arose from nothing of its own accord without any supernatural interference, the ultimate Prime Directive. Harvard genetics professor Richard Lewontin recently confessed what critics of this position have always known, that materialism must be an a priori commitment for scientists— that is, materialists must begin with materialism before doing any science.[3] This is why materialist scientists remain steadfast in their materialism, even when they are forced to resort to their own deus-ex-machina explanations. For example, Nobel laureate Francis Crick, the discoverer of DNA, who has his doubts about the old naturalist formula "time-plus-chance" producing even one-celled creatures, recently suggested that space aliens devised life and sent it to Earth. Oddly enough, we find the same sort of materialist-designer motif in both Carl Sagan's novel *Contact* and the *TNG* episode "The Chase." All of which only postpones the question, who designed the designers? The explanation remains materialist because that's where it begins.

Under Gene Roddenberry, the supernatural on *Trek* is always depicted as gods with machines: starship crews are constantly encountering would-be deities, witches, or devils, only to see these creatures debunked by the end of the episode as charlatans whose "supernatural" powers come from some fully explainable technological means. The old Hollywood production code insisted filmmakers could not show that crime paid. The Roddenberry code meant *Trek* writers could never depict the supernatural as real.

Again, we must note that such a view is a presupposition. And one has to wonder if the Great Bird's a priori rejection of religion stemmed less from any well-thought-out objections than from his characteristic aversion to authority, especially a God who might suggest limits—God being, of course, the "guy who knows you masturbate." (Incidentally, this was Lewis's objection to God as well: "No word in my vocabulary expressed deeper hatred than the word Interference. But Christianity placed at the center what then seemed to me a transcendental Interferer."4) Yet Roddenberry's critique of theism and defense of materialism, as seen in interviews, was terribly uninformed, relying primarily on the equivalent of dismissive technobabble. The book *Gene Roddenberry: The Last Conversation* is astonishing in the lack of the Great Bird's insight into his own creation, and embarrassing in his attempts to critique alternative views.

Of course, what Roddenberry actually believed was, some would say, very much like a religion: like many who embraced a glib Enlightenment optimism, Roddenberry evinced a romantic faith in progress—the belief that science would create a just society. For someone remembered as a seer, Roddenberry seemed to have many blindnesses: he never gave any indication he saw the leaps of faith and logic required to legitimate *Trek*'s notion of ethics, humanity, the value of the individual, or reality. He was apparently blind to the fact that his own gods—especially progress— had already been declared dead by many even as he embraced them. Worse, Roddenberry seemed oblivious to the implications of the Enlightenment understanding of man as machine: the utter emptiness of materialism, the spiritual hunger it could not fill. Nowhere in any of Roddenberry's many comments about *Trek* and his pronouncements about humanity do we find any sense of sympathy or even comprehension of the deep despair of those who have struggled with the lack of human meaning and value in the face of existential nothingness—the end of an entirely scientific view. Dealing with this kind of despair with glib optimism, it must be said, is like giving characters spaceflight capability and engaging the enemy with grappling hooks.

It's no surprise, then, that as Roddenberry was launching his materialist vision, the culture of the sixties exploded around him in violent revolt against materialism. The Age of Aquarius was a rebellion against the "plastic society" and against the stifling authority of science; the counterculture sought freedom from "the cage" of the closed Enlightenment view of reality. The spiritually starving masses in the sixties welcomed an invasion of spirituality: a revival of drugs, an interest in the paranormal, religious cults, Satanism and the occult—much of what was later institutionalized (loosely) as New Age.

The phenomenon of the materialistic *Trek*'s appeal at a moment of intense reaction against materialism is an intriguing one; we'll offer a possible explanation for such doubleness in a moment.

Meanwhile, we must observe that even the materialistic *Trek* could not remain long unaffected by changes in the culture. The

first chapter of post-sixties *Trek,* the 1979 *Motion Picture,* opened
with Vulcan mysticism—couched, to be sure, in the language of
logic, but presented in that typical "illogical," quasi-religious
Vulcan way. The conclusion of that film—the confession of a
need to go "beyond logic"—opened the door, as we noted in our
chapter on Spock, to any number of places one might go if one
were to go beyond logic. The religious overtones of the ending of
TMP, a veritable spiritual transfiguration—suggested that some
manner of spirituality might begin to find a welcome in the hitherto materialist cosmos of *Trek.* Sure enough, in the next film,
Spock's *katra* makes spirit the key to keeping *Trek* alive, as it is
passed from one movie to the next.

Gene Roddenberry lost control of the *Trek* films for a variety
of reasons, among these his difficulty in letting *Trek* go places
other people seemed intent on letting it boldly go. The Great Bird
turned his attention to TV *Trek,* a throwback in more ways than
one. And while *TNG* also paddled away from the shores of logic,
into the therapeutic world of the nondirective, nonjudgmental
Counselor Troi, the supernatural was still stubbornly excluded.
One of the early *TNG* episodes was "Who Watches the
Watchers?" a vehicle for restaging the old Enlightenment-versus-
religion fight. In this story, Picard is taken for a god by otherwise
rational natives, who had long abandoned religion; he applauds
their rationality and urges them to keep on that path. In an interview with *The Humanist,* Roddenberry expressed surprise and disappointment when the episode didn't generate the heated controversy with religious types he apparently expected. It is no wonder
that, cloistered in the humanist fraternity, Roddenberry never
noticed that humanism was already passé.

Meanwhile, real-life astronaut Edger Mitchell stayed in the
headlines with his think tank for the study of the paranormal.

Baby Boomers were spending piles of money on spiritual quests, fueling the business of spiritual advice to the status of a growth industry: from Shirley MacLaine, reincarnation, and crystals, to channeling, astrology, ESP, Scientology, holistic healing, neopaganism, and the nascent goddess movement. And that catalyst to the cinematic space-alien revival, *Star Wars*, had as its centerpiece a space religion; the unexpected success of the Lucas film was what made possible the resurrection of *Trek*.

One thing the infinite diversity of New Age spirituality had in common with the *Trek* vision was the absence of the interfering sort of God that Roddenberry had long detested. Indeed, certain later statements by the Great Bird indicate he, too, perhaps, found room in his own personal cosmos for the sort of amorphous, unknowable "force" god popular among this spiritual counterculture. At last, maybe he thought, a god who strictly observes General Order Number One.

Be that as it may, the Great Bird would be horrified at the extent and implications of the revival of religion on *Trek* which followed his final departure from the series with his 1991 death.

On *Deep Space Nine*, religion is absolutely central to the story, and seems to be somewhat derivative of the SF religion of Frank Herbert's *Dune* series. On Bajor, the planet nearest the *DS9* station, lives an extremely religious race, whose church and state are indivisibly mixed. The Bajoran religion revolves around the Prophets, beings said to inhabit a Celestial Temple, which turns out to be a nearby wormhole. The Bajoran religion is far from monolithic, featuring conservatives, liberals, hypocrites, decent folk (some of whom struggle with doubt), total freethinkers, and plenty of true believers. There is concern for knowing and doing the "will of the Prophets," but for the most part the Prophets are pretty laid-back: the liberal Bajoran cleric Vedik Bareil regularly visits the *DS9* station to spend the night with Kira, the station's Bajoran liason. As with all religions, Bajor's can sometimes function as a thin cover for political-power grabbing and maneuvering. A continuing character is the Eddie Haskallesque cleric Vedik Winn, who one suspects functions as the writers' stand-in for the Reverend Pat Robertson.

An interesting wrinkle in the *DS9* subplot involving the Bajoran faith is the fact that station commander Sisko becomes—against his own wishes or better judgment—a figure of major importance in the religion. Sisko is uncomfortable to find himself the subject of prophecies by the clerics: he is the long awaited Emissary who is to play a role in shaping the destiny of Bajor, and has to perform various ceremonial functions. Reluctant at first, perhaps like a *Trek* actor facing his first *Trek* convention, Sisko is the skeptic who eventually makes his peace and grows less skeptical as he goes on—especially when he, too, begins to experience visions and prophecies, and even speaks with the Prophets.

Here the schizoid *Trek* perspective works to its advantage: often there is some ambiguity as to whether or not the supernatural experiences are real, with room left for a naturalistic explanation for various phenomena. This approach has worked well for the *X-Files*, which divides its own schizoid approach into the two characters of Agents Scully and Mulder. Freud, in a famous essay on the uncanny, says that this sort of ambiguity actually heightens the heebie-jeebies. Nevertheless, also like the *X-Files*, *Trek* can't resist supernatural chills and special-effects thrills that come with a little visual and sonic evidence for unexplainable phenomena. Thus, on *DS9*, prophecies come true. The Prophets turn out to be actual disembodied beings living in the wormhole who *do* guide the destiny of Bajor, and *do* have a will. In fact, these literal gods in the machine save Bajor and the entire Alpha Quadrant from an invasion by the evil Dominion. Yet whether they are actually spiritual beings, or just another form of alien intelligence, is left intentionally unclear.

On *DS9*'s sister series, *Voyager*, we likewise see cracks in the hitherto strict *Trek* brand of scientific materialism. With the introduction of the character of Commander Chakotay, we see the Hollywood reverence for the mysterious powers of Native Americans. Chakotay has a spirit guide he gets in touch with; on occasion he has gone into shamanlike trances, had visions, seen the future, etc. Again, despite the requisite bone thrown toward entirely naturalistic explanations for the phenomena, the viewer, at least, gets "objective" proof of their reality in the form of effects-laden visuals. (That's the advantage of TV and film: these media can "prove" assertions still in debate in the real world, from evolution to shamanism, to the existence or nonexistence of the soul. V'Ger can travel the whole universe and still be unable to find God. All you need are special effects, sound effects, and the appropriate music.)

Of course, if materialism is wrong, and if the soul does survive beyond death, and if he hasn't had more pressing things to think about or do, Gene Roddenberry must have rolled over in his grave after the *Voyager* episode "Sacred Ground." In this story, the crew visits a planet run by a religious order similar to the priests of Bajor. The away team observes monks passing in and out of a shrine—an energy field—which we learn is similar to the Bajoran Prophets' Celestial Temple in that it is home to the monks' "ancestral spirits." *Voyager* crew member Kes is a typical nonbeliever and empiricist, so she enters the shrine and is knocked unconscious. When the ship's doctor can't revive her, the monks tell captain Janeway that the only way to save Kes's life is for the captain to participate in a religious ritual.

Janeway agrees, though she is still the complete skeptic.

CHAKOTAY: Of course there's the possibility that the ancestral
spirits really do control what happens at the shrine. . . .
JANEWAY: To each his own, Commander. But I imagine if we
scratch deep enough, we find a scientific base for most religious
doctrines.

In hopes of reviving her crewman, rationalist Janeway patiently
goes through the motions of the ritual. Predictably, nothing
happens. The monks are on to her. They gently mock her over-
confidence in rationality and science. The captain must surrender
logic, they say, along with her need to be in control; she must
believe. In the end, Janeway *does* surrender logic, and she, too,
experiences a vision. The spirits she meets in her vision debunk
her nearly religious confidence in science: a criticism to which
materialist science is vulnerable, as we have seen. The spirits also
tell Janeway how to save Kes—not by just going beyond logic,
but by outright defying reason: she must again pass Kes through
the energy field—which the ship's sensors read as deadly. So
Janeway ignores her devices and follows the monks' instructions;
Kes is healed. The Doctor offers an ironclad naturalistic explanation for what they've just experienced, but as the episode comes to
an end, the camera plays over Janeway's face and we can see she's
not so sure.

"Sacred Ground" marks another blow against *Trek*'s traditional
antisupernatural materialism. But it also raises some questions
with regard to *Trek*'s view of the nature of faith. These are very
similar to the earlier questions we raised about *Trek*'s notion of
intuition. Was Kes healed because Janeway let go of reason, or
because the captain used her reason to conclude that the most
rational thing would be to trust someone who could see more than
she? In other words, did Janeway go beyond logic to illogic, or did

she go beyond empiricism to personal trust? Did she learn to have faith in faith, or did she have faith in the character and vision of the ancestral spirits?

Here we can see the contrast between the existential, irrational notion of faith and the traditional notion of faith—the very one criticized by *Trek* in its earlier, materialist incarnation. For no doubt the commands of the biblical Deity sometimes defy reason: the order to sacrifice one's only son, to conquer a city by marching around it blowing horns, to walk on water. But in these cases, the apparent leap of logic was not the sine qua non, but the Person who commanded. In the *TNG* finale "All Good Things . . ." Jean-Luc Picard travels through time, and so gains a much broader perspective than the rest of the crew. When he gives a command that *seems* irrational to the others, they hesitate. "You've got to *trust* me," he says. In this case, faith is a reasonable response to a person: it acknowledges the limits of sensory evidence without having to jettison reason.

Then again, a personal faith raises the spectre of divine will, or interference in personal freedom. Faith in faith, or faith in feelings, offers a way to bypass a Cosmic Interferer. Yet it likewise bypasses the interference of one's own judgment: there are no criteria for judging feelings, nothing to say to the mental patient whose inner voices and feelings urge him to harm himself or others. As noted in connection with Major Kira's take on her Bajoran faith, this is the inbuilt difficulty in dealing with someone who has accepted a faith that requires them to abandon reason—there is no way to talk reasonably about it with them.

So the new *Trek* perspective on the spirit world introduces yet another internal split, another unresolved love/hate relationship. And, as with *Trek*'s ethics, resolution of this conflict seems unnecessary: *Trek* leaps beyond contradictions by going beyond logic, and so is able to escape "hard" materialism.

But *Trek* always had a positive/negative relationship to matter.

MATTER/ANTIMATTER

"Brain, brain. What is brain?" ("Spock's Brain," *TOS*)

Trek's interstellar vessels are powered by the explosion created when matter is brought into contact with antimatter. Late twentieth-century physics has actually succeeded in creating small amounts of antimatter, but manipulation of this volatile material on the scale of Federation science seems a long way off.

Meanwhile, there is a different kind of matter/antimatter dynamic at the heart of *Trek*, pulling it in opposite directions.

At issue in the old mind/body or mind/brain debate is whether human consciousness is simply a matter of matter—that slab of meat we call "brain"—or whether sentience also requires an immaterial component, a mind or a soul which operates that slab of meat the way a man might operate a personal computer. On *Trek*, the self-consciousness of the android, Commander Data, would seem to indicate the debate has been settled—with matter beating mind. (Shhh. We're tiptoeing past a can of worms involving how we know whether Data has consciousness or he's just simulating it. The book *The Metaphysics of Star Trek* opens that one.)

The creation of machine intelligence will no doubt be the end of the debate on this issue for some. Yet we see that not every race in *Trek*'s cosmos has lost their soul. Bajorans believe themselves to possess an immaterial essence called a *borhyas* ("The Next Phase," *TNG*). The souls of dead Klingons, it is said, travel to a place that race knows as Stoval Core. Ferengi believe, albeit somewhat tongue-in-cheek, in an afterlife in the Great Treasury. Vulcans consider the individual's katra no laughing matter. Indeed, without a disembodied katra, the immaterial essence of his being,

Spock could not have survived the death of his body in *The Wrath of Khan* and his subsequent transplantation of being to another body in the next film, *The Search for Spock*.

The fact that *Trek* humans are shown as able to make such transfers would suggest that Vulcans aren't the only species with a *katra*. Kirk and Dr. Janice Lester change bodies in "Turnabout Intruder" *(TOS)*. In "By Any Other Name" *(TOS)*, human "life-entities" are stored while aliens borrow their bodies. Such disembodied intelligence would seem to contradict the notion of the material basis of self-consciousness "proven" by Data.

The nature of this katra, Vulcan or otherwise, is unresolved: is mind merely matter, or psychological information, or Something Else (an eternal soul?). The question makes for a fascinating frisbee to toss around, one that gets flung in both the *Physics* and *Metaphysics of Trek,* especially in connection with another device, *Trek's* teleporter, "the transporter." Lawrence Krauss *(Physics)* asks what is actually "beamed"—*atoms* (the actual matter composing a body) or *bits* (the digital information connected with a particular individual).[5] *Trek* techies would answer that both atoms and bits are beamed, but those notorious transporter accidents have proven that the same set information (bits) can be combined with what must be additional matter (more atoms) to create exact duplicates. Which means that matter (atoms) is secondary to information (bits). So why not just send the bits, he asks, using the atoms available at the destination to reassemble the body in question? (This option gains currency after Krauss makes it clear that the beaming of atoms makes the transporter *Trek's* single most implausible bit of technology.)

Of course, using the matter available on arrival means vaporizing the original body on departure—which means the end product is a replicant. Which was, no doubt, always the sneaky suspicion of Dr. McCoy, who saw "beaming" as a threat to the integrity of his person. Richard Hanley *(Metaphysics)* wonders what difference a replicant would make. As a professor of that branch of philosophy concerned with reality, Hanley wants to know what is crucial to personal survival: matter (atoms), or psychological data (bits), or a third element—the allegedly immaterial soul. Dr. Krauss thinks teleportation would prove the nonexistence of the soul.[6] Dr. Hanley says not necessarily, though with that all-too-common a priori commitment to materialism, Hanley says he disbelieves in the existence of the soul regardless.[7]

Hanley notes that McCoy's objection to transporting is based on the assumption that integrity of identity depends upon continuity of body—rather, of matter. But which matter? he asks. *Trek* characters typically have no problem with artificial organs—but only to a point, drawing a line at artificial brains. Which seems funny, since they accept the personhood of Data. Spock's "being" moves into a new body, and they're okay with that. But any scientist who moves his "being" into a machine must be "mad." Hanley has no problem with this and says *Trek* should lighten up—it's just bits of information. Right? (And here we pass into the stuff of that recent SF evolution—cyberpunk—featuring disembodied intelligences, soulless data preserved in computers.)

As usual, though, *Trek* can't decide. The title of one episode says it all: "The Schizoid Man"; this is a *TNG* episode where Data's "grandfather" transfers his personality (life-entity?) into Data's brain. Typically, the *Trek* humans accept artificial intelligence in machines, but not human intelligence in machines.

This love/hate relationship with the soul is the flip side of *Trek*'s love/hate relationship with the body. The characteristic attitude of cyberpunk is a "relaxed contempt for the flesh," a view shared by gnosticism, an ancient religion which (no surprise) is enjoying a recent revival. Gnosticism is a cluster of beliefs involving some form of secret knowledge and the idea that flesh (matter, the organic element of humanity) is bad, and spirit (in this case either data or soul) is good.

The Gnostic bent of *Trek* begins with a de-emphasis on the organic. To normal TV unnaturalness (nobody goes to the bathroom, or gets zits), add the science-fiction component: food is created in replicators (no animals were slain to make those steaks!), surgery is noninvasive surgery, blinking doodads cure internal injuries, and there are all those squeaky-clean, bloodless phaser battles. (A notable exception is in *The Undiscovered Country* when disgusting globs of purple Klingon blood drift to the camera.)

One could take the argument several ways about those bloodless phaser battles. The lack of gore on *Trek* seems to make it fairly kid-safe. On the other hand, the no-fuss-no-muss approach to death common to *Trek* and most action-hero shows tends to abstract violence in a way some find equally disturbing.

The de-emphasis of the body on *Trek* includes the strategic retreat from "the natural" we discussed last chapter, when nature is seen as an oppressive limitation on self-determination. *Trek* characters seem able to overcome this limitation by changing species at the drop of a hat—with as much trouble as changing a hat—when they need to go undercover. *Trek* is somewhat vague as to how this is accomplished, though apparently it involves some combination of makeup and surgery.

Moreover, in the life-entity transfer episodes, the particular body a katra occupies often seems irrelevant. Sometimes lovers resume relationships after their beloved has switched to a new body. Dax has no problem with this ("Rejoined," *DS9*). Beverly Crusher doesn't mind when her lover switches male bodies, but she draws the line when he lands in a female body ("The Host," *TNG*).

In sum, while the delusion of slasher films is that to be human is to merely be a body, a meat puppet, so much guts—or, in the words of the Velarians, "ugly bags of mostly water" ("Home Soil, *TNG*)—*Trek* exhibits the opposite tendency: the suggestion that being human has little to do with a physical body. One almost wishes for an episode where a crewman falls down and splits his gut, intestines rolling out in a big, bloody mess—just to remind everybody in the future what's still inside. ("Whoa, I guess the human body isn't merely a social construct after all. . . .") Our bodies are full of squiggly, gelatinous organs and rubbery worm–like things, and stringy fluids—very much the alien. Here is an Other *Trek* does not always embrace, an alien that is, after all, paradoxically, central to what it means to be human.

Meanwhile, along with the de-emphasis on the organic, *Trek* also projects an assumed sense that pure mind, freed from the limitations of either bodies or computers, is the real goal of evolution.

Like the Krell of *Forbidden Planet*, various *Trek* species have gone beyond the necessity of flesh. The telepathic Talosians communicate mind to mind, their bodies withering away ("The Menagerie," *TOS*). The Organians, the advanced energy-beings in "Errand of Mercy" *(TOS)*, force the Federation and the Klingons to make peace. Other incorporeal beings in *TOS* include the parents of Trelane in "The Squire of Gothos," the Companion in "Metamorphosis," Sargon in "Return to Tomorrow," the Medusans in "Is There No Truth in Beauty?" and the Zetars in "The Lights of Zetar." As Richard Hanley points out, there's no such thing as disembodied information, so these beings are apparently truly incorporeal: spirits (which his a priori commitment to materialism does not allow him to accept).

On *Trek*, disembodied beings differ in their attitude toward flesh: some prefer their existence as bodiless intelligence; others seek a body to be their vehicle. In March of 1997, thirty-nine members of the Heaven's Gate religious cult participated in a mass suicide. They, too, believed their bodies were unnecessary vehicles, that gender was irrelevant (especially so, apparently, after some of the male members were castrated). Killing themselves was their final effort to overcome all "human-mammalian behavior," to go "beyond human" to the "Next Evolutionary Level." They believed their disembodied spirits would then be picked up by a UFO following in the trail of the newly discovered comet Hale-Bopp. The Heaven's Gate cultists were big fans of science fiction, especially *Trek*. In interviews and their written material, they made continual reference to *Trek*, using terminology and concepts from the show to illustrate their own beliefs—that, for instance, the world of the senses was merely a holodeck projection. The dead wore patches identifying themselves as a part of a cosmic away team.

Yet Heaven's Gate had to pick and choose among the *Trek* mythos for ideas that already fit their religious beliefs; as we noted, *Trek*'s relationship with the flesh is love/hate. Gnostic cultists may have appreciated the hate part. But guess where the love begins and *Trek*'s Gnostic tendencies end. Like most New Age dabblers, *Trek* has always had a weakness for one particular manifestation of "human-mammalian behavior": that is to say, sex.

In the future, along with all that other stuff humanity has left behind are primitive sexual taboos and hangups. Nature may be bad, but casual sex is the most "natural" thing in the world. Starfleet service makes it easy to have families, but most crew members don't. The atmosphere at times is an interstellar Club Med. Skimpy-costumed aliens, girls/guys in every port, pleasure planets, and we haven't even gotten to the holodeck yet. Again, everything seems to depend on that evolved sensibility that *Trek* of late is having second thoughts about: sexual relationships among Federation peoples never seem to be fractured by jealousies, adulteries, or violence. Just like the Federation economy: all that was needed, it seems, was plenty—and everybody's happy. With presumably flawless birth control, no unwanted pregnancies, abortions, complications, birth defects, sexually transmitted diseases, *Trek* offers the ultimate in safe sex: sex freed from all the negative consequences that caused so much pain in the past.

The "safest" possible sex takes place on the holodeck. This device works on the same principle as the transporter, rearranging atoms to create "holomaterial," blurring the line between the real and the unreal. Here, crewmen can go on their off hours and dial up any fantasy they choose. There exist such things as "holonovels," but the participatory element makes the holodeck more like a game than a narrative directed by an author. And since pornography has been in the vanguard of every new image and information technology introduced so far, there's no reason to suppose it won't be the first and most popular game on the holodeck.

It's great for shy guys: Lieutenant Barclay ("Hollow Pursuits," *TNG*) and Geordi LaForge have better luck with holodeck-generated women. Even "real-life" lady-killer Commander Riker is not above the occasional holodeck fling, as in "11001001" *(TNG)*. ("What's a knockout like you doing in a computer-generated gin joint like this?") Like other casual sex, "holosex" seems to be an accepted part of future life, part of a healthy lifestyle.

But how safe is this "safe" sex? Depends on what one wants to be safe from. Sex would seem fundamentally about union: driven by the same longing for personal relationship that sent *Trek* humans to the stars, the individual seeks contact of the most intimate kind. There are dangers in such intimate contact, and sex has been hedged traditionally with protections, a framework for safety: to contain powerful instincts and maintain mutual dignity and respect. The inherent dangers of sexual intimacy have led some to renounce it entirely; Gnostics and semi-Gnostics have declared war on bodily pleasures and sought complete safety from human emotions in the manner of Spock seeking purity of logic.

And pornography has always introduced a peculiar fracture into the old mind/body split:[8] it combines Gnostic abstraction with physical pleasure—sex without contact with the Other. Such detached sexual experience means dehumanization of the object of sexual gratification: sex goes from "I-thou" to "I-it." In the episode "11001001," Riker and Picard talk about a holodeck babe in the third person, admiring her beauty and realism, even though she's sitting right there at the table with them. You have to wonder how somebody who gets used to treating "virtually" real women on the holodeck as "it" can shake off that habit when they get back to the nonvirtual world. The connection between the abstracting of persons in pornography and violence has been documented in ways only a tobacco industry lawyer could deny. And here, the supposedly liberal *Trek* seems to be oblivious to something on which even conservatives and feminists can agree.

Trek rarely asks questions about what effect new technologies or changes in individual or social morality will have on society. So it is not surprising that neither the practice nor the institution-alizing of virtual sex on the holodeck has ever been seriously treated as anything other than harmless fun. The possibility of addiction is suggested in the *TNG* episode "Hollow Pursuits," but Barclay's problems seem to be depicted as the exception, not the rule. Here we also learn there is some sense of propriety, a taboo against using images of real people in holodeck fantasies—though how we get such primitive things as sexual taboos in *Trek*'s ultra-nonjudgmental environment nobody explains. As if a mere taboo would really be enough to slow down some horny spaceman in his own private dream machine.

In this case, *Trek* avoids hard questions (and criticism) by stacking the deck. Barclay's fantasies are not whips and chains but a chivalrous romancing of ladies, along with some bloodless swordplay with holodeck projections of his superiors. Geordi LaForge falls for the computer-generated image of a real-life woman named Leah Brahms ("Galaxy's Child," *TNG*). He later meets the real Brahms, who turns out to be different from the program; she resents having been used by LaForge as a fantasy object—though Geordi insists that "nothing happened." Thank goodness for those evolved sensibilities.

But is it the sensibilities, or those pesky network censors? Once asked what he would write about if he was free to write about anything on *Trek*, producer Brannon Braga replied, "That's easy," he says. "I've always wondered what people really do on the holodeck."[9] Extrapolating from what is known of human history —especially the recent history of the smorgasbord of sexual options on the relatively primitive Internet—the possibilities for Braga's fantasy episode begin with images from the steamy ancient Roman *Satyricon* to some pre-AIDS San Francisco gay bathhouse and go to places we'd best not imagine. It is insinuated that Ferengi holoprograms offer more creative options than most: in "Meridian" *(DS9)*, Quark makes a holosex program featuring Major Kira, who discovers what he's up to and threatens, basical-ly, to reduce *him* to an object (i.e., a corpse).

Trek seems blissfully oblivious to the holodeck's systematic degradation of human beings by making them abstract objects who exist merely for someone's pleasure. Likewise, *Trek* seems unaware of the self-degradation involved in abstracting sex from personal relationship (which, even if *real* people *are* involved, can be pretty abstracted and degraded!). Once again, the advantage of television: protection from real-life consequences.

Since *Trek* itself is a sort of holodeck, then, it should be no surprise that there is no clear line in sexual matters between where fantasy ends and "real" life begins. Indeed, the real-life women of *Trek* have always been treated as sex objects. Here's another dirty little secret of the supposedly advanced *Trek:* there may be women on the bridge, but they're wearing mini skirts. From the scantily clad space-bimbo, girl-in-every-port fantasy of *TOS* to the bikini'd holobabes of *Voyager* (which, commanded by a woman, you'd think might be a little more enlightened), the vision of the nonsexist future presented by *Trek* has always veered toward over-sexed heterosexual fantasy.

This is one aspect of the *Trek* vision that *was* manifested in the personal life of its creator. Various kiss-and-tell accounts of *Trek* depict Gene Roddenberry as personally crude, his language full of sexual references. He was legendary for his sexually oriented practical jokes (often extremely antiwoman), his affairs with actresses, his script descriptions—packed with details about busty women with a smoldering passion for the leading man. He was always coming up with sex-obsessed alien races: the Deltans of *TMP,* for example (depicted in even greater sexual detail in the Roddenberry-penned novelization). *TNG*'s Counselor Deanna Troi was originally conceived as "a four-breasted oversexed her-maphrodite"[10] (The version of Troi that finally *did* air was known for her low-cut, skin-tight jumpsuits.) The Ferengi, as envisioned by Roddenberry, "have prodigious sexual appetites . . . ," and we'll skip further disgusting detail.[11] Roddenberry's sex scenes were cut by those network censors he took pride in battling; in fact, as we earlier noted, this was the censorship he complained about most.[12] One has to wonder if Roddenberry wasn't lost on his own private holodeck program.

We have one final fracture in the mind/body split that must be considered. In the discussion, "Atoms, Bits, or Something Else," we need to consider the flip side of the existence of the soul, the possibility of a malignant Something Else. As noted, the border between what used to be called spirits or demons and the disembodied alien intelligences of the Prophets on *DS9* is rather vaporous on *Trek*. Disembodied ETs "borrow" material bodies— by mutual agreement ("By Any Other Name," *TOS*) or by force ("Power Play," *TNG*). In "Power Play," bodiless aliens "possess" crew persons, claiming to be ghosts. Disembodied aliens also pose as ghosts in "Subrosa" *(TNG)*, and "Coda" *(VOY)*. In the latter, Captain Janeway has a near-death experience and meets a bodiless alien posing as her dead father, who tempts her (unsuccessfully) into joining him in the "afterlife." (Would that the Heaven's Gate crew had shown such caution to a similar invitation!)

As we were reminded when our panel discussion of SF and fantasy was interrupted by the Aleister Crowley fan, there has always been a dark side of romanticism. W. B. Yeats was a member of Crowley's occultic Hermetic Order of the Golden Dawn. And even more so than in Yeats's time, it is possible today to be a true believer in the supernatural without necessarily surrendering the scientific point of view. More than one scientist has crossed the great divide between physics and metaphysics in response to the bizarre descriptions of reality given by the New Physics; among these, the phenomenon which suggests that the observer of an experiment can affect the outcome just by observing, has led some to give scientific credence to the Eastern idea of "All is One."

Such converts seem to be fine examples of Screwtape's "perfect work" in C. S. Lewis's book of letters between an elder devil and his apprentice. Here we learn of the tempters' catch-22: if devils hide, they can make no believers in black magic. If they reveal themselves, they can make no materialists. The ideal goal, says Screwtape, would be to create "the Materialist Magician," the person who believes in "what he vaguely calls 'Forces' while denying the existence of 'spirits.'"[13]

In C. S. Lewis's *That Hideous Strength*, the N.I.C.E. seeks the same goal as Spock does in the first scene of *TMP*—a final victory over nature, and absolute freedom from humanity. In this story about the mind/body split, the N.I.C.E is led by a disembodied head in a tray.[14] "The Head" speaks with a voice the scientists attribute to "extraterrestrial intelligence"—which is quite true, except the ET is spiritual, not physical. Believing only in atoms and bits, the scientists at the N.I.C.E. seek to recover the comatose body of the magician Merlin to utilize his powers—like the Nazi scientists seeking to master the supernatural powers of the lost ark in the first Indiana Jones film. And just like the climax of that film, the effort to control nature by the use of "forces" ends in releasing something more than atoms or bits—and in being controlled by the very forces they sought to use to control (or conquer) nature.

This has always been the objection of some religious believers to New Age channeling and other "spirit" contact. Such "magic" has always been traditionally forbidden, because it is an attempt to acquire power outside the legitimate forms, i.e., as delegated by God. All power—fire, for example—can be both creative or destructive, depending on the context. And so the rejection of sorcery is similar to religious strictures against extramarital sex: something deemed good in one context, released from that context, degenerates to chaos—and releases Something Else. Those who attempt to conquer nature, says Lewis, may be in for a surprise; they may find that the violent separation of mind and body, in addition to abolishing man, sets free unexpected things.

The title *That Hideous Strength* is a reference from an old poem about the Tower of Babel—another effort to achieve absolute control which ended in chaos and the breakdown of language—as does the novel, where meaning (content) is severed from the flesh (form) of words. In Lewis's story of the Gnostic division between mind and body, the central image of healing is matrimony: a marriage of abstract and concrete, unity of mind, body and spirit.

And for all the gratuitous, disembodied, and abstracted sex one finds on *Trek*, there is at least one Roddenberry-produced *Trek* adventure where sexual union plays an absolutely critical role in the story—perhaps, in its way, in the entire series itself.

MARRIAGE AS METAPHOR: OUT OF MANY, ONE

In *Star Trek: The Motion Picture*, sexual union is employed as a metaphor for unification, a bringing together of opposing sides. The conflict in question is perhaps the central one in *Trek*, the famous Spockian split between impersonal logic and humanity. As mentioned in chapter 3, Spock begins the film trying to drive an irrevocable wedge between his logical and human halves. When he returns to Starfleet, however, and meets up with V'Ger, Spock realizes that the purest logic is barren and empty next to simple human pleasures like (to cite his example) friendship.

V'Ger has already accumulated all the *facts* of the universe—and finds that information alone is just so many cold equations.

So V'Ger is driven across the galaxy, then, not to simply gather more data, but to make *personal contact* with "the Creator." The effects-laden climax of *TMP* involves a mystic union between the machine V'Ger (who has taken over the body of a sexy Deltan female) and a human male, a member of the crew who represents the Creator (V'Ger turns out to be the old Earth probe *Voyager*, souped up by well-meaning aliens). This union results in the creation of a new life-form, and makes for an appropriate end to a story about fragmentation and healing, much in the same way the union of Kirk's two halves in "The Enemy Within" healed his split. The picture is twofold: the uniting of logical fact with human value, which we discussed earlier, but this unity also signifies personal experience over abstract knowledge.

Such a connection between between sex and salvation could never be found in any of the bodiless Gnostic religions *Trek* honors, but, ironically, in the very tradition to which Gene Roddenberry most strenuously objected. For Roddenberry, Christianity was the enemy of bodily pleasures, a hateful, life-denying superstition. In the same interview with *The Humanist* where he complained about the lack of controversy generated by the antireligious "Who Watches the Watchers?" the Great Bird recalled going to church as a young man. He said he didn't usually pay much attention to the sermons ("I was more interested in the deacon's daughter and what we might be doing between services"), but one Sunday he was astonished at what he heard:

> They were talking about things that were just crazy. . . . It was Communion time, where you eat this wafer and are supposed to be eating the body of Christ and drinking his blood. My first impression was, "This is a bunch of cannibals they've put me down among. . . ." How the hell did Jesus become something to be eaten?"[15]

From this moment, Roddenberry says, he lumped Jesus Christ with Santa Claus and, like *Trek*'s advanced civilization, left religion behind with other rejected obstacles to personal gratification.

It's too bad the Great Bird couldn't have kept his mind on this particular sermon. Perhaps, then, he'd have come to understand the message of Communion: that the Christian God is not a flesh-despising, amorphous force, but rather a God who *becomes* flesh, experiencing physicality to the death, and beyond, to physical resurrection. The heart of the Christian faith is the doctrine of the Incarnation: the embodiment of the spiritual in matter. ("God likes matter," says C. S. Lewis. "He invented it.[16]) Whoever preached this sermon may have even noted that sexual union is actually the Bible's favorite image for the sort of unity God seeks with humanity. The New Testament writers use metaphors like bride and bridegroom, marriage supper, lover and beloved in a downright Freudian way to describe Christ's relationship with the Church. And you don't have to be Freud to find sex in the Old Testament symbols in the Song of Solomon, used to the same end. For *TMP* to make nuptial union a metaphor for reunification between the Creator and his lost children was to echo, even unwittingly, the biblical picture of diversity-in-unity of which human marriages are just an image.

To the list of ways *Trek* deals with doubles, we can add to integrate, and segregate, *marriage:* unity without loss of diversity. Indeed, the most realistic sexual union on all of *Trek* is the long-running marriage of Chief Miles and Keiko O'Brien. The couple's wedding was performed by Captain Picard on the fourth season of *TNG* ("Data's Day"), and the marriage has carried on now through five seasons of *DS9:* compared to holodeck flings, the ballad of Miles and Keiko is a full-bodied reality, sustained through fights, temptations, separations, struggles with career, and the raising of children; his facing middle age; her being told he was dead, being kidnapped by aliens, and having the school where she works closed. Says Miles: "Marriage is the greatest adventure of all." The presence of even this TV representation of the many-dimensioned adventure that marriage truly is exposes all the illusory relationships of holodeck as cheap imitations.

Of course, one may well take the idea of "marrying" opposites and seek to apply it in the case of the above-mentioned "materialist magician." However, such a "marriage" would be possible only if we first overcame the obstacle of the law of noncontradiction by marrying A to non-A. In other words, as Lewis implies in his book of the same name, there remains a need for a Great Divorce. This need can be seen no clearer than in the example of the next duality we're going to explore, that of fantasy and reality.

But divorcing that particular "couple" is not always so simple.

8

Get a Life
(Or a Reasonable Facsimile
Thereof)

THE PROBLEM WITH SEQUELS (PART 1)

Writing for a successful TV series must sometimes be like being sent to some *Twilight Zone* hell, where your worst nightmare is having your fondest wishes come true—forever. For no matter what sort of trouble your heroes run into today, you know everything's got to be put back in order by the closing credits. "The *Gilligan's Island* syndrome" is what *Wonder* magazine editor Rod Bennett calls this problem: you can untangle Gilligan's latest crisis, but you can never let the castaways be rescued.

Who can afford to mess with success? A *regular* show needs *regular* viewers, so *regular* characters have to stay *regular*. On *Trek*, occasional Holodeck or "alternative" episodes provide an illusion of change, a simulation of real choices with permanent consequences: characters get married, have kids, even get killed. But still, by the episode's end, everything will be as it was at the start, and next episode, nobody will remember what happened. On a continuing television series, change is necessarily maya.

There are exceptions. Some characters develop as the series goes. On *DS9*, Odo finds his people, gets in trouble with them, becomes human, then turns back into a changeling—over the course of a season. Plot developments such as these make a show more rewarding to the regular viewer, but can be a turnoff for those who miss an episode here and there. There are other kinds of changes: Tasha Yar dies. Worf leaves the *Enterprise* for *DS9*. But notice these changes occurred only because an actor wanted out of the show, or wanted to keep going after one series had ended.

For all the infinite diversity, for all the aliens, *familiarity* is one of the things we like about *Trek:* it's a *family*. This is the feeling behind the obligatory "rounding up the old gang" in film after film. The price paid for keeping the family together, however, is that it is progressively harder to suspend disbelief: either that the old gang is still so easy to round up, or that they are ever in any real danger. For no matter how bad things look, we all know they've got to be available for possible sequels.

It's like a Cardassian show trial: the verdict is rendered before the trial even begins.

Too much familiarity, then, breeds contempt. We have superficial changes. Riker grows a beard. Sisko shaves his head. The holographic Doctor gets a device that allows him to be more mobile. Whatever it takes to keep the audience. One must be careful, though: too much change, too fast, and the show becomes too alien—and viewers surf to someplace more dependable. It's the same old problem, an almost impossible task: balancing unity and diversity, order and freedom, individual and community, many and one.

For all the coming and going, however, the television medium seems to be much more flexible and forgiving: the sum of a particular show can be greater than the parts. After all, there's a new story every week. If this week's episode is subpar, if they didn't feature your favorite character, just wait until next week. Most viewers seem to understand the limitations that come with weekly television production, and so keep their expectations tempered accordingly.

With films, on the other hand, expectations are higher, and so are the stakes. It might take a year to write, shoot, and edit a film. Six months to promote. Cost ten or twenty times as much money for what turns out to be about twice the time of a single television episode. All the regular characters need "screen time," but you also have to throw in a big-name guest villain. Meanwhile, the producers are concerned to make sure the effects are stuff you could never do on TV, that their investment in "the money shots" returns even more money at the box office. Making a dud film is no small matter: there is no "tune in next week."

Storywise, a film must be a complete movement, a self-contained work of art, with a beginning, middle, and end. Unlike a series, a film must DO SOMETHING, cross a Rubicon, some line which cannot be recrossed, a one-way gate. The writers for the original *Trek* theatrical film, Leonard Nimoy recalled, "were preoccupied with this idea that [the first film] must have size and stature."[1]

And yet, if there's any chance at all for a film to generate sequels, the writers are put in a terrible position, a no-win scenario: a fate analogous to that of poor Jake Barnes in *The Sun Also Rises:* You have the desire, but you lack the ability. You long to do the irrevocable, but you just don't dare. That's why films with sequel potential have a tendency to to feel tentative—they have to hold something back for next time.

In the case of *Trek*, though, the writers on the first film were less tentative because nobody as yet knew what a gold mine of sequels *Trek* was going to be. They'd *already* done all the sequels, so to speak, in the form of a weekly television series. Now, with this film, it was time to go out with a bang, do something irrevocable. As we already discussed, what they decided to do, that first time around, was let Spock pass through a one-way gate, with his life-changing experience with emotion.

When Paramount decided to do another *Trek* film, Leonard Nimoy started getting nervous: he was ready to move on to better things. This dovetailed well with the needs of the writers, who, again, needed to do something irrevocable—even more so than last time. So what they decided to do the second time was *really* transform Spock, i.e., kill off the character. (It wouldn't be the first time somebody chose murder as a means to validate their existence.) This film was originally titled *The Undiscovered Country*, after Hamlet's musings on the *real* final frontier. Later the film was renamed *The Wrath of Khan*, and offered up Kobayashi Maru as a metaphor for cheating death. *Trek* was finally going to face the no-win scenario without cheating. Such self-reflexive ambitions made *TWOK* the overall best of the *Trek* films. An aging Admiral Kirk allows that "galavanting around the cosmos is a game for the young." The plot leads, of course, to the brink of disaster. But this time, in order to save the ship, our dear friend Spock sacrifices his life. With an epic tragedy, *Trek* finally lives up to its longstanding Shakespearean pretensions.

Until the sequel. For unlike the first *Trek* film, *TWOK* had been a smash at the box office. Now Leonard Nimoy had some second thoughts about killing off Spock, especially when they offered him the chance to direct *Trek III*. Luckily, the producer, Harve Bennett, had hedged all their bets by adding in some cryptic dialogue at the end of *TWOK* that left open the possibility for the return of Spock. And, sure enough, in the 1984 *Search for*

Spock, viewers are introduced to the hitherto unknown idea of katra: now, we learn, the Vulcan soul can be extracted from one body and placed into another. One small deus ex machina and Spock is resurrected to be in more films, and even in *TNG*. So much for the irrevocable: with sequels, *nothing* is irrevocable.

TNG also killed off a regular character, Tasha Yar, amid plenty of sober self-congratulation and talk of death—once again with "the tragic sense of life." And, once again, the life-changing experience of attending one's own funeral seemed to change an actor's mind. For Denise Crosby was soon resurrecting the character of Tasha Yar via various contorted ruses for the duration of the *TNG* series (for example, as a Romulan "evil twin," as an "alternative" Tasha within a temporal anomaly . . . .)

By far the most cowardly attempt at fulfilling the human need for irrevocability on *Trek* is when validation by killing is aimed not at regulars, but at innocent bystanders. Classic *Trek* was notorious for killing off any extra who beamed down to a planet wearing a red shirt. The worst example in the films is when Kirk's newly discovered son is suddenly murdered without warning in *Trek III*, basically just to show how really bad the bad guys are. The *Enterprise* itself keeps being killed—with diminishing returns of shock and sadness each time—and then getting resurrected: as with the titles of the sequels, all you really have to do is add another number or letter to the name.

Cheating death is, of course, the bread and butter of an action show. But *anybody* would feel guilty about using some of these methods—especially a show with the guilty conscience of *Trek*.

In the film *Generations*, we see one more crack at the irrevocable—and, perhaps, an effort toward penance for past sins against the irrevocable—in the decision to kill the most central icon in all of *Trek*: Captain James T. Kirk. Truthfully, this choice wasn't really all *that* daring: Kirk *is* by now, indeed, too old to continue gala-vanting around the galaxy. And, with the katra of *Trek* passed on to *TNG* even Kirk has become expendable. Nevertheless, the death of Captain Kirk, said one writer, would be the real thing: "none of this Spock stuff."

In the story of *Generations*, Kirk becomes trapped in an energy field in space, the Nexus: the ultimate cheat of death, the final Kobayashi Maru. Here, inhabitants are kept in a timeless bliss, unable to die—a metaphor, perhaps, for life everlasting in sequels. This is a very self-knowing story: Kirk is able to cheat death in his fantasy world, but finds this to be a hollow pursuit. One day out riding his fantasy horse (that ancient symbol of freedom), Kirk jumps a ravine—and is frustrated because he doesn't experience any sense of thrill. The reason, he realizes, is because there was never any real risk—because in the Nexus, neither horse, nor ravine, nor even death, is real. Kirk's choices are meaningless because they have no permanent consequences. So, like *Trek* writers, Kirk longs to be able to do the irrevocable—to "make a difference," in his words. We recall that's just what William James said was the test for significance. And that's the one thing linear time is good for: change, making a difference. Viewers who have been watching Kirk jump ravine after ravine over the years, knowing he was never in any real danger, could sympathize with this longing.

In *The Mind of the Maker*, Dorothy Sayers analyzes deus-ex-machina solutions from a theological context: the sovereignty of the Author (God) versus the essential dignity of the characters' (human beings') free will. As in the case of the Prime Directive, Sayers concludes that arbitrary intervention by God would be an act of violence against the dignity of a particular character. The plot problem may be solved with hocus-pocus, but only at great cost to the work: "The effect is to falsify the story."[2] Robbed of the dignity of free choice, the character is left an automaton. In a good story, says Sayers, "consequences cannot be separated from their causes without a loss of power. . . ."[3] This explains Kirk's dissatisfaction at his inability to "make a difference" within the limbo of the Nexus. Reinhold Niebuhr says human beings need to believe "life is a critical affair": that their choices have meaning.[4]

The irony of *Generations*, though, is that in their determination to kill off Kirk, the writers shipwrecked the most thoughtful *Trek* film since *The Wrath of Khan:* for, unlike Spock's death, which rose naturally out of the action of *TWOK*—and was actually demanded by everything else in that story—Kirk's demise in *Generations* is shoehorned uselessly onto the end of the film. In other words, his death actually makes no "difference" at all. Captain Kirk, in the end, becomes only the ultimate "red shirt."

And you gotta wonder how the galaxy will survive without Captain Kirk. Of course, we really have no guarantee that Kirk will actually stay dead—not as long as they keep making *Trek*. It is, on the other hand, true that actor William Shatner will eventually die. And so, it would seem, short of passing Kirk's katra to another actor to play James T. Kirk (à la Dr. Who) the only God in the machine left to save the Shatner Kirk at that point would be some advanced computer technology that allows dead actors to appear in new films. In fact, we get a glimpse of such technology in the *DS9* episode "Trials and Tribble-ations," in which *DS9* regulars were dropped into old footage from the original *Trek* series. Perhaps the thought that the old swashbuckling Captain Kirk (and Kirk in his prime beats other *Trek* heroes hands down) might have new adventures in the future—even after William Shatner is dead, buried, and (who knows?) forgotten must be of some consolation to the aging actor.

On the other hand, like Woody Allen says, Bill Shatner would probably much rather achieve his immortality by "not dying."

In general, it seems that *Trek* works much better as weekly TV series than as film series: they do best when they think smaller, going slow and steady—with no frantic compulsion to save the galaxy, just make Keiko happy after the *DS9* school closes and she feels her sense of self-worth threatened. There are some gems among those hundreds of one-hour episodes. And the clinkers are not so irrevocable. *Trek* films, on the other hand, for all the agonizing about interfering with the timeline, keep making "irrevocable" botches in the past, present and future (maybe the Federation needs to hire more "Time Cops.") Perhaps in future sequels *Trek* can come up with a ruse to undo some of the unfortunate choices made in past stories. Then again, you can't make much progress in the future if you keep going in circles.

The problem with sequels, like the problem of deus ex machina, is the lesson Kirk learned in his final episode and Pike already knew in the first: unreality is ultimately unsatisfying. "Food in dreams," says Augustine, "is exactly like real food, yet what we eat in our dreams does not nourish: for we are dreaming."[5]

Of course, reality has its own problems.

HOW DO YOU DEAL WITH DEATH?

"You haven't experienced Shakespeare until you've read him in the original Klingon," says one of the Bard's Klingon fans in *TUC*. In that film, Hamlet's phrase about the "undiscovered country" is translated by everybody concerned as a reference to the future. A more careful reading of the play in the original English reveals that the country Hamlet is referring to is *death*—which is "undiscovered" because dead men tell no tales. (Except for Mr. Spock, but, apparently, he isn't talking either.) Perhaps both *death* and *the future* are interchangeable, in a sense: the one thing we can predict with certainty is that we will die.

Here is an irrevocable change we would do anything to revoke. It is certainly one of the things that separates humans from the rest of the animal kingdom: humans *have* a future; that is, they can picture what's coming in the sequential revelation we know as time. Probably the most compelling thing about being able to picture the future is knowing in advance about one's own mortality. Most of the time, that particular picture, our own death, is another alien "Other" to repress. So we fill our lives with diversions: not just watching television shows, buying products, and memorizing trivia, but also *making* television shows, getting rich, hurling our ashes into space, which is where our science says we and all we've done will end anyway.

Somber stuff. The kind of stuff we like to forget about by watching action shows where the heroes cheat death. Yet despite all the cheating, *Trek* has made some attempt to face death.   Jean-Luc Picard is always making speeches, in that Shakespearean voice of his, about human mortality, the need to face death without resorting to superstition, the preciousness of life, the need to live each moment to the fullest (see, for example, "The Bonding," "Sarek," and "Interface," *TNG*). In the film *Generations,* amid some crew R and R, Picard receives word some relatives have been killed in a tragic fire. During the course of the rest of the film, Picard must come to terms with this terrible event. When it comes to death, *Trek* counsels coming to terms, i.e., acceptance; *Trek* has always had a low view of any attempts at immortality: both the religious versions and those bad guys who attempt to prolong their existence artificially, by stealing organs and/or dumping their consciousness into computers, or losing themselves in the eternal illusions of the Nexus. These dodges of the inevitable human fate are viewed on *Trek* with the same contempt most of us hold for those passengers who escaped the sinking Titanic in various dishonorable ways. "How you deal with death," says Kirk, "is at least as important as how you deal with life" *(TWOK)*.

Of course, such bold talk of accepting death is cheapened somewhat when we remember that it comes from within a vicarious projection of human life into the distant future and across the galaxy, spoken by actors who deny their own mortality with makeup and hairpieces and other remodulations, and then live forever in reruns.

Moreover, the constant flirtation with, then denial of, the "undiscovered country" is like writing a check that keeps bouncing. As with the case of the much-lauded transformation of human nature in *First Contact*, the wiser course might have been simply avoiding the issue. But, like the lady in horror films who walks down into the basement alone, *Trek*'s instinct for staring into the face of death, trumpets blowing, then pulling back with a "Just kidding," threatens to make even death a cliché. As Spock himself might say, "Been there, done that."

Yet it's that old *Trek* guilty conscience that keeps dragging them back, trying to get them to face painful realities. In this way, how *Trek* deals with death is as ambivalent as everything else about *Trek*. And, as usual, it is up to the more self-reflexive incarnations of *Trek* to come nearest to facing the issue clearly.

In the *DS9* episode "The Quickening," an away team encounters a planet whose inhabitants are born with a terminal disease: when blue lesions on the aliens' faces turn red, their "blight" is said to have quickened, and certain death is not far behind. Dr. Bashir, with typical Federation hubris, combined with the hubris traditional to his profession, orders advanced medical gear beamed down, and immediately sets up both a clinic and the expectation that he will cure the blight by episode's end.

For once, however, deus ex Starfleet is not so effective. After some initial progress, Bashir's patients continue to die. The episode is almost a *Trek* version of Albert Camus's existentialist novel *The Plague*, which is, of course, a metaphor for death and our inability to finally find a cure: "Each of us has the plague within him; no one, no one on Earth is free from it." The closing credits of the "The Quickening" roll on an ending not entirely happy: Dr. Bashir is unable to cure the people living on the planet—but he does discover a way to make sure their next generation will be born blight-free. The hope of this ending is the hope of *Trek* itself: that "the next generation" will defeat death. In this light, the many speeches about accepting death seem truly hypocritical. For Camus, on the other hand, it is the plague that is "a never ending defeat." And so *Trek*'s effort to have it both ways—facing the truth about death, yet finding cause for hope in defeating death—touches, but ultimately avoids, the anxiety underlying *Trek*'s instant cure: the failure of even Federation science to cure humankind's ultimate limitation.

A far better effort is *Voyager*'s incredible episode, "Real Life." Here, the holographic Doctor, in an effort to better understand his patients, creates a holographic family. He brings several *Voyager* crewmen to his "home" to meet the family. The forthright B'lanna Torres is so disgusted by the perfection of the Doctor's fantasy family, she offers to adjust the program to make it more real. Soon the episode is crosscutting between what are now the Doctor's nightmarishly real family problems and the doings on *Voyager*'s nonholographic version of real life. Needless to say, the Doctor's "reality" makes the space-opera problems of *Voyager* seem ridiculous. Tom Paris gets himself in trouble with some dopey space anomaly, and we all know he'll be saved in the nick of time before episode's end. Meanwhile, the Doctor is having trouble communicating with his teenage son, and is alienating his wife and daughter with his insistence on controlling their lives.

A heated discussion between the Doctor and his son—over the son's choice of friends and lifestyle, and over the nature of moral authority, and the father's claim to it—are all too real for an escapist television show. One longs for the simplicity of nonholographic reality, where such a no-win scenario would be solved with a cheery bit of technobabble. Especially difficult to watch are the scenes after the Doctor's daughter is injured playing a school sport. Unlike nearly every other injury faced by Starfleet omnipotence, this injury is untreatable. In an excruciating scene, the daughter lies in a hospital bed, blind, unable to move her legs, crying pitifully, "What's going to happen? When will I be able to see again?" The Doctor turns away in anguish, shouting, "Computer! End program!"

And so the episode cuts to a commercial. What a relief!

When the story resumes, the Doctor has had *enough* reality, and decides not to go back to his holodeck family. He's already gained a new appreciation for the preciousness of life. He lectures a crewman: "People like you who court danger should be thrown into the brig. You never think of the consequences of your actions." Talk about boldly going: the writers are clearly zeroing in on the fundamental weaknesses of a regular action series. For thirty years, the characters on *Trek* have been saved from facing the consequences of their actions.

After an unconvincing lecture on reality by classic action hero Tom Paris, the Doctor finally decides to go back and finish his scene with his holographic daughter: it is the most heartrending and realistic scene in all of *Trek*. He tells her she is going to die. She asks him to stay with her. Her entire family is there when she goes. No escapism here, just a very painful reality.

Yet it seems self-defeating that all the critical choices and irrevocable actions *Trek* makes must take place on the holodeck.

TREK'S LOVE/HATE RELATIONSHIP WITH REALITY

In some ways it's ironic that *Trek* fans would be the ones told to "get a life!" For, in a sense, that has been the show's message from the start. There is a venerable tradition of *Trek* plots involving the rejection of some pleasant illusion in favor of accepting reality, even a harsh one. This tradition goes all the way back to the "liberty or death" theme in the maiden voyage of the *Enterprise* in the original *Trek* series pilot, "The Cage."

Produced to sell the series to NBC, "The Cage" was set in a *Trek* cosmos that was still evolving: Christopher Pike (played by Jeffrey Hunter, Jesus in the 1961 film *King of Kings*) was in command as the story opened, with the *Enterprise* responding to a distress call from an unexplored planet, Talos IV. As with the Kobayashi Maru, the alarm turns out to be bogus. The space-crash survivors we meet on Talos IV are actually illusions created by the telepathic Talosians as bait to lure in a human to capture for their zoo.

Pike is taken below the planet's surface to be mated with a female human specimen, Vina—the sole survivor of an actual crash. Though locked in a cage with Vina, Pike is given the opportunity to experience any fantasy of his choice. The Talosians provide several options, yet Pike refuses them all. Vina's puzzled response is best encapsulated in the phrasing found in one of the episode's earliest script outlines:

VINA: Why not relax and go along with the illusion? It's pleasant, isn't it? Everything looks real, feels real; the pleasure is equally real. [6]

But after Pike makes it clear he prefers death to captivity, even a pleasant captivity, his keepers release him. Pike invites Vina to come along, to escape Talos IV, but she refuses to go. She reveals her terrible secret: all her beauty and youth are illusions provided by Talosians. Without them, she bears horrible scars of shipwreck and age. Sadly, Pike leaves her behind.

And so *Trek* blasts off with a satire of its own chosen medium: the Talosions ("Televisions"?) possess superior intellects, yet have lost all vigor and discipline, unable to maintain their advanced civilization. They stare blankly at "televisors," reliving their ances-tors' experiences and emotions, and those of the creatures in their zoo. The theme is quite similar to that of "The Gamesters of Triskelion" *(TOS)*, in which an *Enterprise* landing party is forced to fight in contests staged to amuse "the Providers"—beings who turn out to be disembodied brains kept in a glass bubble: their only interest is in being entertained.

After *Trek* provoked its unprecedented fandom, and though it surely benefited from the amazing intensity of that fandom, the satire seemed to be increasingly directed at the fans themselves— though this was denied by the producers. In *TNG*'s "Hollow Pursuits," shy Crewman Barclay lives out his dreams of being a hero and lover on the holodeck, a machine to which Barclay has become addicted. In the *DS9* story "If Wishes Were Horses," Quark thinks the station's grouchy constable doesn't have any fun. So the Ferengi offers to customize his upstairs holosuite (basical-ly, a holographic brothel) with a special "changeling" fantasy.

> ODO: I have no time for fantasies.
> QUARK: Hmph. No imagination, eh?
> ODO: Waste of time. Too many people dream of places they'll never go. Wish for things they'll never have instead of paying adequate attention to their real lives.

Is *Trek* directing these comments at the most rabid *Trek* fans?

There's an obvious contradiction here: a fantasy show criticizing fantasy, a television show criticizing television—both of these being either subversive or hypocritical. The latter would seem the truth here, especially when one recalls that the main character of this TV show is a father figure whose characteristic pose is sitting in an easy chair facing a large TV-like screen.

This thematic tug of war creates a paradox within the content of the series itself, another of those patented *Trek* inner conflicts. We see this immediately with the later rewrite of "The Cage" as "The Menagerie." When NBC added *Trek* to its fall 1966 lineup with a revamped cast, Gene Roddenberry devised a plan to utilize his original pilot: as a two-part episode, with the "Cage" story shown in flashback, set in a "present-day" frame. The new story was this: due to the dangerous illusion-making powers of the Talosians, visits to Talos IV are prohibited under penalty of death. Spock, however, commandeers the *Enterprise* from its current captain, Kirk, to transport his former captain, Pike, to this forbidden planet. Why? Due to an accident, and in spite of all the medical wizardry of the future, Pike is now paralyzed, confined to a wheelchair. As expected, when he arrives on Talos IV, Pike assumes the appearance of a virile young captain, joining Vina in eternal beauty and youth. And happily, Starfleet drops its charges against Spock. The story's new moral: a pleasant fantasy *may actually be preferable to a harsh reality after all.* "The Menagerie" was Roddenberry's best-written story, winning a Hugo award, science-fiction's top honor.

This "alternative" attitude toward fantasy on *Trek* may also be seen in the *TOS* episode "Shore Leave," in which Kirk's crew enjoys recreational make-believe on an fantasy amusement planet.

Finally, of course, beginning with *TNG*, a fantasy-creating device that reproduces both the "Shore Leave" planet and the Talosians' power of illusion becomes a standard feature of all starships and space stations: the holodeck is the ultimate god in the machine, an advanced technology designed to help people truly get away from it all, the need for which remains even, it would seem, in the midst of having exciting adventures in outer space.

In a typical example of holodeck fun, *Trek* heroes get to pretend they're heroes, according to personal taste: Sherlock Holmes, a Raymond Chandleresque hardboiled detective, a James Bond–like spy (see "Elementary, My Dear Data" and "Long Goodbye," *TNG*, and "Our Man Bashir," *DS9*). On *Voyager*, characters relax at the holographic Sandrine's Parisian Bar, or the holodeck equivalent of MTV's beach house. On *DS9*, private "holosuites" offer pleasures of an undisguised sexual nature. And a malfunctioning holodeck is one of *Trek's* favorite "devils in the machine."

Thus, we see *Trek* is ambivalent (as usual) with regard to what might be generally classified as therapeutic illusion—and well they should be. For art itself is, in a sense, a form of therapeutic illusion. To experience fiction is to enter an alternative universe. In *reality*, the *Enterprise* is plywood. Our heroes are merely repeating words written by someone else—perhaps standing in front of a blue screen *pretending* to see the monster that will be added to the shot in postproduction. Yet this combination of unrealities can produce a different sort of reality: the "lies" of art that tell their own sort of truth.

Indeed, the traditional idea that truth might be found in the fictions of literature or film is how some would account for the fact that *Trek* has acquired such rabid fans to begin with. From this perspective, many of those who seem most lost in the fantasy of *Trek* are shown as those most desperately seeking "a life."

And yet, while the lies of art have traditionally been viewed as a means for discovering truth, we saw in the previous chapter that truth—to paraphrase the title of one book on the subject of post-modernism—"isn't what it used to be." It's one thing to say art is an illusion that conveys human truths; but what if, as many believe, human truth is one more illusion? Wouldn't that mean that art is just an illusion of an illusion?

The problem with some people, says Joseph Campbell, is that they take the symbols of their mythology literally—as if the symbols pointed to some actual reference or truth "out there." Such behavior, says Campbell, is "like going to a restaurant, asking for the menu, seeing beefsteak written there, and starting to eat the menu." [7] Of course, what Campbell doesn't spell out so clearly—a chronic problem for Campbell—is that he also believes that there is no such thing as beefsteak, or any other kind of food, *that there is only the menu.* In which case, gobbling down the menu seems an understandable course of action.

And so one can identify two diametrically opposed responses to our twentieth-century human predicament vis-a-vis reality. These roughly parallel the approaches of what we might call the early Pike ("Give me reality or give me death") and the later Pike ("Better the illusion of health than the reality of disease").

Science-fiction writer Kurt Vonnegut would probably put himself in this latter category. Vonnegut has written about what he calls "foma," those harmless lies we tell ourselves to make it through the cold, dark night of existence. [8] A false hope is better than none; better to eat the menu than to starve. So go ahead and pick your favorite fantasy: faith in the future, a better world, a happy ending, something to fight for, something to progress toward, an ideal, the Grail, Shangri-la, a place somewhere over the rainbow—follow your dream, even if you know its just a dream.

On the other hand, the tough guys of contemporary philosophy, like Albert Camus, have echoed the earlier Pike—i.e., better to face the hard truth about our species' inherent meaninglessness than embrace a pleasant fantasy about "the intrinsic value of the individual," etc. All true philosophy, says Bertrand Russell, must begin nowadays with the fact that human beings are nothing but particles in motion and end with the unpleasant reality that we and our many accomplishments will vanish and be forgotten.

One wonders why *Trek*, boldly jaunting through time, has never visited the farthest reaches of the future to the heat death of the universe, when all the energy has been used up and nothing remains but the cold eternity of the silent spaces (with perhaps a "Beam me up, Scotty" button drifting absurdly through the void.)

If such a perspective represents the life scoffers urge us to get, one sympathizes with those who seek to avoid this "reality."

Casting about for a bright side, we recall there is, of course, the possibility that what some people maintain is real is actually just another bit of foma—an illusion.

HOW DO WE KNOW WE'RE NOT DREAMING?

In the *TNG* episode "Ship in a Bottle," Sherlock Holmes's arch-nemesis Dr. Moriarty comes to holographic life and, through some devious means, escapes the holodeck into the world of reality. Later we realize that Moriarity has never really left the holodeck: rather, he's just programmed his own holodeck illusion of leaving the holodeck and fooled everybody. In the end, though, it is Moriarity who is fooled: he thinks he's *really* escaped the holodeck, but he's actually trapped into another computer-generated reality, one more illusory but comfy "cage."

At least, the crew *thinks* Moriarity is the one in an illusion, and they're the ones left in reality. But how can they be sure?

It seems very striking that one of the most-used plots in *Trek*, used more than once in every one of the series, involves a regular character who wakes up to find himself transported, inexplicably, to a radically new existence claiming to be real.

The *TNG* episode "Frame of Mind" features Commander Riker waking in an insane asylum, where doctors try to convince him that his entire Starship career was just a delusion. In "Non Sequitur," Ensign Kim wakes to discover he never joined the crew of *Voyager*, but instead had an alternate Starfleet career on Earth. Once again, it is Riker who awakens in "Future Imperfect" *(TNG)* to find that sixteen years of his life have passed—sixteen years of which he has no memory. Captain Picard wakes up in "The Inner Light" *(TNG)* to find himself with a wife and family, living an entire lifetime on some hitherto unknown planet—his Starfleet career apparently just a dream. In the film *Generations*, Picard, just like Kirk, is sucked into the Nexus, and once again finds his heart's desire—a home and family. James T. Kirk gets a new life the old-fashioned way: in "The Paradise Syndrome" *(TOS)*, Kirk gets amnesia following an accident, so he, too, "goes native."

Such plots are another way of doing the "alternative" episodes fans love so much. In these, one can experience the alien and return home, all in one story. At issue in such stories is also the quest for identity with which viewers find so easy to identify.

Yet this business of suddenly finding one's identity in question, of being transported to an alien reality, is used so frequently, it's funny to see the various *Trek* characters so transported try to act surprised. It's funnier still to hear them run down the ever longer list of possible explanations for their plight.

JANEWAY: We'll have to consider every possible explanation.
KIM: Oh, believe me, I have been. Space-time anomalies. Alien

telepathy. Alternate realities. The list gets weirder as it goes on."
(*VOY*, "Favorite Son")

Indeed. Weirder as it goes, and sillier.

Most characters who find themselves in an alternate reality at first refuse to accept the new reality; they'll do anything to get back where they belong. Even Ensign Kim turns down a chance for a pleasant alternative to being lost in the Delta Quadrant, preferring instead to return "home"—i.e., lost in space.

On the other hand, after a few *years* of living in his alternative reality, Jean-Luc Picard accepts the fact that this reality must be the real one, and he gradually forgets about Starfleet ("Inner Light," *TNG*). Kirk, under the narcotic sway of the Nexus fantasies, very nearly loses touch with external reality—until Picard appears on the scene to reconnect him to the outside world.

After all, this *is Trek*, and all this reality confusion must eventually be resolved in a happy ending—which in this case means a return to "real" reality for the individual involved. Thus, even those characters who have given in to the illusions, "gone native," eventually must come to their true selves.

There are several ways that this is accomplished.

Sometimes it begins with a vague sense that something is wrong. Inside the Nexus, Picard sees a strange flicker in a Christmas-tree ornament. "This isn't right," he says, snapping out of his trance. "This can't be real." In "Yesterday's *Enterprise*" *(TNG)*, the ship and crew are trapped in an alternative reality until the mystic Guinan "senses"—using Kirk's "gut feeling" no doubt—that something is wrong with the reality they find themselves in and convinces Picard to take action that finally sets things right.

On other occasions, there is not just a vague sense, or intuition, but—and this would please Spock—empirical proof. In

"Cause and Effect" *(TNG)*, the ship is caught in a "temporal causality loop"—like in the movie *Groundhog Day*, only, unlike that story, the crew doesn't remember any of the past repetitions. There is only an annoying sense of déjà vu. What solves the problem is Doctor Crusher, who begins to hear "echoes" of previous conversations, records them as evidence, and, based on that evidence, they come up with a plan to break out of the loop. Likewise in "Future Imperfect," Riker *senses* something is wrong when the ship's computers are cagey about answering his queries; but what settles things for him is when the computer identifies his late "wife" as what he knows to be an old holodeck program. He then realizes he's on an alien holodeck and makes his exit.

In short, the only way out of these various "wrong" realities is a deus-ex-machina escape. Because, again, nobody ever asks if their sense, or flickers, or evidence—or even the experience of returning home to the "right" or "real" reality—*are not also part of the illusion.* Christopher Pike, for example, has no real way of knowing *he ever truly left Talos IV.* And how could he? How could he ever truly know that what he perceived was an escape, a subsequent career, and the later accident that brought him back to Talos IV weren't all just illusions created by the Talosians to help him come to terms with life in the Cage?

"How do I know I'm not dreaming?" asked the philosopher Descartes. And, of course, there's no way to answer that question in a way that may not also be part of the dream.

The *TNG* episode "Frame of Mind" explores these difficulties. After Riker has awakened in a mental hospital and been diagnosed as delusional, a doctor helps him call up his alleged memories of the past. These memories appear as images of the people we recognize as being part of the *Trek* "real world." But the doctor tells Riker these images are not real—they're just *symbols* for psychological states. The urgent message that these "symbols" bring to Riker is that they are *more* than just symbols, that everything he is experiencing in the hospital is the illusion, that his real life still awaits him on the *Enterprise*.

Nevertheless, Riker tries to reconcile himself to what he has been told is reality. "You're all just delusions," he says to the "symbols." One image, that of Lieutenant Worf, replies, "Do not listen to [the doctor], Commander. He is trying to trick you." For awhile, though, Riker is able to do what Captain Picard in *Generations* could not: by sheer act of will, Riker resists these sirenlike "flickers in the Nexus."

> DOCTOR: You've taken a big step today. You've finally turned your back on those delusions and all they represent to you.

Yet unlike Picard in "Inner Light," when time has gone by, Riker finds he still cannot shake his doubts: primarily because he is tormented by the reappearance of these illusory "symbols." At one point, Riker sees images of persons who claim to be a rescue party from the *Enterprise,* yet he refuses to leave the mental hospital and go with them. As they plead with him, Riker decides to perform the ultimate test of their so-called reality. He points a phaser weapon right at these "symbols."

> RIKER: If I'm right, you're not really here. This isn't a real phaser. It's all a fantasy. And I'm going to end it, no matter what it takes.
> PICARD: What if it isn't a fantasy? Are you willing to take that chance?
> RIKER: You're right. I won't. (He lowers the weapon.) But I'm going to find out what's real and what's not.

Now Riker points the phaser at himself—and fires. Luckily for him, this really *was* an illusion. The phaser turns out to be illusory, the "symbols" were not real people after all. And Riker finds himself back in the hospital—"reality." But now Riker begins to wonder how he can know if any "reality" is real.

The members of the Heaven's Gate cult, steeped in this sort of reality-questioning atmosphere of *Trek,* came to believe that the "real" reality was this: that they were actually an away team from space, and that their existence on planet Earth was—their words—a holodeck illusion. They sought to escape (again, in their words) via "the true '*Enterprise*' (spaceship or 'cloud of light')," that is, the alien spaceship they had been told by their leader was traveling behind the comet Hale-Bopp. And the cult members put their reality to the test by killing themselves.

And who among those of us in what is popularly referred to as the "real world" could *prove* the Heaven's Gate "reality" was wrong?

Aye, there's the rub. Hamlet, we recall, took the opposite course of Heaven's Gate. He'd been told that bad things happen to people who take the "escape" of suicide. And since no one could *prove* he would not face a worse situation on the other side, in the "undiscovered country," Hamlet postponed his trip.

In "Frame of Mind," Riker tries his reality check again later. This time he grabs a weapon and points it at his captors. Once again, they tell him that what he thinks he is holding is not a phasor. He tests this assertion by firing at one of the doctors, who is instantly vaporized. Riker demands an explanation.

> DOCTOR: It's very complicated. I'll answer all of your questions. But first, I want you to put that down.

But instead of complying, Riker keeps blasting away with his phaser—and the entire scene before him shatters and scatters like a broken mirror. There is a marvelous sequence as Riker keeps firing his phaser and one "reality" after another shatters apart—to reveal endless new layers of "realities." What is also shattered in this sequence is the Enlightenment confidence in "seeing is believing," as well as the modern optimism that all of reality might be explained and brought under rational control.

In the end, however, as always on *Trek*, at the deus-ex-machina moment, Riker figures out that he's being held prisoner by aliens, kept inside a holodeck-like illusion. He escapes and is able to identify the "real" reality, and so get home. The final scene of this episode is an attempt at closure. Among the layers of "reality" Riker had been experiencing in the story was his constant shifting between the mental hospital and a play taking place in the *Enterprise* theater. The last shots of the episode show Riker tearing down the phony walls of the play set with his own hands. This is his way of finally dispensing with illusion. Yet it is also a cowardly ignoring of the still-unsolved problem. Namely, how can Riker know that this "real" *Enterprise* is not just another phony "set"?—which, as we know, it is! And how can we know whether our living room where we're watching *Trek* on television isn't also part of an alien holodeck?

It's a no-win scenario. Human beings are starving for reality. Yet they apparently have no way of telling the dream food from the real. Descartes finally decided that, since God created the real world, God—being good—would not deceive us. Short of that kind of literal deus ex machina, the *Trek* viewer has an even greater problem than knowing if the *Trek* characters have found reality. *The viewer has no way of knowing that he or she isn't just another brain in a plastic bubble on the planet Triskelion.*

Despite the impossibility of proving that one is not dreaming, the final assurance of reaching "real" reality is always possible on *Trek*. The end of the *TNG* episode "Parallels" is similar to that spectacular shattering of layers of realities in "Frame of Mind": in this story, though, it is Worf who has been lost in an alternative universe. At the climax, Worf flies a shuttlecraft through various realities in a mad dash for his true home—which he finally reaches, of course. And as the credits roll, there doesn't seem to be any question that this reality is home.

Like the crew of *Voyager*, lost in the Delta Quadrant, who keep turning down chances to settle someplace, everybody on *Trek* takes it for granted that there is a real reality to get home to.

The closest *Trek* ever seems to come to raising the horrifying questions of being certain about finding the real reality are at the end of *TNG's* "Ship in a Bottle." Once again, we replay a variation of that journey through multiple realities to at last get home. In this episode, at last, we get a little nervous joking about the finality of the reality we finally end up in:

> PICARD: Who knows? Our reality may be very much like theirs, and all this might just be an elaborate simulation running inside a little disc sitting on someone's table.

Everybody has a good laugh. Lieutenant Barclay is left alone in the room, and we see a doubt creep across his face. He speaks out loud, "Computer. End program"—just to make sure. Nothing changes, Barclay smiles sheepishly, and it is a happy ending. (Of course, in "Inner Light," Picard tried the same thing—and subsequent events proved that Picard's "reality" was a dream.)

Yet even if Barclay's final "reality" was also "an elaborate simulation"—like Dr. Hanley says about the possibility of the transporter creating replicants—what difference would it make?

In his book, Thomas Richards cites other sorts of *Trek* episodes where characters are trapped in a false reality. The lesson of "The Royale" and "Darmok" *(TNG)*, says Richards, is that no reality exists outside stories.[9] Knowing this may seem empowering, he says, but it means that, in the midst of *Trek*'s optimism are hints of contemporary despair: there is no ultimate reality beyond the lies we tell ourselves. *Trek* appeals to the homeless modern by offering a home; that such a home is merely an elaborate simulation doesn't seem to bother Richards, either.

Yet this view makes for a deeply unsatisfying "meaning" of *Trek*.

THE NEXT GENERATION

It is all a dream—a grotesque and foolish dream. Nothing exists but you. And you are but a thought, a homeless thought, wandering forlorn among the empty eternities. (Mark Twain, *The Mysterious Stranger*)

The logic of postmodernity results not just in the end of all grand unified theories of morality and humanity, but also in the end of any norm for reality. All notions of a single reality are exploded into an infinite diversity of arbitrary metanarratives, social constructs, or other such fantasies. All claims of truth are fictions. "Going home" or "getting a life" means picking a place and persona to visit, staying as long as you like, going elsewhere whenever you choose. Postmodernity, then, brings not just the end of *ought*, but also of *is*.

This new way of looking at things means exchanging the exploration of what is objectively real for the admitted constructions of what one prefers: artificial generations of reality.

The film *Star Trek: Generations* was self-consciously postmodern in attitude, using the illusions of the holodeck and the Nexus as metaphors for postmodern role-playing and reality shifting. The film opens on an eighteenth-century sailing ship, which turns out to be make-believe, "just good fun." Later, when Jean-Luc

Picard follows James T. Kirk into the unrealities of the Nexus, Captain Picard is finally able to convince Captain Kirk to abandon his pleasant illusion—not because losing oneself in illusion is morally wrong, but because it wasn't any fun anymore. The chance to save the galaxy one last time, though, Kirk says, "sounds like fun." Indeed, these are the last words of Kirk as he exits the pages of *Trek* history: "It was fun". Yes, but was it good? or right? or meaningful? Or do any of these things matter anymore?

So even the once solid and dependable James T. Kirk fades into the sunset as the horizon blurs into postmodern shapelessness.[10]

This late-developing metaphysical humility on *Trek* shows up elsewhere, as evidence *Trek* has now made peace with illusion.

In the *DS9* episode "Shadowplay," members of a society are aghast to discover they're not real after all, just mere holographic projections. If they leave a certain valley, as with the magical Shangri-la in *Lost Horizon,* they will vanish. The creator of these illusions actually lives among them, and often forgets his home and community are merely figments of his own imagining. When he finally decides it's time to turn off the hologram and get a life, Odo (the shape-shifter who usually seeks after absolutes) talks him out of it, arguing that reality is relative:

> ODO: Don't you see? She's real to you. They're all real. You can't turn your back on them now.

(Perhaps this episode functions as a subliminal argument against any possible future threats to cancel *Trek*!)

In any case, we're many light-years indeed from the early Pike's indignant refusal of the seductive illusions of the Cage. Even the latter Odo (who, while losing his shapeshifting abilities for awhile, has of late regained them) shows signs of abandoning his search for solidity, and sounds a lot like Vina: "[I'm as] real as you wish. Relax and enjoy the illusion." Or Joseph Campbell, who urges us to "Follow your bliss." Captain Pike was finally set free from his Cage, his keepers told him, because their research showed humans have a unique hatred of captivity: "Even when it's pleasant and benevolent. You prefer death." They didn't do their homework very well. Patrick Henry to the contrary, if the fantasy is more pleasant and benevolent than reality, most humans will choose the fantasy in a nanosecond.

Especially if it turns out that fantasy is all there is anyway.

The chilly wasteland of cold equations has proven incapable of supporting human life. Voices in the materialist wilderness tell us of late that proper care of the soul requires myth, poetry—we need stories in order to find our place in the cosmos. Pop myth-meisters have made a killing selling baby boomers books and tapes on the power of myth. And these ideas have helped shape the recent renaissance of science fiction. Joseph Campbell's own series on myth was filmed on the ranch of one of his biggest fans, George Lucas. The pro-myth view pervades Thomas Richards's book *The Meaning of Star Trek*. But what Richards and the others do not face very unflinchingly is the fact that stories are different: the smorgasbord of available realities includes religious cults and right-wing conspiracies. If we follow our bliss to Aztec mythology we may come to believe, like them, that the sun won't rise without a daily human sacrifice. The mythmeisters are cagey about the "truth" of myth, leaving fans with a lot of double-talk about the relation of myth to reality.

This seems an especially dangerous frame of mind in which to leave people in a world where the choice of bliss people choose to follow can be the difference between life and death. Christopher Pike may come to believe he's off having fun with the beautiful young Vina, but somewhere under there is a biological organism that still requires maintenance. If Pike loses too much touch with reality, the mechanically challenged Talosians will soon face a challenge even greater than giving a paralyzed man the illusion of mobility: that of giving a dead man the illusion of life.

Despite its own double-talk about the value of fantasy, *Trek*'s warnings about illusion are worth considering carefully. The "holodicted" Talosians, said Vina, learned that illusions are a trap, like a narcotic, because when dreams become more important than reality, you give up traveling, building, creating. You even forget how to repair the machines left behind by your ancestors. You just sit living and reliving other lives left behind in the thought records.

It has been speculated that the triumph of postmodernism will ultimately spell the end of the scientific enterprise. It seems a fair question: who will go exploring space if such adventures are available at home, minus all the risk? It's all too easy to imagine a holodeck-addicted human society, lost in some orgiastic fantasy, sliding into social anarchy as their mechanical skills atrophy: like Talosians, having given up all science for fiction.

Maybe it's too late: maybe we're already too busy watching pretend heroes pretend they're heroes to do much of anything else.

But perhaps it's just as well: reality may turn out to be much less fun—and less livable—than fantasy. The physics and metaphysics of *Trek* are certainly based in make-believe. *Trek*'s entire utopian future could well be as illusory as Vina's beauty, covering equally ugly and unalterable truths—about humanity and our ability to find certain knowledge, along with the resulting moral quandary of that particular limitation, and the unfortunate limitations of the laws of physics. At least the technology for producing fantasies is becoming more sophisticated all the time.

In conclusion, the evidence suggests human beings need to believe "life is a critical affair": that their choices have meaning. Yet the primary choice before us now seems to be between false hope and real despair. Here is a no-win scenario indeed: man cannot live on dream food alone. But real food does not exist.

And yet—one must ask—what are we to make of *hunger?*

Could our very longings—for significance, goodness, beauty, and reality—actually be "flickers in the Nexus," clues to a "real" reality "out there"? Or are these merely psychological phenomena that can be explained away as just so many illusions?

We share that familiar predicament of *Trek* characters: we find ourselves in a confusing world where the phenomena of existence are interpreted for us by various authorities who would presume to outline the borders of what they insist is reality. We can either accept the reality we find ourselves in or try to escape. But that "escape" has its own problems: how can we know that the reality we escape to is any more real than the one we left?

If there exists any true hope, it would seem logical that the only way to find it would be to resolutely refuse to surrender to illusion. The prerequisite to finding a real happy ending would mean rejecting glib optimism and steadfastly facing real despair. But if there's one lesson *Trek* teaches in every episode it is that one must go through the darkest moment to reach the dawn.

In our next chapter, we're going to step back and view *Trek* in a much wider context, broadening the scope of our survey to include a variety of sources from literature, poetry, science, philosophy and popular culture.

9

A Starship Named *Desire*

HOW I WONDER

Look at the stars! look, look up at the skies!
  O look at all the fire-folk sitting in the air!
(Gerard Manley Hopkins, "The Starlight Night")

Ah, the double pleasures of stargazing! Who on earth has not looked into the twinkling nighttime sky and wondered? There's the first sense of wonder—letting the infinite simply wash over you—and the second sense—where wonder provokes the questions: Is anybody out there? Are *They* looking down at us, wondering, too? And will we ever make *contact*? *Trek* was born under the stars, according to Gene Roddenberry's first wife, Eileen. On family camping trips, she says, Gene made up stories for his daughters snuggled in their sleeping bags, bedtime stories of beings from Out There.

Of course, many people think some of those beings from Out There have come "down here": that we've already made contact. Our culture has long been gaga over the idea of visitors from space. In the last two decades especially, space aliens have conquered television, the tabloid media, and Hollywood movies.

But why this obsessive interest in Others from space by beings who have been so chronically intolerant of Others in their own midst? Here is one more phenomenon about which to wonder.

Various explanations have been suggested. Carl Jung claimed UFOs rang common chords in humanity's collective unconscious. Carl Sagan said we long for the stars because we're made of "star stuff." Others are attracted to space aliens by the hope that they might teach us the secrets of the universe—human origins, new technologies. Then there is the popular dream that simply *knowing* somebody is Out There will bring us together down here.

One suspects, however, that the real reason behind our obsession with extraterrestrials is less practical and more primal: it is that old stab of "infinite, indeterminate longing" that comes of wishing on a star, or dreaming of "somewhere over the rainbow."

The Wizard of Oz opens with Dorothy running from that mean old witch threatening to turn Toto into a newt. But nobody listens to Dorothy's cry for help; not Auntie Em, not Uncle Henry, not even her farmhand friends. They're too busy with grown-up troubles. Dorothy is brushed aside with a gruff, "Find yourself a place where you won't get into any trouble." So she walks off in her black-and-white world, sighing, "A place where there isn't any trouble. Do you suppose there is such a place, Toto?"

There's more than mere escapism going on here. A whiff of the same desire can be detected in that most beloved movie about space aliens, *E. T.: The Extraterrestrial.* Elliot, the young hero, is a deliberate echo of Dorothy: brushed aside, ignored, lonely. "If Dad was here, he'd believe me"—but Dad has escaped his own troubles with a new girlfriend. So when Elliot leaves an angry dinner-table exchange and looks out the window into the night sky, we know what he's looking for: not merely an escape from his troubles, but Somebody Out There who will listen—i.e., contact.

Awakening this sense of bittersweet desire, said J. R. R. Tolkien (who should know), is the best thing a fantasy story can do.[1]

Such longing, like Joseph Campbell's "hero," has a thousand faces—and at least as many places: Middle-earth. Narnia. Barsoom. Pellucidar. El Dorado. Shangri-la. Brigadoon. Camelot. Atlantis. Avalon. Utopia. Eden. Never Land. Arcadia.

One finds Arcadians in the strangest places. "Project Ozma" (Ozma was a princess of Oz) was the original name for the Search for Extraterrestrial Intelligence (SETI) program, begun with radio telescopes forty years ago. "Like [fantasy author L. Frank] Baum," confessed SETI pioneer Frank Drake in his autobiography, "I, too, was dreaming of a land far away, peopled by strange and exotic beings."[2]

The SETI scientists are true believers, undaunted by continued negative returns for their increasingly sophisticated efforts. They tend to cut themselves slack they wouldn't think of giving to religious believers. For example, there's no way to prove the *non—existence* of something, they tell naysayers. Dr. Drake stood firm with his colleague Carl Sagan on their "Sagan-Drake equation," a row of letters and numbers that proved, they said, that our galaxy is teeming with life just waiting to be found.

Yet the naysayers are many. Critics of SETI have produced their own equations to prove the galaxy is bereft of intelligence (with, perhaps, a single planetary exception). Some charge that the entire SETI enterprise is fired by quasi-religious motivations.

And no doubt our attraction to Somebody Out There is entangled with religious emotions. We recall that genre of films devoted to the alien messiah. In *E.T.*, citing just one example, a being from Out There, childlike and innocent, possesses mystical healing powers, is misunderstood by the authorities, and finally lays down his life for Elliot—only to be resurrected and so ascend to the heavens. Steven Spielberg, the film's Jewish director, claims any Christlike elements of his story are purely coincidence—as have the makers of other alien-messiah films.

How very strange! One wonders if wonders will never cease.

WHEN I HEARD THE LEARN'D ASTRONOMER

Carl Sagan was passionately involved in SETI his entire career. In his final days, he must have felt he was on the verge of seeing his heart's desire fulfilled: recent months had witnessed new planets found outside our solar system, the discovery of water on the moon, revised theories about the conditions under which life might develop, and a meteorite found on Earth offering new hope for the ever-tantalizing possibility of life on Mars. Surely these astonishing developments must have given Sagan strength as he battled the blood disease that finally killed him in 1996.

Sagan sometimes identified himself as an "exobiologist," an expert on extraterrestrial life. He modeled conditions under which alien life might have developed as he waited for specimens to be discovered. Actually, he wasn't just waiting: Sagan actively encouraged SETI on all fronts. He sat on panels and committees and organized debates on the subject. He helped create the various greetings sent on NASA satellites bound for points beyond our solar system. He was the founder of the Planetary Society, a group dedicated to the search for extraterrestrials. And whatever Sagan might have thought of any quasi-religious aspects of this quest, the Planetary Society was the grateful recipient of a $100,000 donation from Stephen Spielberg, some of the profit generated by the success of *E.T.*

In the mid-eighties, Sagan wrote his own novel about ETs, *Contact*, whose main character was Ellie (à la Elliot), a female SETI scientist on her own quest for contact. The book was made into a film directed by Robert Zemeckis *(Forrest Gump, Back to the Future)*, released in 1997, after Sagan's death. The story of *Contact*, book and film, begins with a SETI project that picks up a message from space—plus plans for building an interstellar spaceship—and climaxes with a mind-bending cosmic journey reminiscent of *2001:* the hero confronts the mysteries of the universe, learning that not only were Sagan and Drake right and we humans are not alone, but that we have some catching up to do before we can take our place in galactic society. The good news is that there is a galactic society in which we can take our place.

The story of *Contact* features a key secondary character, a religious leader, Palmer Joss, portrayed (in Sagan's novel more so than the film) as an enemy of SETI, of science in general, and of any discovery that might threaten his own version of reality. Carl Sagan had little patience for what he identified as fundamentalist religion, creationism, or any other example of what he lumped under the category of pseudosciences. He carried his battle against "superstition" to his death bed—brave words as he lay dying, facing nonbeing, with tragic courage.

Yet it seems unfair to characterize an ancient antagonism between those who "wonder" at the stars in the two different senses we have noted as solely between religious fundamentalists and science.

Indeed, *those who wonder*—in the nonscientific sense—also includes those we might lump together under the catchall name of *poets*. In the view of the poets, the scientists are missing the forest for cataloging the trees. Walt Whitman wrote of being bored by the "learn'd astronomer," with his maps and graphs, and sneaking out of his lecture to contemplate the stars. Wordsworth urged his readers to leave behind their books and the ways of analysts who "murder to dissect." One recalls the scientists in *E.T.*, a faceless army bristling with flashlights and metal detectors, whose aim seemed wrapping mystery in plastic, suffocating wonder—murdering to dissect. Poet John Keats said philosophy—his word for science—"will clip an Angel's wings:"

> Conquer all mysteries by rule and line,
> Empty the haunted air, and gnomed mine—
> Unweave a rainbow. . . .

And we all know how hard it is to get over an unwoven rainbow.

From the poets' point of view, the history of science is a progressive desertification of the imagination. Once upon a time, the woods were filled with fairies, the oceans with dragons, the earth with Dark Continents and Lost Cities. The unknown "Out There" was much closer: a trip down the Nile could be as exotic as an adventure to the stars. Yet in seeking to fulfill their longings, human beings climbed the unclimbable, passed the unpassable, and reached the unreachable. Spaces on maps once labeled "Terra Incognita" were filled in, given names, paved over. And so the fairies were eventually chased off the Earth into nearby space. As late as 1938, rumors of an invasion from Mars seemed plausible enough to panic the nation. But sixty years later, scientists cross their fingers and hold their breath hoping to find life on Mars about on the level of shower fungus: no more bug-eyed monsters, but *maybe* bugs. As our telescopes continue to reach ever further, the "somebodys" Out There keep packing up and moving on; from Mars to distant points beyond.

Fairies, Martians, and Metalunans seem to represent an unshakable human conviction that the cosmos is *not* all there is: that dancing among the stars, creeping in the shadows, are intelligence and will; that we are *not* alone; that somebody *is* indeed Out There.

Of course, that's just one side of the story. The history of science, from the scientists' point of view, is much different. In this version, the world was once filled with suffering, ignorance, and abusive manipulation of its peoples. Through science, there has been progressive elimination of these. "We can pray over the cholera victim," wrote Carl Sagan, "or we can give her 500 milligrams of tetracycline every 12 hours."[3]

Furthermore, the charges of murdering to dissect and destroying wonder are unfounded: science can also provoke wonder, said Sagan. "Any protozoology or bacteriology or mycology textbook is filled with wonders that far outshine the most exotic descriptions of the alien abductionists."[4] Nobel Prize–winning physicist Stephen Weinberg says that knowing why Betelguese is red only enhances our pleasure of viewing the sky.

And the scientists have their own warning: that what we don't know will hurt us. Humanity's failure to give up its beloved fantasies and accept the scientific perspective will bring on a new Dark Age: Aum Shrinkyo and Heaven's Gate are just the start.

If this tug of war sounds familiar, that's because it's another variation on humanity's love/hate relationship to the Other. In this case, the conflict is between a love of knowing and understanding the Other, and a love of encountering the Other as an *unknowable mystery*. And, despite some critics' assertions, this Ping-Pong match is not simply a replay of the stereotypical "Galileo versus the Church," i.e., "science versus superstition." It has more to do with two different ways of viewing the unknown: as a disease to be cured, or as an endangered species to protect.

Perhaps knowing why Betelguese is red *does* enhance our pleasure; but knowing there aren't really any Martians has been a painful disappointment. Percival Lowell, the Boston aristocrat who founded the Lowell Observatory, insisted that the lines on Mars called by an Italian astronomer *canali* were actually canals designed by intelligent beings. When newer, more powerful telescopes proved there weren't really canals on Mars after all, Lowell defended the use of smaller telescopes, with theories about atmospheric disturbance to explain the disappearance of this "proof" of ETs.[5]

And *that* sort of behavior was the biggest mystery of all for Carl Sagan: "Whose interest does ignorance serve?" he asked.[6]

A very good question. But do we really want to know the answer?

THE ANATOMY OF WONDER

British sage Samuel Johnson defined wonder as "the effect of novelty upon ignorance." In Chesterton's view, wonder was "Divine ignorance"—a sort of ignorance which *is* bliss.

And yet while wonder may depend upon ignorance, not all ignorance results in wonder—especially ignorance concerning wonder. In the movie version of *Contact*, director Robert Zemeckis subversively reinterpreted Sagan's material to suggest that perhaps strict materialism was one more form of ignorance. The film *Contact* included a character not found in the novel: a blind astronomer who hovered over the action—an astronomer who looked suspiciously like Carl Sagan. And without a doubt, there were some things Sagan just couldn't see. "Seances occur only in darkened rooms, where the ghostly visitors can be seen dimly at best," he wrote. "If we turn up the lights a little, so we have a chance to see what's going on, the spirits vanish."[7]

Absolutely. But the same holds true for wonder, mystery, and romance—all of which require a careful combination of light and shadow to thrive. (That spirits prefer darkness, says Chesterton, no more disproves their existence than the fact that lovers prefer darkness disproves theirs.[8]) The magic of romance—or of poetry—works not in stating directly, but through *suggestion,* the irresistible flickering of ambiguity. Conjuring the mysterious requires distance, strategic obscurement, blurred focus—not bright lights, full views, and clinical dissection.

Even the makers of *Alien Autopsy*—who were neither poets nor scientists—understood this. Their sensational "documentary" featured "real" footage of a purported extraterrestrial. Of course, the camera never held still long enough to give the viewer a stable, unobscured, *clinical* view of the subject: no real dissection. But what the bogus footage *did* manage to convey was the deeply satisfying experience of the power of *suggestion.*

Possibility steals one's breath in a way actuality falls short of. Idea is almost always better than execution. And hope springs eternal that what we've just barely glimpsed in the shadows, out the corner of our eye, we'll someday catch—whatever it is.

"This X of ours . . ." is how German theologian Rudolf Otto tried to define the undefinable, the shiver down the spine one feels in the presence of the uncanny. In his book *The Idea of the Holy* (1923), Otto named the source of all spine tingling "the numinous": the rush of creature-consciousness, the sense of overwhelming nothingness in the presence of a "wholly other." The object of this encounter by definition defies definition; the numinous, said Otto, is what remains stubbornly inexplicable.

The numinous is what puts the *X* in the *X-Files,* a show that always seems in danger of being done in by its own success. For with too much light the spirits *do* vanish. The monsters are scary until we get a good look at them; then we're disappointed to realize those rubber masks couldn't possibly be the real object of our spine-shivers; they're not *Other* enough. The best any fan of the numinous can hope for, it seems, is the merest *suggestion* of the unfathomable; anything more than a suggestion, and the object is revealed to be much less than unfathomable.

So we love *unsolved* mysteries, urban myths and ancient legends that fill the tabloid press. Freud, writing about the "uncanny," said the more realistic the setting, the greater the sensation. Thus, we see sober hosts of pseudodocumentaries, fictional FBI agents chasing UFOs, ghosts, and other assorted unfathomables.

This mix of pseudo and science is the kind of stuff Carl Sagan found so frustrating. For materialist science operates on the assumption that nothing is ultimately unfathomable. James T. Kirk echoed the mind of his own maker, Gene Roddenberry, here:

> KIRK: The greatest danger facing us is ourselves and our irrational fear of the unknown. But there is no such thing as the unknown. There are only things temporarily hidden, temporarily not understood. ("Corbomite Maneuver," *TOS*)

The *Trek* calendar on my desk features a photo with this caption: "Kirk, Spock and Uhura, whose job is to understand the unknown." Such an attitude seems especially hypocritical on *Trek*, which lures us with the promise of encountering "strange, new worlds."

Of course, the problem with strange, new worlds is that once they've been mapped, measured, and quantified, they stop being strange and new. The alien becomes familiar; the familiar breeds contempt; too much light makes the spirits vanish. The first real-life moon landing riveted the world's attention from blastoff to splashdown. The only later moon shot to draw any kind of crowd was Apollo 13, and that was because something went *extraordinarily* wrong: at some point even trips to the moon can become routine—can anything be more dull than that Howard Johnson's in orbit in *2001*—and so no longer strange and new.

Living with aliens becomes old hat. So *Trek* heroes themselves must *become* aliens, fish out of water, experiencing *alternative* adventures. Just having an onboard android is no longer enough, so we must dress him up like Sherlock Holmes. ("Elementary, My Dear Data," *TNG*, etc.) And after a while, all this talk of going "where no one has gone before" seems less noble as it comes to resemble the cry of an addict; it begins to smack of desperation.

Walker Percy, in his book *Lost in the Cosmos*, describes a long list of bizarre items people have used as coffee tables. His observation was that human beings have an odd propensity for sucking the life out of the familiar. This is what drives the relentless march from the avant-garde to the status quo—and then to the cliché. We recall the *Star Trek: Voyager* episode "Death Wish." In this story, a member of the godlike, immortal Q Continuum longs to become mortal so he can die. Why? Because he's found immortality boring. Life everlasting has meant simply hanging around long enough to solve *all* mysteries, answer *all* questions, and reduce all experience to a stultifying "been there, done that"; no more countries left undiscovered, and no room for what Chesterton called man's "chief pleasure": surprise.

The benefits of ignorance become a little more clear. For suppose a man could forever fill his hunger with one meal, asked Robert Louis Stevenson, take in all knowledge with a glance. What then? Alexander the Great wept when he realized he had no more worlds to conquer. Thus we have the popular picture of heaven: listless angels plucking harps, or the "Heaven Room" at Wheaton College's museum of evangelism, white walls and a mirror. So much for happily ever after. Lucky for us, thought Stevenson, who himself never stopped moving, the universe is infinite: we can chase the horizon till we drop. "To travel hope-fully," he concluded, "is better than to arrive." (Something maybe the producers of *Star Trek: Voyager* should keep in mind!)

The *TNG* episode "Where No One Has Gone Before" featured an alien with the limitless powers of Q, but who hadn't yet exhausted the unknown possibilities of infinite space. Asked by the humans about his ultimate destination, this "Traveler" was confused:

> TRAVELER: Destination?
> PICARD: Yes. What place are you trying to reach?
> TRAVELER: Ah—place, no—there is no specific place I wish to go.
> PICARD: Then what is the purpose of your destination?
> TRAVELER: Curiosity.
> PICARD: That's not an answer.
> TRAVELER: I don't know if I can put this in terms you can understand.

And why bother spoiling anyone's pleasure with the finality of an *explanation*? Wouldn't it be better just to "travel hopefully"?

So we meet again at the crossroads of *Trek*'s double vision: the desire to know, to understand, versus the desire for the Unknown. We all love a mystery. But we also love to learn "whodunit." We love magic, but also being let in on the secret. To turn against either mystery or knowledge is to be half human. Reason without mystery, says Chesterton, makes madmen. The poet puts his head into the heavens, but science tries to put the heavens into one's head—which can only result in splitting it.[9] But Carl Sagan's warnings about scientific ignorance seem equally compelling.

As we have seen throughout our investigation of *Trek*, the dif-ficulty in being fully human is navigating our own extremes.

Trek fans are often adept at playing both sides of this duality. A regular feature of conventions is the famous "blooper reel"—a collection of outtakes from various *Trek* shows: missed cues, doors that won't open, forgotten lines, etc. And a screening of bloopers may be followed by a demonstration of the secrets of stage fights or makeup or special effects. The fans dress like aliens, but they had to master some practical skills to do so. Bearing this in mind, I've been fairly confident this analysis of *Trek* has not been perceived by fans as "murdering to dissect."

Fans just wouldn't want me doing it in the middle of watching the show. For it's very annoying to have somebody trying to explain something while you're suspending disbelief and experiencing.

But wait a second. In the last few chapters we've seen how science has presumed to explain away all that makes us human, our values, our meaning, even our longings; our "wonder." How can we still enjoy "the show"—that is, the experience of being human—even as we're being told it's all just a trick? Should we just work all the harder at suspending our disbelief? As we saw in the last chapter, the "realists" of philosophy would say, No, better to face facts, even if the truth hurts. Those who can't live with that kind of pain recommend "therapeutic unreality"—"foma"—saying, Pay no attention to that man behind the curtain; suspend disbelief in human value and meaning, even at the cost of truth. If the cold facts of humanity and its place in the universe as presented by materialist science are correct, the answer to the question Who does ignorance benefit? becomes ever longer: it includes not just lovers of mystery, but also anyone who believes in human rights, dignity, purpose, meaning, ethics—even "humanity."

And these are some "spirits" most of us don't want to vanish. The faded beauty queen of Tennessee Williams's play *A Streetcar Named "Desire,"* Blanche DuBois, is surprisingly clearheaded and calculating when it comes to her own need for a few dark shadows:

I don't want realism. I want magic. Yes, yes. Magic. I try to give
that to people. I do misrepresent things. I don't tell truth. I tell
what ought to be true. But if that is sinful let me be punished for
it. Don't turn the light on. . . .

Socrates said the unexamined life is not worth living. These
days, many have concluded the opposite: that the overexamined
life is the one that's not worth living—that it's possible to know
too much for one's own good, certainly for the good of one's
"humanity."

Even Carl Sagan seemed reluctant, in his own fictional quest
for *Contact,* to blast the bright light of science into every dark corner of the Unknown. The climax of his novel depends not on discovering all the answers but in learning new questions: the sense
of wonder depends, as always, on encountering the Unknown.

Then again, Sagan never took his "candle in the dark" very far
into examining the contradictions of his own moral assumptions.
Likewise, Sagan died before he had the opportunity to find out if
discovering an ET was the sort of contact he had been desiring all
along; here again, he traveled hopefully and never arrived.

Others who stake so much on finding ETs would be wise to
consider carefully the possible consequences of actually finding
one: that is, the possibility that having is much less satisfying than
wanting. We can see this by trying on another mask of desire.
Suppose, says Walker Percy, somebody should actually find the
Holy Grail,

> dig it up in an Israeli wadi, properly authenticate it, carbon date
> it, and present it to the Metropolitan Museum. Millions of visi-
> tors! I would be as curious as the next person and would stand in
> line for hours to see it. But what difference would it make in the
> end?[10]

One wonders. What if there *is* somebody out there? What if they *are* like us? What if they've been channeling their loneliness and longings into their popular arts, dreaming of visits from aliens, pinning their hopes on contact—with somebody who might turn out to be us? Wouldn't *that* be a cosmic joke? If such contact wasn't a disappointment for us, it surely would be for them. Maybe the best thing such contact would provide would be an opportunity to exchange alien-messiah movies. And so both races could keep dreaming about contact with Somebody Else Out There.

It could be we won't even be that lucky. The more scientists do learn about the uniqueness of life, and intelligent life, on planet Earth, the more improbable those equations "proving" the likelihood of ETs become. And where shall we go next? Where, if there is nobody out there, will the insatiable longing that drove us to look for the source of the Nile and shoot off into space locate a new lost horizon that we might travel hopefully toward?

What if it turns out we can't get there from here?

THE SWEET POISON OF THE FALSE INFINITE

This, some would say, is the real tragedy of the human condition: "We are so constituted that our hopes are inaccessible, like the stars. . . ."[11] Perhaps the truest picture of our plight is Judy Garland, that real-life Blanche DuBois in her drug-addicted hell, still pouring her soul after so many years into a song about going over the rainbow, trying until the bitter end to conjure the old magic: "Birds fly over the rainbow. Why can't I?"

Indeed, it seems cruel to awaken desire—with a fantasy story or anything else—if there is no real object for such a desire. A few sturdy souls claim to be able to handle an occasional sip of absurd, objectless hope—traveling hopefully—in moderation. But it's hard to be moderate with an infinite desire.

The poet Yeats certainly knew the agony of unfulfillable desire. The hero of his poem "The Man Who Dreamed of Fairyland" could have found happiness in this world if only he'd not once glimpsed "a woven world-forgotten isle." Ever after, he felt no peace, not even in the grave. Such longings seem out of place in a world that is, as Yeats said elsewhere, "so full of weeping."

Plato presumed to banish all poets from his ideal Republic in order to keep them from creating any such mischief in his utopia. Better total abstinence than painful longing without any hope of fulfillment. Buddhists would say the wise man is the one who gives up all desires. If that is true, we may add to our list of mystical lands Nirvana—the land where all desire is extinct.

For, clearly, traveling hopefully isn't for everybody. In the end, the only thing weary F. Scott Fitzgerald was able to capture was the futility of the chase. In *The Great Gatsby,* he wrote,

> believed in the green light, the orgiastic future that year by year recedes before us. It eluded us then, but that's no matter— tomorrow we will run faster, stretch out our arms farther. . . . And one fine morning . . . . So we beat on, boats against the current, borne back ceaselessly into the past.

The risks of futility can be much worse than mere disappointment. Chasing an ever elusive quarry can drive one to madness. Witness Captain Ahab, who destroyed himself in an insane quest for the ungraspable great white whale. Strangely, the ever questing *Trek* invokes Ahab more than once. Khan, in *TWOK,* quotes *Moby Dick* as he seeks his vengeance on Kirk: "To the last I grapple with thee; from hell's heart I stab at thee. . . ." This classic-dropping is probably not much more than garnish, as it is in *First Contact,* when Picard, with a personal score to settle with the Borg, lets his desire for justice degenerate temporarily into a mad lust for their destruction. But neither of these stories follow very far the questions raised in shadowing the noble quest of *Trek* with mad Ahab and his uncatchable whale.

Herman Melville's whale, on the other hand, is a deliberate metaphor for all the things human beings chase:

> It is the image of the ungraspable phantom of life; and this is the key to it all. . . . All visible objects, man, are but as pasteboard masks. . . . If man will strike, strike through the mask! . . . That inscrutable thing is chiefly what I hate. . . . And of all these things the Albino whale was the symbol.[12]

(There's an episode of *DS9* which offers a lame attempt to invoke Melville. Three Klingons swear vengeance against an alien "Albino"—but somehow this story doesn't quite conjure the same sense of desperation.)

This is where our love/hate relationship with the Other slides fastest from love to hate. Agent Mulder on the *X-Files,* chasing his elusive mysteries, is often compared with Captain Ahab and his whale. Mulder's partner Agent Scully's nickname is Starbuck, which was the name of Ahab's first mate. Again, we can see how easily what begins as an earnest desire for contact—to discover truth Out There—becomes an irrational wish to destroy that which is able to elude our attempts at control.

"We push over the verge of the creation," says George MacDonald; "*we damn*—just because we cannot embrace. For to embrace is the necessity of our deepest being. That failed, we hate."[13]

In C. S. Lewis's novel *Perelandra,* the hero, Ransom, has an insight about the nature of man's itch for control: our desire to so command our circumstances that we can replay them at will is, he sees, the root of all evil, including the love of money.[14] One commentator has seized upon a particular phrase in *Perelandra* to give a name to this temptation: "the sweet poison of the false infinite."[15] The character in that novel who falls hardest for this "sweet poison"—Weston—is the perfect embodiment of Wellsian scientism: he wants humans to spread through the galaxy, conquering and bringing everything under control. Ransom watches in horror as this lust for a false infinite becomes, for Weston, the path to dehumanization. Indeed, Weston becomes "the Un-Man"—the end result of fruitless pursuit of the infinite. This sort of hunger is, in fact, precisely what makes "mad scientists."

No doubt, for all of us, our lands of heart's desire include some element of security; and most security that we know about includes the element of *control*. In the Christian vision, a surrender to divine control is the key to the Edenic utopia. The later expulsion from Eden was a result of an attempted assertion of human control, and has been the issue ever since: a never-ending cycle of revolution and counterrevolution. With the Enlightenment came the idea that control of human destiny was possible by means of rational human effort. It is interesting to reflect that our efforts at rational control of our environment, while they have raised cities and driven forward the march of progress, have also released ever more boundless horrors; the most "controlled" (by "cold equations") regimes have let loose the most unbridled violence and destruction of the environment.

Lewis predicted (as did Nietzsche) that the end of belief in some universal moral pattern for humanity, i.e., "the tao" would unleash continuous and violent collisions of unrestrained lusts. "When all that says 'it is good' has been debunked, 'I want' remains."[16] Against that ultimate unfathomable, the threat of annihilation presented by the ungraspable whale or the deeps of space, lies only the assertion of Self. Here is the basic human impulse, said Nietzsche: the will to power, all other alleged motivations or desires being merely "masks" for this. "Make it so"—the seduction of instantly being able to conform reality to one's wishes: point and click. Think of the power-mad glee of a little kid with a squirt gun: his will, the utter domination of everyone, at a distance, in an instant—it's just like magic!

Indeed, in this case, science and magic are two means to the same end: the control of the elements, to be exercised for good or for ill. Tolkien contrasts good fairy magic with the "scientific magician," who "desire[s] power in this world, domination of things and wills."[17] Faust sought the knowledge to manipulate reality: "All things that move between the quiet poles shall be at his command." Remember Frodo's ring: the longer one possesses the ring, the harder it is to let go—merely having it around works a dark magic on the possessor. On *Trek,* the ancient Klingon relic, the Sword of Kahless, works the same dark magic.

Trek, of course, repeats all the old warnings about absolute power corrupting. In "Where No Man Has Gone Before" and "Charlie X" *(TOS),* humans are given superhuman powers and quickly rendered un-men. In "Hide and Q" *(TNG),* that omnipotent space imp grants Commander Riker the gift of absolute power—even over life and death. But after some disturbing experimentation, Riker wisely returns the power to Q with a speech about humanity being defined by its limits. (We note again, in passing, the appeal to some unspoken universal moral standard in these episodes, since without the tao, power could not be seen to corrupt, since there would be no "corruption" to speak of.[18])

The warnings against power are ironic in view of the power of *Trek* humans: to instantaneously move, change, heal, create, destroy—all very much like magic. Again, the weakest element of this utopian fantasy is the prospect of our easily tempted species assimilating all these technological expansions of individual power so effortlessly with little or no social consequences. But the *Trek* vision for the future raises the same old questions, presenting a picture of humanity borne ceaselessly back into the past. One recalls Gene Roddenberry's own Gollum-like confidence in science and in the rightness of his own vision. Or the tolerance-loving *Trek* fans who love to dress like *Trek*'s least tolerant villains. Or that constant judgment in favor of nonjudgmentalism, dispensed from the end of a phaser.

This is much the same schizoid attitude, in fact, expressed by certain scientists who love to speak of the "objectivity" of science and then issue moral imperatives or make moral judgments about those who disagree with them. When, for example, the late Carl Sagan spoke for "science," you never knew if he was referring to a method for research or an elite body of certain individuals.

Yet it doesn't take a rocket scientist to figure out that killing that whale would never have made Ahab happy. Picture him on the bow of the *Pequod*, exultant over the bloated white carcass. Not likely. The mad Captain is more likely to be weeping, like Alexander, devastated that the one thing he thought for sure was unfathomable turned out to be very fathomable after all. Better, for Ahab, as for Carl Sagan and his ETs, to travel hopefully, than discover that—after all the effort—what one grasps is merely another stand-in for an ungraspable Something Else.

Aye, and there's another rub. What if the truth *is* Out There, and we can't catch it?

LOST HORIZONS

C. S. Lewis hated the "travel hopefully" mentality—just like those "hard" realists who would have us wean ourselves of false hopes, but for a different reason. Lewis knew only too well the stab of inconsolable longing—such experiences became benchmarks of his life, scattered clues to a puzzle he finally believed he'd solved. In Lewis's allegorical autobiography, *The Pilgrim's Regress,* his protagonist gets a tantalizing glimpse of an island. But unlike Yeats's man who only dreamed of fairyland, Lewis's pilgrim follows his longings and *reaches* his island.

This next section will feature an unlikely comparison of Lewis's fantasy *The Great Divorce*—wherein he directly addresses the notion of "traveling hopefully"—with the *Trek* stories "The Cage" and *Generations.* Then we'll compare all these with *Lost Horizon* — a novel by James Hilton, but we'll rely more on the film version by Frank Capra, with Ronald Coleman and Jane Wyman (who, trivia buffs note, played Spock's mother, Amanda, on *Trek*).

In *Lost Horizon* a planeload of Western refugees from that all-too-familiar world of power struggles and violent conflicts crash-lands in a hidden valley of the Himalayas. The survivors are taken by passing Sherpas to a Buddhist lamasery, Shangri-la. Like much of the mysticism in *Trek,* the Buddhism of *Lost Horizon* is purely cosmetic: the inhabitants of Shangri-la have found true happiness: not, however, as true Buddhism would insist, in the renunciation of desire, but because in Shangri-la, all their desires have been fulfilled. The lamasery has books, beautiful architecture, gardens, art, horseback riding, romantic love, music, conversation, delicious food, and fulfilling labor. The inhabitants do not grow old, nor is there conflict amongst them. Yet Shangri-la isn't entirely conflict free: the struggle is against certain values of the outside world; the peace is an active peace, combined with a sense of mission: to preserve mankind's highest and best works against the coming apocalypse.

One of the passengers of the downed plane, a world-weary English diplomat, Robert Conway (Coleman), falls under the enchantment of Shangri-la. Conway's brother George, however, is deeply unnerved by the place: George seems to *need* conflict and noise. "We don't belong here," he tells his brother, eventually convincing Bob the whole thing is an illusion and a trap; so they make their escape.

We see the similarities to *Trek*'s "The Cage" and *Generations*. In those stories, characters find themselves in veritable Shangri-las, mysterious lands where their dreams come true: Captain Pike on Talos IV and Captain Kirk in the illusions of the Nexus. Both Captains are tempted to stay, but they too become convinced that their utopias are illusion; both, like the Conways, choose to leave. Pike's conversations with his Talos IV dream girl, Vina (when he refuses to surrender to her illusory charms) and Jean-Luc Picard's speeches to James Kirk (where he tries to wake the older *Enterprise* captain from his pleasant dreaming) are reminiscent of George's argument with his brother: we don't belong here, our place is out there, we need to escape.

The Shangri-la of "The Cage" features Vina (the Blanche DuBois of space), who refuses to leave Talos IV, since that would mean the end of her magical youth and beauty. *Lost Horizon* features the likewise young and beautiful Maria. Like Vina, Maria has been warned that if she leaves, she'll assume her true age and appearance: again, ancient and decrepit. Unlike Vina, however, Maria refuses to believe this warning. She abandons the hidden valley with the Conway brothers, and eventually—right before their very eyes—ages in an instant and drops dead in the snow.

Here is a critical difference between two utopian visions: in both cases, a beautiful young woman's sudden and instant aging provides objective proof—in Vina's case, proof that Talos IV is a dream world, and in Maria's case, proof Shangri-la is real. (Of course we can jump back into the radical skepticism of the last chapter and wonder if the fate of both Vina and Maria weren't also illusory, but for the sake of avoiding that nasty downward spiral, let's go with the validity of sense evidence.)

We observe that the brothers Conway have different responses to objective proof of Shangri-la: George, who was much too restless to be happy in Shangri-la, would now rather die than face its reality—so he jumps off a mountain to his death. Robert Conway, on the other hand, who loved Shangri-La, now realizes he's made a terrible mistake in leaving; and *he'd rather die than live without that place of peace*. Robert Conway spends the rest of his days trying to get back to Shangri-la—like a man possessed, someone says. He shares Captain Pike's determination to live in reality: only in Conway's case, his utopia *is* reality.

Lost Horizon indeed raises compelling questions.

Why, first of all, if it *was* possible to find true contentment in Shangri-la, would Maria leave? Especially when (a) she had personal knowledge of her own great age and miraculous youth, and (b) she'd been warned of the consequences of leaving? Did she disbelieve the warning? But doing so would mean she had to not only reject what she'd been told, but also what she knew. Could it be that in some twisted desire for "freedom," Maria was led to actually *deny* what she knew was true, and *will* herself to believe a fiction? A twisted demand of "liberty" or death?

And what about George Conway? Why couldn't he find happiness in Shangri-la? His unhappiness lends credence to the notion that human beings need conflict in order to be happy. *Trek*'s utopia certainly couldn't survive without human conflict, even when Gene Roddenberry tried to make it illegal. And certainly both Captains Kirk and Pike were unable to find happiness in their respective Shangri-las. But in both these cases, it wasn't the lack of conflict that drove them out, but *the lack of reality*.

The possibility of a *reality* in which human need for conflict has been somehow permanently resolved is almost impossible to picture.

On the other hand, Pascal says *too* much reality is the real reason men hate prison. In a cage, men must *face themselves:* where they're from, where they're going, their own sense of naughtness. Rather than do so, men seek to drown the cry of their empty hearts and unfulfillable longings with noise and diversions. Earth men take pleasure in diverting themselves from themselves with visions of adventure in space; spacemen seem to have an equal need for diversion via holodeck, in which they can drown out their unshakable emptiness with fantasies of life on Earth.

So was it that George was perhaps afraid to live without his diversions, to face his own nothingness? He did not want to arrive, apparently, if it meant giving up the sense of *control* of destiny afforded by traveling. Did George prefer death by his own choice to submitting to reality on any terms other than his own? The Milton quote alluded to by Khan in "Space Seed" *(TOS)* would apply: "Better to rule in hell than to serve in heaven. . . ."

Or "Better to travel hopefully in hell than arrive in heaven." That would certainly be the motto of certain characters in C. S. Lewis's story *The Great Divorce,* which is strikingly similar to both the *Trek* stories and *Lost Horizon.* The visitors in this utopia, though, don't arrive in a starship from space or an airplane from the West. In Lewis's story, the visitors arrive on a bus from hell—and they can stay at their destination—heaven—if they choose. But just like the visitors to those other Shangri-las, *almost nobody wants to stay.* "We don't belong here," many say, echoing all those previous utterances of that line. One visitor actually announces, with great pomposity, that "to travel hopefully is better than to arrive." And in Lewis's tale, we meet the unforgettable character of the artist who would much rather *paint* the object of his longings than *possess* it.

Apparently, some people *would* rather just eat the menu, even if it means pushing aside the food. In his interview with Bill Moyers, Joseph Campbell waxed symbolic about the mythological significance of the number thirteen in conjunction with the original American states. Moyers had to point out (apologetically) that there were, *in fact,* thirteen states. Yet Campbell seemed less interested in history than in metaphor. To hunger hopefully, for Joseph Campbell, was better than to eat.

Two unfortunate twists on the human double-need for both the known and the infinite unknown seem to be these: to apply that infinite longing to a quest for infinite control, and thereby become "un-men," and to choose deliberate ignorance, to refuse to *un*suspend disbelief.

Lost Horizon ends with an aristocrat in his club commenting on the inspiring story of Conway's single-minded search for his utopia: "I believe in Shangri-la," he says, "because I *want* to." Just like the poster on Agent Mulder's wall: I *want* to believe. But what does that mean? People can say "I want to believe" and mean different things, all of which may agree on premise (ETs, utopias, or some other object seem to correspond on some level with the heart's deepest desire) but differ in conclusion:

a. They are real and I believe in them.

b. I will believe in them, real or not.

c. Although I'd like to believe, I cannot.

Your dreams are real if they're real to you, says Odo. "I'm as real as you want," says Vina. Are human values real because we want them to be? or are human values real even if we believe otherwise? Does a fulfillment for our longing exist? or are we just traveling hopefully, without any real reason for our hope?

Is anything as real as we *want*—that is, *as real as our longing?*

THE ILLUSION OF A FUTURE?
(I WANT TO BELIEVE)

Longing was the fundamental reality of C. S. Lewis's life. Like Rousseau, "consumed by desires of the object of which I was ignorant," or Augustine, who in his own *Confessions* "longed for a happiness of which I had no idea, and of which I neverthe-less felt the want," Lewis felt the irresistible pull of Otto's "X."

It was his training as a logician which facilitated Lewis's analysis of an experience of longing he called joy. His conclusion: every desire must have an object. When astronomers or nuclear physicists observe some heavenly or subatomic body behave in unexpected ways, they look for the cause. Yet for Lewis, whatever object his desire led to proved inadequate to the desire—which by then had already flown away and come to rest on some other, more distant object. Lewis's logical conclusion was, "The human soul was made to enjoy some object that is never fully given—nay, cannot even be imagined as given—in our present mode of sub-jective and spatio-temporal experience,"[19] and yet "our experience is constantly suggesting it, and we betray ourselves like lovers at the mention of a name."[20]

This otherworldly object may suggest itself in this world, under a thousand "masks," says Lewis; our imagination salutes this desire "with a hundred images"[21]—new pictures in every age—from stories of lost cities to tales of alien messiahs. All these wake in human beings a desire for something beyond this world. After his strange evening with William Butler Yeats, who believed in fairies, Lewis found his own way to bridge the gap in his experience between the "real world" of the senses and the "other worlds" he grasped after in imaginative works. Lewis credited pioneer science-fiction writer David Lindsey, author of *Voyage to Arcturus* (1920), for helping him to see "what other planets"—that is, "outer space stories"—"were good for." They were not, decided Lewis, just exotic settings for fiction, but windows into other dimensions. "To construct plausible and moving 'other worlds,' " wrote Lewis, "you must draw on the only real 'other world' we know, that of the spirit."[22] For Lewis, iconic art forms such as fairy stories and science-fiction tales were not merely iconic in conveying concept, but iconic in a religious sense: "inklings" of spiritual reality; "a real though unfocused gleam of divine truth falling on human imagination."[23]

This mythic approach to science-fiction criticism would probably be Lewis's explanation why *Trek*, for all its materialism, became popular even as confidence in materialism faded in the sixties, and why *Trek* has remained popular in spite of its materialist foundations.

Those materialist presuppositions create an inner conflict at the heart of *Trek*, of which the episode "Frame of Mind" is a picture. Commander Riker is told by a prison psychiatrist (who could easily be Joseph Campbell) that the recurring pictures of that "other reality" he keeps experiencing are not real, but symbols—symbols for ultimately nothing. Riker, he is told, is mistaking menu for food. But there is only menu.

So Riker faces a most critical choice—as do we all. For despite the cheerful relativism of Joseph Campbell or Gene Roddenberry—the celebration of infinite diversity, "Follow your bliss"—it makes a difference which story one believes.

It certainly makes a difference to Robert Conway whether Shangri-la is real or merely a pleasant fantasy: he gives up everything in his Ahab-like persistence to return. And without a doubt it made a difference to Maria whether or not Shangri-la was real. Heaven's Gate certainly staked their lives on their choice. Likewise, all those times when Spock has been confronted with identical Kirks—one real, one an imposter—it clearly makes a difference which one he shoots with his phaser. It makes a difference both to Kirk, obviously, and, no doubt, to a galaxy whose fate has been so often dependent upon rescue by Kirk. Two colorless liquids may both *look* like water. But if Willy can't tell H_2O from H_2SO_4, goes the lab ditty, Willy will be "no more."

One can only wonder. Is *desire* a flicker in the Nexus? or part of the illusion? Is everything a metaphor for sex and death, as Freud suggested? or are even sex and death metaphors for Something Else? Is Christ just another Christ figure? or are all Christ figures figures of Christ? Which is sign and which is signified? Which is changeling, which original? Which is flicker, which is Nexus?

Are these mysteries the sort for which we really want answers, or are they mysteries we would perhaps do best to leave unsolved? Dare we arrive? or is it, after all, better to travel hopefully?

10

The Voyage Home

IS THERE NO TRUTH IN BEAUTY?

Overnight, a carnival appeared in the empty school yard next door to the apartment building where I live. Right outside my window, in fact, was every kid's dream: lights, color, motion, sound—possibilities and magic. I gotta say, though: it got old *real* fast. That was the week I developed a theory as to why so many carnies look like their faces have been run over by city buses: after five days of continuous wheezy-organ skating-rink renditions of "Snowbird," "Edelweiss," and "Scarborough Fair," I myself felt like wandering into the traffic on Wilson Avenue.

Then I saw them—on the sides of those very city buses—bright, colorful ads for the new Viacom Entertainment Store down on Michigan Avenue, in the heart of Chicago's "Magnificent Mile." Viacom, Inc., is the media giant which owns, among other things, MTV, Nickelodeon, Paramount Pictures, and *Star Trek*. The Magnificent Mile is Chicago's toniest shopping district—Nike Town, Saks Fifth Avenue, and Water Tower Place. To keep from going under a bus, then, I got on one, dragging my family along.

Unfortunately, my memories of the Viacom Store are pretty much my memories of that carnival—only more so: every kid's dream and every parent's nightmare. The place must have been two or three stories tall, about a city-block wide, and filled with clever and carnivalesque attention-getting gimmicks, lots of TV- and Hollywood-themed displays, and loud sitcom music playing in the backgound. Oh, and there was some stuff you could buy, too.

In short, what had taken that lousy carnival at least three days, the Viacom store managed to do to me in fifteen minutes. (I left vowing never to return.) In fact, my visit to Viacom's *Trek* department was my second-lowest moment working on this book—the lowest being at a convention, sick as a dog, in a men's room full of Cardassians and Klingons, wondering if I really *did* need a life. On both occasions, I prevented myself from doing anything rash by calmly talking myself down.

There must be *something* here, I reasoned, or there wouldn't be so many people wanting to watch, buy, or emulate *Trek*. Indeed, Viacom, Inc., has hit upon—in a way the rest of our media purveyors can only envy—one of the most profound manifestations of "what the people want" ever offered in the mass market. Almost thirty years after that original five-year mission ended, people are still hoarding *Trek* paraphernalia in astonishing quantities. More than with any other series in television history, people want to *identify* with *Trek*. They wear the costumes. Learn the languages. Surround their everyday lives with calendars and mousepads and seek to recapture the experience in sequels and reruns and discussion groups and even theme parks. Fans long to breathe the special atmosphere of *Trek* as if they would die without it. They'll do or purchase almost anything they think will bring them further inside the universe of *Trek*.

It is this need to be "inside" *Trek* which, I believe, is the key to understanding the duration and intensity of the show's appeal. At the same time, the "insideness" of *Trek* reveals an assumption of the series which is in conflict with the official *Trek* doctrine of celebrating infinite diversity. For *Trek*'s celebration of diversity is framed by an unacknowledged unity—even if this unity amounts to little more than subsuming the diverse impulses it presents under a single name: e pluribus *Trek*.

In the same way, if our discussion here is to find a unity any more substantial than being published between the same covers, we're going to have to grasp the infinite diversity of phenomena we have explored, and bring them together to see where they lead.

ALL'S WELL THAT ENDS WELL

I've always wanted to do one of these (indulge me):

Captain's log. We are nearing the end of our survey of the Star Trek *cosmos. We don't delude ourselves that we have made much of a dent in mapping the vastness of these infinite spaces: one can't raise cosmic questions and hope to begin to answer them either in a single episode or a brief book. Yet on our survey we have seen wonderful, unexpected, and even disturbing phenomena. What would seem a satisfying conclusion to such a voyage would be the return home. Yet this has been our most disturbing discovery: we have no home to return "home" to. We have met the aliens and "they are us." We have learned that what it means to be human is to be lost in the cosmos, exiles, fragmented souls —alone. We are strangers wherever we find ourselves; the fact that we cannot be satisfied with our lot only proves the point. We scour empty space for meaning, we span time to overcome mortality. Our quest to find ourselves is actually an effort to escape ourselves.*

And I led you to believe our ending would be happy.

But so does *Trek*. That promise is what draws to *Trek* its many rabid fans. Yet even the most rabid fans would not deny that the happy ending in many *Trek* episodes depends upon a Kobayashi Maru. Much of this book has been a blast against the slick facade of *Trek*'s unity to reveal what goes on behind the scenes: deus ex machina—which make possible the happy ending, not just for certain episodes, but for the background of *Trek*'s bright future.

Trek has often been accused of presenting a unified philosophy, sometimes called secular humanism. And for the sake of this discussion, we have treated the *Trek* point of view, though created and developed by multiple writers, directors, and more, and affected by countless economic and other considerations, as a unified perspective—as it is sometimes perceived by the fans.

But rather than presenting a true unity, a framework in which human conflicts, inner and outer, might be resolved, the messages of *Trek* are as mixed up and contradictory as you'd expect to find in such a randomly evolved cosmos. Listen to your head. Listen to your heart. Conquer the Unknown. Submit to the Unknown. Seek unity. Celebrate diversity. Embrace the alien. Judge the alien. Never intervene. We owe it to them to intervene. Resist dehumanization. Be open to dehumanization. The unified philosophy of *Trek* seems to mean agreeing with everybody, talking out of all sides of the mouth at once, and so justifying anything the writers happen to prefer or the audience happens to expect.

Such a complex network of shifting allegiances means that the boldly going forth must often be yanked abruptly back: *Trek* is Gnostic until it remembers the body, pantheistic until it remembers the individual, individualistic until it remembers community, relativistic until it needs moral outrage, moralistic until it remembers its own failings, and antiauthoritarian except when it comes to the authority of its own unexamined assumptions. Like Constable Odo on *DS9*, *Trek* is a shape-shifter that has difficulty holding solid form.

Some may defend *Trek*'s contradictions as being in line with the unimaginable dualities of subatomic physics, which are thought by many to prove reality is itself, at bottom, contradictory. Others might defend *Trek*'s lack of coherence as an example of postmodern thinking, which resists "totalizing" unities in favor of diversity. And all the confusion certainly seems to be a fine embodiment of *Trek*'s own celebration of infinite diversity.

And yet, always, alongside infinite diversity *Trek* has valued unification, an impulse to "embrace the Other." And so *Trek* has embraced others—other races, other species, other genders, other value systems, other realities. Yet the uncritical championing of all Others necessarily leads to an inability to make distinctions, to exclude or choose. And though such a predicament would make logic impossible, the logical end of such an approach means calling evil good, blurring the lines between *me* and *not me*, between reality and fantasy. Such a monistic Great Link threatens those *Trek* values which depend upon exclusion: logic, individual identity, and the significance which is contingent upon meaningful, irrevocable choice and consequences.

Torn between unity and diversity, the *Trek* universe is a reflection of our own: our existence depends upon an unresolved tug-of-war between the explosive forces unleashed by the Big Bang and the implosive attraction of gravity. Scientists disagree on which side will ultimately win, whether our final destiny is scattered flux or final crush, bang or whimper. But there is little disagreement that neither ending makes for a happy one.

Trek's happy ending depends on a similar unresolved tension, one maintained not by the discovery of some grand unified theory, but on an external integrator, a deus ex machina, the subjective "gut" of the producers. Bouncing between extremes, *Trek*'s unresolution is less a happy ending than a no-win scenario. And, following its own venerable tradition of characters who find themselves facing the no-win scenarios, *Trek* cheats: time after time, the need for hard choices is magically removed, via instant cures, last-minute rescues, mushy logic, and touchy-feely technobabble. For this reason, *Trek*'s superior attitude toward the viewers' "less advanced" world may be reassuring, but it is hypocritical and illusory.

Trek's own attitude toward illusion, like its attitude toward everything else, is ambivalent. If the truth hurts, *Trek* admits, a therapeutic fantasy can become an acceptable alternative. In recent years, *Trek* has drifted into the laid-back attitude of postmodernism: the "truth" that there is no truth, that the best thing to do is pick a favorite fantasy and enjoy the illusion.

This attitude would seem the only reasonable strategy left for those who wish to retain their "humanity" while accepting the conclusions of materialist science: that our species is a cosmic accident, that our lives appear and vanish without significance, that all our achievements—even if we do reach Federation splendor—will ultimately vaporize into the endless night of nothingness. Add to all this the comparatively trivial news that the moral and technological machinery of *Trek*'s bright tomorrow are physically and metaphysically implausible, and we realize *Trek*'s deus ex machina is our deus ex machina, or an illusion thereof. And it is a smooth diversion indeed that pretends to boldly face and then solve humanity's most unsolvable problems.

In concluding this summary "log," we are reminded there are good reasons that venturing away from our own small world requires the admonition to be "bold." And we also realize that the dangers of chasing through the universe asking Who am I? may include finding an answer: like Odo, who—when he finally discovers his people—realizes he could never be happy in his true "home," we may conclude that the examined life isn't all it's cracked up to be.

TREK IS ONLY HUMAN

Yet *Trek* fans, of all people, should know better than to give in to the despair that threatens to overwhelm at the darkest moment. The double-vision vision of *Trek* is too complicated for a simple "Get a life" dismissal. For one thing, as we've noted, "Get a life" presumes there is a "life" to get. For another, *Trek*'s double-talk solutions lead clearly to *contradictory* conclusions.

On the one hand, the smooth and constant juggling of meanings within the *Trek* cosmos may leave the unsavvy viewer open to a bait and switch. Along with the otherwise omniscient Q, such viewers may find no contradiction in seeing dehumanization as a victory for tolerance. Or they may give credit to science for awakening desires science can neither account for nor fulfill.

Those who abandon logic will not be able to see: that *Trek*'s urging of viewers not to judge is itself a judgment between judging and not judging, that absolute tolerance requires celebrating all that humankind has traditionally identified as "evil" as so many examples of "diversity," that the claim that there are no absolutes is itself an absolute. Such talk is reminiscent of the loopy logic Kirk used to employ to drive alien computers crazy. Remember those pretty androids in "Mudd's Women"—the ones with the blank looks on their faces and the smoke coming out of their ears: permanently open minds.

Thus the dangers of unreflective viewing include following the logic of *Trek* to inhuman conclusions, or the heart of *Trek* to an unreasonable, impossible future. *Trek* can in this way be the biggest obstacle to its own bright tomorrow. While fans are lulled by the fantasy of thinking hard problems can be easily solved, the resolution of humanity's inner conflicts is left to whoever is powerful enough to impose their own preferences.

Yet even though there is this sense in which *Trek*'s double vision makes for an unreliable, even dangerous, guide to navigating the future, there is another sense in which double vision is the most human way of looking at things. Certain internal inconsistencies actually turn out to be the *glory* of *Trek:* for many of these dualities match our own peculiar double-jointed human needs.

To steal a line from *Trek*'s favorite classic author: "What a piece of work is man!" How confused in all his aims! As contrary as anything Dr. Heisenberg ever tried to measure, he is both particle and wave. Man dreams of finding a safe utopian haven, yet is unable to imagine a happiness that excludes danger and struggle. He is so desperate to know, yet even more so to reverence the Unknown. He ever seeks explanations, yet always secretly hopes to find a wonder that can't be explained away. Drawn to infinity *and* boundaries, uniqueness *and* predictability, freedom *and* justice *and* community, man longs for a country to explore that will somehow remain always undiscovered. How clearly in need is humankind of one compensator or another!

Some might argue that our only compensator, the only way to experience the wholeness of our humanity is in the alternative worlds of art; dancing on the tension points of the human condition makes for a contradictory, but compelling, experience.

Certainly, despite our human contradictions, and despite *Trek*'s own occasional flirtation with either Eastern or postmodern rejection of distinctions, *Trek* continues to treat this bundle of diversity as a unified identity, as if there were a human essence. Without this assumption, there could be no appealing vision of living "humanly" with technology. Furthermore, *Trek*'s notion of *human* transcends mere Earth origin or biological classification to designate moral and spiritual values, a moral unity to defend, emulate, and contrast against *alien* values.

In spite of all the lip service to absolute relativism, and with no defensible grounds—illogically, Spock might say—*Trek* has stood stubbornly for moral norms; the happy ending would not be happy unless the *good* guys won, and "good" still had meaning. Politically correct speeches to the contrary, *Trek* heroes act on the basis of norms which include objective, transcultural, and disinterested notions of justice (as opposed to the "might makes right" of autocratic alien races). The *Trek* ideal promotes altruistic values such as mercy and self-sacrifice (against the selfish greed of Ferengi or bloodthirst of Klingons). With no solid philosophical basis, *Trek* makes the sanctity of human life and the inherent dignity of the individual issues to die for. Finally, *Trek*'s much-needed vision of a multicultural future is shown not merely as practical necessity, but as just, as *ought*.

Despite its setting in the distant future, then, *Trek* remains somewhat behind our own "advanced" times, philosophically speaking. (Ironically, *Trek*'s appeal may be based in part on nostalgia for a simpler time!) Perhaps the "compensator" offered by the fiction of *Trek* can help us keep from surrendering to the dehumanizing logic of the cold equations of our science.

Yet who integrates the integrator? *Trek* seems permanently fixed at the crossroads, trying to follow both paths. If one were to venture an easy prediction about the future of Roddenberry's future society, it would be that such ambidextrousness will be harder to maintain as time goes by. In our own time, the once "self-evident" values which grounded human rights and dignity have increasingly fallen under suspicion. To show good triumphing over evil means to identify certain practices as evil; this would seem to put limits on tolerance. If *Trek* gives in to its confused guilty conscience and follows its logical premises of relativism and materialism, it will destroy its happy ending.

Meanwhile, the optimism of *Trek* seems cause to label the glass half-full. For while *Trek* provides no grand unified theory for gluing together human dualities or "the just society," it offers *the experience of living as a whole person in a just society,* an experience at times so winsome it renews both the hope that such a grail exists and the courage to keep looking. "Without a vision, the people perish." In an age when visions have perished, *Trek* offers that most precious of anachronisms: hope.

And as Tolkien says, it may not be *better* to travel hopefully than to arrive, but we must travel hopefully if we *are* to arrive.

Of course, a pessimist would still insist that even dressed up, we have no place to go: that *Trek* is a merely holodeck for a certain carbon-based species, a place where various bundles of "accidental collocations of atoms" might occasionally and temporarily escape their tragic predicament and pretend to be "human."

Our final question is whether the optimists or pessimists are right, or whether each is only half right, or if an alternative view might exist to break this stalemate in *Trek's* double vision.

THE GOD IN THE MACHINE

We have observed that the utopian cosmos of *Trek*, like those utopias *Trek* heroes have encountered, is held together by an external integrator. In the case of the alien utopias, the integrator was usually some literal "god in the machine," a computer or alien deity. In *Trek's* case, the integrator is the writer and producer—the "alien messiah" of *Trek*'s moral and metaphysical cosmos. Perhaps this accounts for the religious zeal of many fans; their hopes for a better tomorrow are founded upon the existence of an unseen, benevolent, and omnipotent *being*.

This is ironic, given the anti-interference, antireligious, and antiauthority (other people's, at least) bent of *Trek*'s creator. Gene Roddenberry, like all secular humanists, hoped to salvage what he deemed were the highest values of religion while discarding the Being behind them. In the post-Roddenberry era, the New Age religiosity explored by the show has presented variations on Roddenberry's bias, the benefits of religion without a deity.

This is understandable. For if a transcendent moral pattern does exist, human beings, with their bad record, have good reason to feel uneasy. Better some amorphous cosmic "force" than a Judge before whom creatures with such a bad record must answer. One would hope that in such a scenario the defendant might truthfully be able to say, "We're not like that anymore." And one would hope such a defense would really be good enough for such a judge.

But how could it be? What happens to justice if there are exceptions? In the *TNG* episode "Justice," an alien god demands the death of a crewman who has broken a local law. Picard's defense in this case is, "There can be no justice so long as laws are absolute." It's hard to know what Picard means by this. Is he arguing that there can be no justice when abstract laws (a.k.a "cold equations") are applied mechanically, without regard for the dignity of the individual? That is exactly what happens in the coldly mechanistic cosmos of scientific materialism, where there can certainly be no justice. However, it seems far from likely that Picard is arguing against scientific materialism. Given the overall relativistic tendency of *Trek*, it seems more likely Picard is *making an attack on the notion of absolutes.*

And once again, we observe *Trek* stacking the deck: the crime in question is breaking a window. How would Picard's impassioned defense sound if the crime had been murder, rape, the attempted extermination of an entire race, gunning down a kindergarten class, pushing a car with children in the back seat into a lake?

It would seem that Captain Picard has confused the definitions of *justice* and *mercy*. Justice is what we are due. Mercy, by definition, is *undeserved*. And there can be neither mercy nor justice *unless, at bottom, the moral law is absolute*. If, as *Trek* often suggests, there is no "evil," only "different," that moral judgments are all relative, that "Embrace the Other" must necessarily mean that right now embraces wrong, the result is a collision of alternative universes which, as in the case of matter and antimatter, will result in the obliteration of both. The theory of relativity has been commonly misunderstood to mean that all things are subjective—yet this very theory is based on the speed of light, which is an absolutely fixed reference.

Thus, Picard's attempt to separate actions from consequences is the very thing that makes deus-ex-machina solutions ring false, the "cheat" which makes illusion so ultimately unsatisfying. A successful imaginary or secondary world, argued Tolkien, depends upon internal coherence, including an internal moral coherence. There is a sense, then, in which Picard's solution is an attack on reality itself—and further, a violation of the individual's right to choose and face the consequences of those choices.

The scenario of human utopia seems no-win from the start if it includes this impossible combination: a society founded upon a genuine moral order (admitted or not), whose inhabitants are given freedom—which presumably includes freedom to reject that order and to experience the consequences for doing so. The scenario becomes even more dubious when those inhabitants have already demonstrated a propensity for choosing against any moral order. *Trek* itself would surely be viewed as an admission of guilt before any cosmic judge: for to presume to offer an *ought* for society and the individual is both to suggest that a universal moral pattern exists and to admit one has fallen short.

There is, of course, a traditional human device for bridging the gap between *is* and *ought*—for meeting the demands of justice without either experiencing the consequences of violating the law or "cheating." This device involves redirecting those consequences onto a ritual sacrifice. It is perhaps the most common theme in all mythology: the sacrificial death of a hero or god that somehow brings about salvation for the community. The mythic value of sacrifice was introduced into this discussion earlier: Spock is "the most human" because his self-sacrifice touches on the core of what humans *ought* to be. In self-sacrifice C. S. Lewis observed a familiar pattern, one "written all over the world": a rising up by going down, the higher descending into the lower to ascend again. We see the pattern replayed in Christ figures in movies, heroes who save the galaxy, death and rebirth in nature, ancient myths of dying and resurrected gods. If a sacrifice could solve the central plot problem of the human story, it would not be a literary deus ex machina: *for it would be what the story has always been about.*

This is one of many suspicious "coincidences" G. K. Chesterton says caused him to abandon his own attempts to design a utopia. Just as he was putting the finishing touches on his own personal creed, Chesterton says, he made that embarrassing discovery astronomer Robert Jastrow talks about as he describes those scientists who discovered the Big Bang: he climbed over the last ridge of the mountain to find the peak already occupied by a bunch of theologians. G. K. C. confesses himself a nearsighted explorer who went not where none had gone before—but "with the utmost daring discovered what had been discovered before." He tried to invent a heresy and discovered it was Christianity.

Chesterton, along with the author of this book, and the other thinkers we have relied upon as our guides through the *Trek* cosmos, came to believe that the Christian view was the most reasonable explanation for the phenomena of human experience, before which both optimism and pessimism are only half-truths.

The Christian view insists the doubleness of man testifies to a broken universe, a separation between humanity and an ultimate Other; and that there can be no integration without a divine integrator who is by nature a diversity-held-in-unity. The paradoxes of the Christian view, Chesterton concluded, have been attacked insanely from all sides because they represent sanity itself: the hyphenated Christian God is, in fact, *the center*. Everything comes together in the collision that is the Cross.

The infinite valuing of the individual person can only be grounded in such a collision of infinite and personal. The Creator of billions upon billions of galaxies, each filled with as many stars, lowers himself to be born a human baby, in an obscure tribe, at a pinprick of time, on a speck of cosmic dust. With the Incarnation, the person of Christ is not artificially imposed on the human story, but is seen as the very heart of the story, a solution rising from *within* the action. And yet the Greek word translated *machine* is used by church father Ignatius to describe Jesus' cross as "the hoist of Christ": God in the machine.

QUANTUM TREK

Yet who can say for sure just where the boundaries of reality lie?

We all find ourselves in the same situation as *Trek* characters

who awaken in a world which claims to be real. We are haunted
by the feeling that something is not quite right. We notice suspicious movement behind the scenes, certain recurring clues that
"reality" as presented is less than real. Like various *Trek* characters
facing this scenario, some may choose to shake off such feelings
and surrender to "reality" as presented. Others may begin to
question whether or not there might be a truth Out There. Our
postmodern jailers may insist that there is no way to get Out
There, that every "truth" is another social or individual construc-
tion, that any story used to judge other stories is, after all, just
another story. Yet "flickers in the Nexus" are undeniable by those
who see with the eyes of the heart.

That such flickers fail to offer conclusive proofs may be one
more "flicker": a hint that the Creator, like those made in His
image, resists being reduced to the sum of an equation, an *It*.
Contact would seem to require attending to the flickers with the
whole person, both intellect and intuition, a double vision that
engages both the reasons of the head and the reasons of the heart.

Since, then, we have charted our course by a fixed reference
after all, we are provided with the requisite context within which
to conclude our conclusions about the double vision of *Star Trek*.

First, *Trek*'s vision is double in double ways. In some ways, the
two-headed impulses of *Trek* match our paradoxical human
condition. In other ways, *Trek*'s double-talk masks contradictions
which pose a threat to maintaining our humanity. It's one thing
to suggest that freedom and order are competing values which
must somehow be held in permanent tension. It's something else
entirely to say both that universals exist and universals do not
exist. Or that to be human is both a meaningful and a meaningless experience. It is the difference between half-humans and evil
twins. In one case, we have opposing tendencies which must be

joined to achieve wholeness. In the other, we have logical contradictions which cannot embrace without destroying logic, breaching the integrity of reality, and canceling our ability to make distinctions, do justice, and, finally, be human.

Therefore, measuring against our fixed reference, we can conclude that the double vision of Star *Trek* is both true and false: measured one way, *Trek* is an *icon*, a vehicle for spiritual reality. Measured another, *Trek* is an *idol*, a false reality posing as a true one. *Trek* presents alternative universes in collision. One is materialistic and human-centered, holding that all values are created by man and absolute beliefs hinder "progress." The alternative universe appears as flickers of an elemental battle where good and evil are part of a transcendent cosmic order, rejection of which leaves one "lost in the cosmos."

Such flickerings of an alternative reality may be seen wherever one looks in popular culture: cracks in the facade, anomalies, and contradictions that can tell us much about ourselves and the nature of our desires, and provide clues to true fulfillment of those desires. The double vision of our stories may well one day be entered as evidence against us, since those stories reveal our knowledge of a real moral order undergirding a universe many claim is random. Even if the characters in our stories *say* such things, their own *actions* are usually at odds with this notion.

The trick would seem to be forging a connection between the hearts of people and their heads, asking questions like, Why do the good guys have to win for there to be a happy ending if "'good" and "evil" count for nothing? Skeptics may agree with our premise here (that goodness would require a transcendent moral order) while disagreeing with our conclusion (that such a moral order exists), and so urge us to "get a life." But any kind of "life," for skeptics or otherwise, requires *hope*, belief in a better future, a happy ending, if human wholeness is more than a myth.

In an earlier chapter we mentioned that J. R. R. Tolkien believed that fairy stories fulfill certain primordial human desires. Along with our desire for contact with the Other, said Tolkien, the most important desire fairy stories fulfill is the desire for a happy ending. He even invented a name for this moment: the *eucatastrophe*. Such a happy ending does not deny the reality of sorrow and failure. On the contrary, the possibility of these is what makes possible the joy of deliverance. What eucatastrophe does deny, says Tolkien, despite the evidence to the contrary, is the universal final triumph of evil. In this way, the happy ending of the fairy story echoes spiritual reality: it is good news, *grace,* a glimpse of "joy beyond the walls of the world."[1]

The gospel, said Tolkien, was the source of all fairy stories, the greatest and most complete eucatastrophe of human history. Happy endings, then, are not merely "what the people want," but, more importantly, what the people have always wanted. If the ultimate reality of the universe corresponds to our deepest desire, then happy endings are what "the people" were made for.

If so, we might well expect to find glimpses of this ultimate reality in myth, in nature, in poetry, in our own desires—even in something as paradoxically idolatrous and iconic as *Star Trek.* "No matter what wonders are described," said Tolstoy, "or what animals talk in a human language, what flying carpets may carry people from place to place, the legends, parables, fairy tales will be true, if there is in them the truth of the kingdom of God."

Notes

Introduction: Infinite Diversity and Unification

1. "Quick Takes," *Chicago Sun-Times*, 26 March 1996, 24.
2. Rhonda V. Wilcox, "Dating Data: Miscegenation in *Star Trek: The Next Generation*," *Extrapolation*, vol. 34, 275.
3. Thomas Richards, *The Meaning of "Star Trek"* (New York: Doubleday, 1997), 60.
4. Robert M. Bowman, "Strange New Worlds: The Humanist Philosophy of *Star Trek*," *Christian Research Journal*, Fall 1991, 22.
5. Vivian Sobchack, *Screening Space: The American Science Fiction Film* (Continuum Publishing, 1987), 136.

Chapter 1: Happy Endings in the Final Frontier

1. Chad Walsh, *From Utopia to Nightmare* (New York: Harper & Row, 1962), 25.
2. *Utopia*, 23.
3. Edward Bellamy, *Looking Backward* (New York: The New American Library, 1960), 194.
4. Walsh, *Utopia*, 77.
5. Susan Sontag, "The Imagination of Disaster," in *Against Interpretation* (New York: Dell Publishing, 1966), 209.
6. Lawrence M. Krauss, *The Physics of "Star Trek"* (New York: BasicBooks, 1995).
7. Robert Heinlein, "Science Fiction: Its Nature, Faults and Virtues," in *The Science Fiction Novel: Imagination and Social Criticism* (Chicago: Advent, 1959), pp. 29–30, cited by John Huntington, "Hard-Core Science Fiction and the Illusion of Science," in Slusser, George E., and Rabkin, Eric S., eds. *Hard Science Fiction* (Carbondale & Edwardsville, Ill.: Southern Illinois University Press, 1986), 46.
8. Gene Roddenberry, *The "Star Trek" Guide*, third revision, 17 April 1967, 3. This is a set of writer's guidelines developed by Roddenberry.
9. Stephen E. Whitfield and Gene Roddenberry, *The Making of "Star Trek"* (New York: Ballantine, 1968), 35.

10. J. R. R. Tolkien, "On Fairy-Stories," in *Poems and Stories* (New York: Houghton Mifflin Co. 1994), 156–157.

11. C. S. Lewis, "On Science Fiction," in *On Stories and Other Essays on Literature*, Walter Hooper, ed., (San Diego, New York: Harcourt, Brace & Co., 1982), 63.

12. Joel Engel, *Gene Roddenberry: The Myth and the Man Behind "Star Trek"* (New York: Hyperion, 1994), 212.

13. Engel, *Gene Roddenberry*, 229.

14. Lewis, "On Stories," 13.

15. Lewis, "On Science Fiction," 64.

16. See John Huntington, "Hard-Core Science Fiction and the Illusion of Science," in Slusser, George E., and Rabkin, Eric S., eds. *Hard Science Fiction* (Carbondale & Edwardsville, Ill.: Southern Illinois University Press, 1986), 50.

17. Tolkien, "On Fairy-Stories," 122.

18. Ibid., 125.

19. Lewis, C. S., *The Silver Chair* (New York: Collier Books, 1974), 207.

20. Lewis, "On Stories," 17.

Chapter 2: Good Guys Versus Bad Guys (And a Few Shades of Gray)

1. Herb Solow and Robert Justman, *Inside "Star Trek": The Real Story* (New York: Pocket Books, 1996), 21.

2. Joel Engel, *Gene Roddenberry: The Myth and the Man Behind "Star Trek"* (New York: Hyperion, 1994), 60.

3. Engel, *Gene Roddenberry*, 125.

4. James Van Hise, *Trek: The Unauthorized Behind-the-Scenes Story of the Next Generation* (Las Vegas: Pioneer Books, 1992), 20–21.

5. Bill Boisvert, "The Federation or the Fourth Reich?", *In These Times*, 1 April 1996, 40–39.

6. Jeff Greenwald, "Write For *Star Trek!*" *Wired*, January 1996, 159.

7. Greenwald, "Write For *Star Trek!*", *Wired*, 159.

8. Richard Zoglin, "*Trek*king Onward," *TIME*, 28 November 1994, 77.

9. See Hugh Ruppersberg, "The Alien Messiah," in Annette Kuhn, ed. *Alien Zone: Cultural Theory and Contemporary Science Fiction Cinema*, (London/New York: Verso, 1990), 32–38.

10. G. K. Chesterton, *Heretics* (1905; reprint, Freeport, New York: Books for Libraries Press), 79.

Chapter 3: The Heart Has Its Reasons (That Reason Thinks "Illogical")

1. George E. Slusser and Eric S. Rabkin, eds. *Hard Science Fiction* (Carbondale & Edwardsville: Southern Illinois University Press, 1986), Introduction, vii.

2. Vivian Sobchack, *Screening Space: The American Science Fiction Film* (Continuum Publishing, 1987), 19.

3. Stephen E. Whitfield and Gene Roddenberry, *The Making of "Star Trek"* (New York: Ballantine, 1968), 30.

Chapter 4: Which Comes First: The Many or the One?

1. Ian Buruma, "The 21st Century Starts Here," *New York Times* magazine, February 18, 1996, 32.
2. William James, "Preface to the Meaning of Truth," in *Pragmatism and Other Essays*, pp. 135, 66, cited in Peter Kreeft, *Love is Stronger Than Death* (San Francisco: Harper & Row, 1979), 49.
3. Stephen Larsen and Robin Larsen, *A Fire in the Mind: The Life of Joseph Campbell* (New York: Doubleday, 1991), 395.
4. Robert A. Segal, *Joseph Campbell: An Introduction* (New York: Penguin/ Mentor, 1990), 142.
5. Joel Engel, *Gene Roddenberry: The Myth and the Man Behind "Star Trek"* (New York: Hyperion, 1994), 49.
6. Engel, *Gene Roddenberry*, 84.

Chapter 5: No Golden Rules Except for this One

1. C. S. Lewis, "Religion and Rocketry," in *The World's Last Night* (New York: Harcourt, Brace and Co, 1960), 89.
2. Stephen E. Whitfield and Gene Roddenberry, *The Making of "Star Trek"* (New York: Ballantine Books, 1968), 40.
3. Nichelle Nichols, *Beyond Uhura: "Star Trek" and Other Memories* (New York: G. P. Putnam and Sons, 1994), 163–165.
4. Michael Okuda, and Denise, Mirek, and Debbie Okuda, *The "Star Trek" Encyclopedia* (New York: Pocket Books, 1994).
5. See H. Bruce Franklin, "*Star Trek* in the Vietnam Era," *Science Fiction Studies*, v. 21 (1994), 24; and Mark Lagon, "'We Owe It to Them to Interfere': *Star Trek* and US Statecraft in the 1960s and the 1980s," *Extrapolations*, vol. 34, 250.
6. David Alexander, "*Star Trek*": Creator: The Authorized Biography of Gene Roddenberry* (New York: ROC Penguin, 1994), 385.
7. James Van Hise, "*Trek*": the Unauthorized Behind-the-Scenes Story of the Next Generation* (Las Vegas: Pioneer Books, 1992), 49.
8. See Wing-Tsit Chan, trans., *The Way of Lao Tzo (Tao-te Ching), Translated, with Introductory Essays, Comments and Notes by Wing-Tsit Chan* (Indianapolis: Bobbs-Merrill Educational Publishing, 1963.)
9. Alexander, "*Star Trek*": Creator,* 370.
10. William Kirk Kilpatrick, *Why Johnny Can't Tell Right from Wrong: Moral Illiteracy and the Case for Character Education,* (New York: Simon & Schuster, 1992), 90, 127.
11. C. S. Lewis, *Mere Christianity* (New York: Macmillan, 1952), 45.

Chapter 6: "We've Got to Save Humanity!"

1. Quoted in Maisie Ward, *Gilbert Keith Chesterton* (New York: Sheed & Ward, 1943), 202.
2. Quoted in Paul M. Sammon, *Future Noir: The Making of "Blade Runner"* (New York: HarperCollins, 1996), 16.
3. Richard Hanley, *The Metaphysics of "Star Trek"* (New York: Basic Books, 1997), 10–11.
4. Joel Engel, *Gene Roddenberry: The Myth and the Man Behind "Star Trek"* (New York: Hyperion, 1994), 48.
5. Herb Solow and Robert Justman, *Inside "Star Trek": The Real Story* (New York: Pocket Books, 1996), 431.
6. See especially Yvonne Fern, *Gene Roddenberry: The Last Conversation* (Berkely: University of California Press, 1994)
7. J. P. Telotte, *Replications: A Robotic History of the Science Fiction Film* (Urbana, Ill.: University of Illinois Press, 1995), 5.
8. Hari Kunzru, "You Are Borg," *Wired*, Febuary 1997, 155.
9. See Michael Ryan and Douglas Kellner, "Technophobia," in Kuhn, Annette, *Alien Zone*.
10. J. I. Packer and Thomas Howard, *Christianity: The True Humanism* (Waco, Tex.: Word Books, 1985), 22.
11. Packer, *Christianity*, 21.
12. Lewis, *The Abolition of Man* (New York: Macmillan, 1947), 69.
13. Carl Sagan, *The Demon-Haunted World: Science as a Candle in the Dark* (New York: Random House, 1995), 268.
14. Norman Spinrad, *The Hard Stuff: Science Fiction in the Real World*, (Carbondale, Ill.: Southern Illinois University Press, 1990), 104.
15. For examples of "posthuman" discussions on the World Wide Web, see "The Posthuman Manifesto" <www.iuma.com/IUMA-2.0/ftp/volume3/Southern/www/03phmgeneral.html>, or "Anders Transhuman Page," <www.aleph.se/Trans>.
16. Richards, *Meaning*, 42–43.
17. Hanley, *Metaphysics*, 149.
18. Ibid., 17.

Chapter 7: Spirits, Bodies, and Other Alien Beings

1. C. S. Lewis, *Surprised By Joy: The Shape of My Early Life* (New York: Harcourt, Brace & World, 1955), 25
2. James Van Hise, *Trek: Next Generation Tribute Book* (Las Vegas: Pioneer Books, 1993), 107.
3. Phillip E. Johnson, "The Unraveling of Scientific Materialism," *First Things*, November 1997, 22.
4. Lewis, *Surprised by Joy*, 172.

5. Lawrence M. Krauss, *The Physics of "Star Trek"* (New York: BasicBooks, 1995), 66.

6. Ibid., 69.

7. Hanley, 161

8. See Dougals Groothuis, *The Soul in Cyberspace* (Grand Rapids, Mich.: Baker Books, 1997).

9. Jeff Greenwald, "Write For *Star Trek!*" *Wired*, January, 1996, 203.

10. Joel Engel, *Gene Roddenberry: The Myth and the Man Behind "Star Trek"* (New York: Hyperion, 1994), 226.

11. Ibid., 245.

12. Ibid., 84.

13. C. S. Lewis, *The Screwtape Letters* (Letter VII) (New York: Bantam Books, 1982), 19.

14. I am indebted here to Thomas Howard's analysis of *That Hideous Strength* in his book *C. S. Lewis: Man of Letters* (San Francisco: Ignatius Press, 1987), 159–175.

15. Engel, *Gene Roddenberry*, 49.

16. C. S. Lewis, *Mere Christianity* (New York: Macmillan, 1952), 65.

17. C. S. Lewis, "On Stories," *Of Other Worlds* (London: Bles, 1966), 12.

Chapter 8: Get a Life (Or a Reasonable Facsimile Thereof)

1. Joel Engel, *Gene Roddenberry: The Myth and the Man Behind "Star Trek"* (New York: Hyperion, 1994), 180.

2. Dorothy L. Sayers, *The Mind of the Maker* (New York: Harper & Row, 1941), 82.

3. Sayers, *Mind of the Maker*, 83.

4. Cited in Christopher Lasch, *The True and Only Heaven: Progress and Its Critics* (New York: W.W. Norton, 1991), 71.

5. Augustine, *Confessions*, Book 3, Chapter 6.

6. Stephen E. Whitfield and Gene Roddenberry, *The Making of "Star Trek"* (New York: Ballantine, 1968), 53.

7. Joseph Campbell (with Bill Moyers), *The Power of Myth* (New York: Doubleday, 1988), 56.

8. Kurt Vonnegut, *Cat's Cradle* (New York: Dell Publishing, 1963).

9. Thomas Richards, *The Meaning of "Star Trek"* (New York: Doubleday, 1997), 145.

10. See Stanley J. Grenz, "*Star Trek* and the Next Generation: Postmodernism and the Future of Evangelical Theology," *CRUX*, March 1994, vol. XXX, No. 1, p. 24–32. Grenz argues that *TOS* represented a modern view, and that *TNG* reflected the cultural shift to postmodernity. In broad strokes this may be true, but I would argue that *TOS* was already well into the struggle between modernity and postmodernity, seen in the divided character of Spock, the championing of Infinite Diversity, the idea that "alien" is not bad but different. My own take on the relation of *TOS/TNG* vis a vis postmodernism is that *TOS* was blissfully ignorant of *Trek*'s own inner contradictions, and with *TNG* we

see an attempt at a more consistent PoMo view—yet this is achieved only by obscuring *Trek*'s debate between absolutes and relativity with self-righteous denial (which may be a postmodern solution!).

Chapter 9: A Starship Named *Desire*

1. J. R. R. Tolkien, "On Fairy-Stories," in *Poems and Stories* (New York: Houghton Mifflin Co. 1994), 149.
2. Frank Drake and Dawn Sobel, *Is Anybody Out There?: The Scientific Search for Extraterrestrial Intelligence* (New York: Delacorte Press, 1992), 27.
3. Carl Sagan, *The Demon-Haunted World: Science as a Candle in the Dark* (New York: Random House, 1995), 9.
4. Sagan, *Demon-Haunted*, 133.
5. William Graves Hoyt, *Lowell and Mars* (Tuscon, Ariz.: University of Arizona Press, 1976), 293.
6. Sagan, *Demon-Haunted*, 12.
7. Ibid., 241.
8. G. K. Chesterton, *Orthodoxy* (Garden City, N. Y.: Image Books, 1908, 1959), 152.
9. Ibid, 18.
10. Walker Percy, *Lancelot* (New York: Avon Books, 1977), 145.
11. Walter Lippmann, *A Preface to Morals* (New York: *TIME* Reading Program, 1929), 139.
12. Herman Melville, *Moby Dick* (Norton Critical Edition) (New York: W.W. Norton & Company, 1967), 14, 144, 170.
13. George MacDonald, "Love Thine Enemy," in *Unspoken Sermons, Series One* (Eureka, Calif.: J. Joseph Flynn Rare Books, orig pub 1886), 222.
14. C. S. Lewis, *Perelandra* (New York: Collier Books, 1944), 48.
15. See Gilbert Meilaender, *The Taste For the Other: The Social and Ethical Thought of C. S. Lewis* (Grand Rapids, Mich.: Wm. B. Eerdmans, 1978).
16. C. S. Lewis, *The Abolition of Man* (New York: Macmillan, 1947), 78.
17. Tolkien, "On Fairy Stories," 161.
18. Lewis, *Abolition*, 78.
19. C. S. Lewis, *The Pilgrim's Regress: An Allegorical Apology for Christianity, Reason, and Romanticism*, "Afterword" (Grand Rapids, Mich.: Wm. B. Eerdmans Publishing Co., 1992 ed.), 204–205.
20. C. S. Lewis, *The Weight of Glory and Other Addresses* (Grand Rapids, Mich.: Wm. B. Eerdmans Publishing Co., 1977 ed.), 4.
21. C. S. Lewis, *Surprised By Joy* (New York: Harcourt, Brace & World, 1955), 221
22. C. S. Lewis, "On Stories," *Of Other Worlds* (London: Bles, 1966), 12.
23. C. S. Lewis, *Miracles: A Preliminary Study* (New York: Collier, 1978 ed.), fn. 134.

Chapter Ten: The Voyage Home

1. J. R. R. Tolkien, "On Fairy-Stories," in *Poems and Stories* (New York: Houghton Mifflin Co. 1994), 175.

Select Bibliography

Those books on science fiction or *Star Trek* most helpful to me I either mentioned in the text or in a footnote. This list is the more general hodgepodge of books I have found helpful in developing a worldview or an approach to culture — a sort of "Imaginarium Must-Read" list for those readers who know what that means, or others who might like help figuring that out. The editions listed are the ones I own, most are still in print.

Carpenter, Humphrey. *The Inklings*. Boston: Houghton Mifflin Company, 1979.

Chesterton, Gilbert Keith. *Orthodoxy*. Garden City, New York: Image Books, a Division of Doubleday Company, 1959.

Forbes, Cheryl. *Imagination: Embracing A Theology Of Wonder*. Portland, Ore.: Multnomah Press, 1986.

Guinness, Os. *The Dust of Death: A Critique of the Establishment and the Counter Culture—And a Proposal for a Third Way*. Downers Grove, Ill.: InterVarsity Press, 1973.

Huss, Roy and Silverstein, Norman. *The Film Experience: Elements of Motion Picture Art*. New York: Dell Publishing Company, 1968.

Kilpatrick, William Kirk. *Why Johnny Can't Tell Right from Wrong: Moral Illiteracy and the Case for Character Education*. New York: Simon & Schuster, 1992.

Kierkegaard, Søren. "What It Means to Seek After God," in *Stages on Life's Way*.

Lewis, C. S. *An Experiment in Criticism*. Cambridge University Press, 1961.

———. *On Stories and Other Essays on Literature*. Hooper, Walter, ed. San Diego, New York: Harcourt, Brace & Company, 1982.

———. *Mere Christianity*. New York: Macmillan, 1952.

———. *The Abolition of Man*. New York: Macmillan, 1947.

———. *The Great Divorce*. New York: Macmillian, 1946

———. *The Screwtape Letters*. New York: Bantam Books, 1982.

———. *Miracles: A Preliminary Study*. New York: Collier, 1978 ed.

———. *The Problem of Pain*. New York: Macmillan, 1962.

————. *Surprised By Joy: The Shape of My Early Life*. New York: Harcourt, Brace & World, 1955.

————. *The Pilgrim's Regress: An Allegorical Apology for Christianity, Reason, and Romanticism*. Grand Rapids, Mich.: Wm. B. Eerdmans Publishing Co., 1992 ed.

MacDonald, George. "On the Fantastic Imagination" (from *The Light Princess and Other Fairy Tales*.

————. "The Imagination: Its Functions and Its Culture", in *The Heart of George McDonald*, Rolland Hein, ed. Wheaton, Ill.: Harold Shaw Publishers, 1994.

McConnell, Frank. *Storytelling and Mythmaking: Images from Film and Literature*. New York: Oxford University Press, 1979.

Monoco, James. *How to Read A Film: The Art, Technology, Language, History, and Theory of Film and Media*. New York: Oxford University Press, 1977.

Niebuhr, H. Richard. *Christ and Culture*. New York: Harper & Row, 1951.

O'Connor, Flannery. *Mystery and Manners: Occasional Prose, selected and edited by Sally and Robert Fitzgerald*. New York: Farrar, Straus & Giroux, 1961.

Otto, Rudolph. *The Idea of the Holy*. New York: Oxford University Press, 1958.

Payne, Leanne. *Real Presence: The Christian Worldview of C. S. Lewis as Incarnational Reality*. Westchester, Ill.: Crossway Books, 1988.

Percy, Walker. *Lost in the Cosmos*. New York: Pocket Books, a division of Simon & Shuster, Inc., 1983.

Sayers, Dorothy. *The Mind of the Maker*. New York: Harper & Row, 1941.

Schaeffer, Francis. *Escape From Reason*. London: InterVarsity Fellowship, 1968.

————. *The God Who Is There*. Downers Grove, Ill.: InterVarsity Press, 1968.

Tolkien, J.R.R. "On Fairy-Stories", in *Poems and Stories*. New York: Houghton Mifflin Company, 1994).

Index

Agar, Goran', 145
Alexander the Great, 233, 242
Alien Autopsy, 231
Allen, Woody, 199
Alpha Quadrant, 173
Amanda, 63, 243
Amin, Idi, 131
Arcadia, 6, 19, 225
Arthur, (king), 36
Asimov, Issac, 33, 42, 166
Athena, 24
Augustine, 199, 248
Aum Shrinkyo, 166, 229

Back to the Future, 227
Bajoran(s), 128, 172–174, 176, 177
Barclay, Reginald, 183–185, 205, 217
Bareil, Vedic, 172
Barnes, Jake, 195
Barrett, Majel, 73
Barry, Dave, 40
Bashir, Julian, 202
Baum, L. Frank, 226
Bellamy, Edward, 20, 21
Bennet, Harve, 45, 197
Bennet, Rod, 167, 193
Beowolf, 47
Berman, Rick, 51–53, 54, 56
Bill and Ted's Excellent Adventure, 56
Billy the Kid, 90
Blade Runner, 21, 140, 141, 151
Blish, James, 72, 120
Borg, the, 23, 41, 47, 48, 56, 57, 59, 75, 89,
    90, 94, 97, 103–106, 109, 132, 134, 145,
    153, 160, 239

Brahms, Leah, 185
Brave New World, 21
Buruma, Ian, 94

Campbell, Joseph, 100, 208, 218, 219, 225,
    247, 249, 250
Camus, Albert, 202, 209
Capone, Al, 90
Capra, Frank, 243
Captain Video, 40, 41
Cardassian(s), 23, 41, 47, 48, 53, 89, 93,
    101, 105, 128, 194
Caretaker, The, 50
Chakotay, 106, 180
Chesterton, G. K., 59, 99, 111, 140, 230,
    231, 233, 234, 263, 264
Christianity, 100, 168, 169, 194, 264
Christianity: The True Humanism, 158
Chronicles of Narnia, The, 32, 84
Clarke, Arthur C., 35, 36
Close Encounters of the Third Kind, 58
"Cold Equations, The," 66, 69, 76
Coleman, Ronald, 243
Companion, the, 181
Confessions, 248
Conrad, Joseph, 92
Contact, 168, 227, 230, 236
Cortez, Hernando, 57
Cosmos, 86
Courage, Alexander, 43
Crick, Francis, 168
Crosby, Denise, 9, 197
Crowley, Aliester, 166, 187
Crusher, Beverly, 180, 212
Crusher, Wesley, 121

Cyborg Manifesto, 155

Data, 7, 9, 25, 35, 82, 87, 98, 100, 104, 105, 107, 110, 121, 122, 127, 128, 143, 150, 153, 154, 161, 177–179
Dax, Lt. Jadzia, 146, 182
Day the Earth Stood Still, 59
Dean, James, 90
Defiant, 51
Delta Quadrant, 55, 103, 211, 216
Deltan(s), 186, 190
Descartes, René, 213, 216
Destination Moon, 66
deus ex machina, 16, 24, 25, 26, 30, 50, 58, 68, 131, 133, 139, 144, 168, 200, 212, 215, 216, 256, 263
Dick, Philip K., 140, 141, 166
Doctor, 7, 175, 194, 203–205
Dominion, the, 173
Dr. Jekyll and Mr. Hyde, 7
Dragnet, 42
Drake, Frank, 225, 227
Drieser, 27
Dubois, Blanche, 236, 238, 244
Dukat, Gul, 53, 54
Dune, 172

Eastwood, Clint, 46
Einstein, Albert, 14, 27, 31
Ellul, Jaques, 103
Encyclopedia of Science Fiction, The, 32
Engel, Joel, 43, 61
Enterprise, U. S. S., 5, 22, 23, 26, 37, 46, 56, 69, 71, 77, 90, 96, 104, 107, 111, 114, 115, 117, 118, 122, 142, 153, 194, 197, 205–206, 208, 213, 214, 215, 244
E. T.: The Extra Terrestrial, 58, 224, 227, 226
Exegesis, 165
Extrapolations, 71, 120

Fantasy and Science Fiction, 33
Ferengi, 47, 48, 51, 127, 146, 177, 185, 186, 206, 259
Fitzgerald, F. Scott, 238
Forbidden Planet, 9, 153, 181
Forrest Gump, 227
Foundation, 166
Flash Gordon, 30

Frankel, Victor, 8
Frankenstein, 47
Freud, Sigmund, 7, 8, 108, 173, 191, 232, 250
Future Shock, 143

Galileo, 229
Garland, Judy, 238
Gawain, Sir, 36
Gene Roddenberry: The Last Conversation, 169
George, Saint, 36
Gilligan's Island, 193
Gnostic, 180, 182, 184, 189, 190, 255
Godwin, Tom, 68
Goldberg, Whoopie, 115
Good News for the Warrior Race, 4
Gorn, 42
grand unified theory (GUT), 14
Great Divorce, The, 243, 247
Great Gatsby, The, 238
Great Link, the, 99, 100, 103, 110, 127, 255
Groundhog Day, 212
Guinan, 212

Hamlet, 71
Hamlet, 196, 200, 201, 214, 215
Hanley, Richard, 82, 142, 144, 164, 179, 181, 217
Haraway, Donna, 155
Have Gun, Will Travel, 42
Heart of Darkness, 92, 118
Heaven's Gate, 5, 166, 182, 187, 214, 229, 250
Heinlein, Robert, 28
Heisenberg theory, 26, 29, 110, 258
Henry, Patrick, 219
Herbert, Frank, 172
Heretics, 59
Hermetic Order of the Golden Dawn, 187
Hilton, James, 243
Hise, James Van, 46
Hitler, Adolf, 97, 105, 131
Holmes, Sherlock, 73, 108, 160, 207, 210, 233
Horta, 41
House of Wax, The, 36
Hubbard, L. Ron, 166

Hugh, 104, 105, 107
Hunter, Jeffrey, 204
Huntington, John, 36
Humanist, The, 144, 171, 190
Humanist Manifesto(s) *I & II, The,* 143, 148, 159
Huxley, Aldous, 21

I Am Not Spock, 98
I Am Spock, 98
Idea of the Holy, The, 231
Ignatius, Saint, 264
Iliad, The, 47
In the Days of the Comet, 59
Independence Day, 41
Infinite Diversity in Infinite Combinations, (IDIC), 3, 5
Inside Star Trek: The Real Story, 42
Invasion of the Body Snatchers, The, 52

James, William, 98, 111, 198
Jameson, Mae, 115
Janeway, Kathryn, 65, 86, 106, 134, 174, 175, 187, 211
Jason and the Argonauts, 36
Jaspers, Karl, 85
Jastrow, Robert, 264
Jem' Hadar, 23, 145, 158
Johnson, Samuel, 230
Jung, Carl, 224
Justman, Bob, 42, 43

Kazon, 23, 47
Keats, John, 228
Kennedy, Paul, 54
Kes, 174, 175
Khan, 239, 246
Kilpatrick, William Kirk, 130
Kim, 210, 211
King, Martin Luther, Jr., 115, 127
King of Kings, 205
King, Rodney, 40
Kirk, James T., 5, 6, 8–10, 23, 25, 31, 37, 47, 51, 52–54, 64, 65, 69, 71, 76, 78–80, 91, 92, 95, 98, 101, 109, 110, 117–121, 127–129, 137, 142, 145, 150, 153, 178, 190, 196–200, 202, 206, 207, 210–212, 218, 232, 244, 246, 250, 257
Klaatu, 59

Klingon(s), 23, 25, 41, 47, 49, 53, 59, 89, 90, 93, 96, 117, 122, 128, 130, 136, 145, 146, 177, 180, 181, 200, 239, 241, 259
Klingon (language), 4
Kobayashi–Maru, 23, 25, 91, 196, 198, 205, 254
Krauss, Lawrence, 26, 178, 179
Krell, 181

LaForge, Geordi, 122, 183, 185
Lagon, Mark, 120
Landru, 50
Laverne and Shirley, 97
Lore, 9, 105, 106, 132, 154
Looking Backward, 20
Lester, Janice, 178
Lewis, C. S., 32, 33, 37, 84, 114, 125, 126, 131, 159, 165, 167, 169, 188, 189, 191, 240, 241, 243, 247, 248, 249, 263
Lewontin, Richard, 168
Lieutenant, The, 42, 43
Logan's Run, 151
Lord of the Rings, The, 33
Lost Horizon, 219, 243, 245, 247
Lost in the Cosmos, 233
Lowell, Percival, 230
Lucas, George, 100, 172, 220

MacDonald, George, 240
MacLaine, Shirley, 171
"Man Who Dreamed of Fairyland, The," 238
Maquis, the, 53, 54, 55, 75, 90, 93, 94, 98, 101
Marx, Karl, 20
materialism, 84, 165, 167, 168, 170, 174, 175, 177, 178, 182
materialist, 27, 29, 37, 38, 86, 136, 152, 167–171, 176, 188, 192, 255
McCloud, Scott, 47
McCoy, Leonard, 10, 25, 69, 70, 79, 85, 95, 119, 134, 179
Meaning of Star Trek, The, 11, 163, 220
Medusan(s), 181
Melville, Herman, 239
Metaphysics of Star Trek, The, 82, 142, 177–179
Milton, John, 246
Mind of the Maker, The, 198

Mitchell, Edger, 171
Moby Dick, 239
Morbius, 9
More, Thomas, 20
Morris, William, 19
Moyers, Bill, 247
Mulder, Fox, 167, 173, 239, 247
Mulgrew, Kate, 6

Napoleon, 105
NASA, 226
Neelix, 70, 96, 97
Nerys, Kira, 86, 98, 127, 172, 176, 185
News From Nowhere, 19
Nichols, Nichelle, 115
Niebuhr, Reinhold, 199
Nietzche, Friedrich, 149, 241
Nimoy, Leonard, 44, 73, 98, 195, 196
Number One, 73
1984, 21, 158

O'Brien, Keiko, 191, 200
O'Brien, Miles, 145, 191, 192
O'Connor, Flannery, 162
Odo, 7, 12, 51, 86, 99, 100, 111, 127, 128,
    135–137, 143, 146, 194, 206, 219, 248, 263,
    259
Organian(s), 44, 181
Orwell, George, 21, 158
Other, the, 10, 12, 42, 88, 95–97, 101, 110,
    113, 132, 136, 146, 153, 164, 201, 224, 229,
    232, 239, 255, 262, 264
Otto, Rudolf, 231, 248

Paris, Tom, 204, 205
Pascal, Blaise, 76, 246
Percy, Walker, 233, 237
Perelandra, 240
Physics of Star Trek, The, 26, 178
Picard, Jean-Luc, 11, 12, 46, 49, 51, 56, 71,
    92, 92, 104, 107, 109, 114, 121–124, 131,
    132, 145, 146, 150, 154, 164, 171, 176, 184,
    191, 201, 210–214, 216–218, 234, 239, 244,
    261, 262
Pike, Christopher, 90, 101, 109, 200,
    204–206, 209, 212, 219, 220, 244–246
Pilgrim's Regress, The, 243
Piller, Michael, 51, 54
Plague, The, 203

Plato, 7, 19, 20, 72, 238
Pon Farr, 64
Pot, Pol, 131
Prime Directive (PD), 11, 57, 66, 67, 91,
    92, 94, 112, 115–118, 120–124, 127, 128, 132,
    168, 199
Project Ozma, 225
Prometheus, 90
Pulaski, Kate, Dr., 122, 123

Q, 24, 37, 46, 51, 104, 110, 113, 114, 116, 130,
    131, 133, 134, 233, 234, 242, 257
Quark, 127, 146, 184, 206

Republic, The, 19
Richards, Thomas, 11, 163, 217, 220
Riker, Thomas, 54, 97, 98
Riker, Will, 10, 49, 54, 96, 98, 122, 183,
    184, 194, 210, 212–215, 241, 242, 249, 250
Robertson, Pat, 173
Roddenberry, Eileen, 223
Roddenberry, Gene, 13, 17, 22, 30–32, 35,
    38, 41–46, 49–52, 55, 56, 58–62, 71, 72, 76,
    79, 80, 86, 89–91, 94, 95, 101, 108, 114,
    115, 120, 121, 128–130, 138, 143, 144,
    147–149, 168–172, 174, 186, 187, 190, 191,
    206, 207, 223, 232, 242, 246, 250, 260, 261
Romulan(s), 9, 23, 25, 41, 89, 93, 96, 105,
    197
Rousseau, Henri-Julien-Félix, 248
Russel, Bertrand, 209

Sagan, Carl, 57, 86, 159, 168, 224–227, 229,
    230, 238, 234, 236, 242
Sarek, 63
Sargon, 181
Sartre, Jean-Paul, 149
Saturday Night Live, 5
Sayers, Dorothy L., 198, 199
Schaeffer, Francis, 75
Scientology, 166
Scott, Montgomery (Scotty), 6, 25, 110,
    209
Scully, Dana, 173, 239
Search for Extraterrestrial Life, (SETI),
    57, 225–227
Search for Spock, The, 52, 53, 101, 109, 178,
    197
Serling, Rod, 43

Sesame Street, 40, 41

Seven of Nine, 7, 134, 153

Shakespeare, William, 71, 153, 200

Shatner, William, 5, 6, 98, 199, 200

Silver Chair, The, 84

Sisko, Benjamin, 44, 51, 53, 54, 130, 136, 146, 173, 194

Six Million Dollar Man, The, 156

Sobchack, Vivian, 13

Socrates, 236

Solow, Herb, 42, 43

Sound of Music, The, 77

Space Jam, 41

Spielberg, Steven, 226, 227

Spock, 7, 8, 9, 10, 12, 25, 31, 63, 63–67, 69, 70, 72, 73, 75–80, 82–88, 95–97, 101, 109, 110, 115, 119, 126, 128, 136, 142, 145, 150, 152–154, 165, 171, 178, 179, 184, 188, 189, 196, 197, 199, 201, 202, 207, 208, 212, 232, 243, 250, 259, 263

Stalin, Joseph, 131

Star Trek (original series—TOS), 8, 9, 25, 41, 42, 44, 47, 50, 54, 64, 66, 69, 70, 90, 101, 102, 109, 117–120, 142, 149, 157, 160, 167, 177, 178, 181, 186, 187, 205, 207, 210, 232, 241, 246

Star Trek VI: The Undiscovered Country, 37, 49, 53, 79, 87, 88, 145, 180, 196, 200

Star Trek: Deep Space Nine (DS9), 23, 44, 51–55, 86, 97, 98, 99, 101, 103, 108, 127, 128, 130, 135, 136, 146, 150, 151, 172, 173, 180, 185, 187, 191, 194, 199, 200, 202, 206, 207, 218, 239, 255

Star Trek: First Contact, 56, 57, 58, 61, 63, 87, 107, 123, 124, 202, 239

Star Trek: Generations, 12, 35, 98, 109, 198, 199, 201, 210, 213, 218, 243, 244

Star Trek: The Motion Picture (TMP), 77–79, 83, 87, 88, 152, 160, 170, 171, 186, 188–191

Star Trek: The Next Generation (TNG), 9, 10, 11, 25, 32, 45, 46, 49–51, 53, 55, 56, 66, 87, 88, 92, 96, 97, 101–104, 108, 109, 113, 115, 117, 118, 121, 130–133, 137, 145, 149, 150, 154, 164, 168, 171, 176, 178, 179, 181, 183–187, 191, 197, 201, 205, 207, 210–213, 217, 217, 233, 234, 241, 261

Star Trek: The Wrath of Khan (TWOK), 23, 101, 109–110, 158, 178, 196–197, 199, 202, 239

Star Trek: Voyager (VOY), 6, 7, 10, 50, 55, 56, 70, 86, 96, 103, 134, 151, 153, 174, 203, 204, 207, 233, 234

Star Wars, 28, 32, 36, 109, 172

Streetcar Named "Desire", A, 236

Stevenson, Robert Louis, 233, 234

Sun Also Rises, The, 195

Talaxian, 70

Talosian(s), 164, 181, 205, 206, 207, 213, 220, 221

Taste of Armageddon, A, 118

Technological Society, 103

Terminator, The, 107

That Hideous Strength, 159, 188, 189

Time Bandits, 123

Toffler, Alvin, 143

Tolkien, J. R. R., 32, 33, 36, 225, 241, 260, 262, 264

Tolstoy, Leo, 267

Torme, Tracy, 46

Torres, B'elanna, 7, 203

Total Recall, 140

Trekkers, 6, 26, 43

Trelane, 41, 181

Troi, Deanna, 122, 137, 150, 171, 186

Tuvix, 96, 99

Tuvok, 66, 65, 70, 71, 96, 97

Twilight Zone, The, 43, 193

2001: A Space Odyssey, 21, 233

Uhura, 115, 232

Ulysses, 36

Understanding Comics, 47

Unforgiven, 46

Utopia, 20

Vaal, 50

Velarian(s), 181

Verne, Jules, 21, 28

V'Ger, 78–80, 83–85, 128, 174, 189, 190

Vina, 164, 205, 207, 219–221, 244, 245, 248

Vonnegut, Kurt, 209

Voyage Home, The, 37

Voyage to Arcturus, 249

Voyager (earth probe), 190

Voyager, 23, 66, 105, 106, 108, 174, 186, 203, 210, 216

Vulcan(s), 3, 4, 25, 31, 63, 63–67, 70, 73, 74,

78, 79, 82, 85, 87, 96, 97, 107, 108, 115, 119, 125, 126, 162, 170, 177, 178, 197

"We Are (Already) Borg," 155
Weinberg, Steven, 229
Weiner, Norbert, 155
Wells, H. G., 21, 28, 59, 150
Whitehead, Alfred North, 100
Whitman, Walt, 228
Williams, Tennessee, 236
Winn, Vedik, 173
Wired, 155
Wise, Robert, 77
Wizard of Oz, The, 36, 133, 224

Wonder, 167, 193
Wordsworth, William, 228
Worf, 25, 105, 121, 130, 136, 194, 213, 216
Wyman, Jane, 243

X-Files, The, 167, 173, 231, 239

Yar, Tasha, 9, 194, 197
Yeats, W. B., 165, 187, 238, 243, 249

Zetar(s), 181
Zemeckis, Robert, 227, 230
Zola, Émile, 27
Zeus, 24

Index of Episodes

These episodes were mentioned or quoted from in this work.

All Good Things. . . , 109, 131, 150, 164, 178
Amok Time, 64
Apple, The, 118, 119
Arena, 42
Ascension, 86

Basics, 151
Best of Both Worlds, The, 104
Blaze of Glory, 101
Bonding, The, 201
Bread and Circuses, 117
Broken Link, 99, 136
By Any Other Name, 178, 187

Cage, The, 90, 205, 206, 248, 244
Captive Pursuit, 130
Cause and Effect, 212
Changeling, The, 160
Charlie X, 69, 241
Chase, The, 168
Circle, The, 128
City on the Edge of Forever, 120
Cloud Minders, The, 118
Coda, 187
Conspiracy, 46
Corbonite Maneuver, 232
Court Martial, 70

Dagger of the Mind, 66
Darmok, 217
Datalore, 9, 154
Data's Day, 191
Day of the Dove, 96
Death Wish, 233

Defiant, 54, 97
Descent, Part 1, 104
Descent, Part 2, 132
Destiny, 127, 135
Devil in the Dark, 41
Devil's Due, 121
Drumhead, The, 92

Elementary, My Dear Data, 207, 233
Encounter at Farpoint, 45, 113
Enemy Within, The, 8, 10, 47, 65, 79, 95, 96, 190
Errand of Mercy, 44, 96, 181
Ethics, 25

Frame of Mind, 210, 213, 215, 216, 249
Future Imperfect, 210, 212
Galaxy's Child, 185
Galileo Seven, 69, 70, 82
Gambit, The, 66
Gamesters of Triskelion, The, 205
Gift, The, 134

Hide and Q, 241
Hippocratic Oath, 51, 145
Hollow Pursuits, 183, 184, 205
Home Soil, 181
Homefront, 52
Host, The, 181

I, Borg, 104
If Wishes Were Horses, 206
Inner Light, 210, 211, 217
Interface, 201
Is There No Truth in Beauty?, 181

Jem' Hadar, The, 146
Journey to Babel, 66
Justice, 121, 261

Lights of Zetar, The, 181
Long Goodbye, 207
Looking for Parmach in All the Wrong
Places, 108, 150

Maquis, The, 53
Measure of a Man, The, 154
Menagerie, The, 101, 109, 181, 206, 207
Meridian, 185
Metamorphosis, 181
Mind's Eye, 145
Mirror, Mirror, 9, 54, 118, 142
Mudd's Women, 258

Naked Time, The, 64
Next Phase, The, 177
Non Sequitur, 210

Offspring, The, 100
Omega Glory, 90, 117
11001001, 183, 184
Operation—Annihilate!, 25
Our Man Bashir, 207

Paradise, 151
Paradise Lost, 52
Paradise Syndrome, The, 210
Parallels, 216
Patterns of Force, 117
Pen-Pals, 118, 121, 122
Piece of the Action, A, 117, 120
Power Play, 187
Prime Factors, 65
Private Little War, A, 117, 120

Quickening, The, 202, 203
Q-Who, 104

Real Life, 203

Redemption, 9
Rejoined, 180
Return of the Archons, 118
Return to Tommorrow, 181
Rise, The, 71
Royale, The, 217
Rules of Engagement, 136

Sacred Ground, 86, 174, 175
Sarek, 201
Schizoid Man, The, 179
Second Chances, 10, 97, 98
Shadowplay, 218
Ship in a Bottle, 210, 216
Shore Leave, 207
Sons of Mogh, 130
Space Seed, 158, 246
Spock's Brain, 177
Squire of Gothos, The, 41, 181
Subrosa, 187
Sword of Kahless, 146
Symbiosis, 9

Things Past, 127
This Side of Paradise, 64
Tholian Web, The, 69, 142
Time Squared, 10
Trials and Tribble-ations, 199
Turnabout Intruder, 178
Tuvix, 10, 96, 103

Ultimate Computer, The, 160
Unification, 87, 88, 96
Unity, 103
Up the Long Ladder, 97

Way to Eden, The, 149
Where No Man Has Gone Before, 241
Where No One Has Gone Before, 234
Who Watches the Watchers, 50, 108, 117,
171, 190
Whom Gods Destroy, 109

Yesterday's Enterprise, 212

Books of related interest from Cornerstone Press Chicago

Christian Mythmakers: Lewis, L'Engle, Tolkien, et al
Rolland Hein

Plunge into the soul of Lewis's Space Trilogy, L'Engle's *A Wrinkle in Time,* and Tolkien's *The Lord of the Rings.* Dwarves, elves, princes and princesses, dark powers, unlikely heros, and fantastic places open up to us in this excellent introduction to Christian mythopoeia. This overview of the major Christian mythmakers explores how they influenced and inspired one another, and identifies the symbols and emblems in their works. Rediscover the characters and worlds of authors such as C. S. Lewis, George MacDonald, John Bunyan, G. K. Chesterton, J. R. R. Tolkien, Madeleine L'Engle, and Charles Williams.

ISBN 0-940895-31-5 • $13.95

C. S. Lewis: Mere Christian, Fourth Edition
Kathryn Lindskoog

One of the best introductions to C. S. Lewis and his writing in print! Lindskoog draws from his fiction, poetry, essays, and radio speeches to explore Lewis's ideas on God, nature, humanity, death, heaven, hell, miracles, prayer, pain, love, ethisc, truth, the sciences, the arts, and education.

"Lindskoog commands an encyclopedic knowledge of Lewis's life and works, and she writes with contagious passion" —*Books & Culture*

ISBN 0-940895-36-6 • 292 pages • $14.95

Finding the Landlord: A Guidebook to C. S. Lewis's Pilgrim's Regress
Kathryn Lindskoog

Finding the Landlord opens up Lewis's classic allegory, *Pilgrim's Regress,* to an audience that may not be familiar with the people and classical allusions that fill the book. Lindskoog has also shown how the journey in the book parallels C. S. Lewis's own quest to find true joy.

ISBN 0-940895-35-8 • 165 pages • $9.95

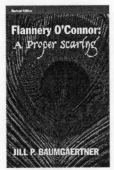